The Query Design Screen

You use the query design screen to create queries that isolate selected records.

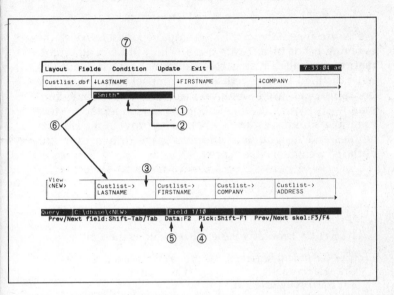

If you want to:	**Here's how:**
① Move highlight left and right	Press Tab and Shift-Tab
② Extend box downward for OR query	Press ↓
③ Add or remove field from a view	Press Field (F5)
④ Select field or operator from menu	Press Pick (Shift-F1)
⑤ See results of query	Press Data (F2)
⑥ Switch between file/view skeletons	Press Previous (F3) or Next (F4)
⑦ Access pull-down menus	Press Menus (F10)

The SYBEX Prompter Series

We've designed the SYBEX Prompter Series to meet the evolving needs of software users, who want essental information presented in an accessible format. Our best authors have distilled their expertise into compact *Instant Reference* books you can use to look up the precise use of any command—its syntax, available options, and operation. More than just summaries, these books also provide realistic examples and insights into effective usage drawn from our authors' wealth of experience.

The SYBEX Prompter Series also includes these titles:

The SYBEX Prompter™ Series

dBASE IV™ USER'S INSTANT REFERENCE

Alan Simpson

San Francisco • Paris • Düsseldorf • London

Acquisitions Editor: Dianne King
Series Editor: James A. Compton
Copy Editor: Michael L. Wolk
Technical Editor: Brian Atwood
Word Processors: Christine Mockel, Robert Myren
Production Artist: Helen Bruno
Screen Graphics: Sonja Schenk
Desktop Publishing Specialist: Charles Cowens
Proofreader: Edwin Lin
Indexer: Frances Grimble

Series Book Designer: Ingrid Owen
Cover Design: Thomas Ingalls + Associates

Screen reproductions produced by XenoFont

Library of Congress Card Number: **89-61320**
ISBN: **0-89588-605-7**
Manufactured in the United States of America
10 9 8 7 6 5 4 3 2 1

To Susan and Ashley, once again
A.C.S.

To my beloved husband, Allan Terry
F.G.

ACKNOWLEDGMENTS

All books are a team project, and this one is certainly no exception. Much credit and thanks are due the following people:

First and foremost, many thanks to Frances Grimble, who was actually co-author of this book.

Many thanks to everyone at SYBEX who guided and supported me through this project, including Jim Compton, series editor; Michael Wolk, copy editor; Brian Atwood, technical reviewer; Chris Mockel and Bob Myren, word processors; Charley Cowens, desktop publishing specialist; Helen Bruno, design and pasteup artist; and Ed Lin, proofreader.

To Dave Micek and Knox Richardson at Ashton-Tate, for providing current software and information.

To Bill, Cynthia, Tara, and Syrus Gladstone, our friends, family, and literary agents.

And to my wife Susan, and daughter Ashley, for their never-ending patience and support.

Table of Contents

Chapter 4
Sorting a Database   53

Chapter 5
Searching a Database   69

Chapter 6
Labels and Reports   **107**

Chapter 12
The Applications Generator

INTRODUCTION

dBASE IV is a very large and powerful database management system. Few of us, including the real "power users," can remember all the details of operations, and menu options. Similarly, few of us need to use the entire set of dBASE IV manuals, which cover all aspects of dBASE IV, when working on a particular project.

For these reasons, this small "pocket reference" was created. This book focuses entirely on those aspects of dBASE IV that beginning and intermediate dBASE IV users use the most—the Control Center and the various screens used for designing databases, queries, reports, labels, forms, and applications. The dBASE Applications Generator is presented in detail here because this important new feature gives nonprogrammers the same ability to develop complete applications, for themselves and others to use as often as necessary, that the dBASE command language offers to programmers.

Who This Book Is For

This book is intended for dBASE IV users who need quick reminders of techniques used in dBASE IV. It is not intended to teach you how to use dBASE IV, but rather to provide quick reference to specific features that dBASE IV offers. (An absolute beginner who has no experience whatsoever with dBASE IV would be better served with a tutorial book such as my own *Understanding dBASE IV*.)

Readers who are looking for information on more advanced topics, such as the dBASE IV programming language, would be better served by a more advanced book such as my own *dBASE IV Programmer's Reference Guide* or *dBASE IV Programmer's Instant Reference*.

How to Use This Book

Each chapter in this book presents a major topic, such as creating reports, forms, queries, and so forth. Within each chapter, topics are divided into the sections described below.

Topic

Each section deals with a particular topic, which is briefly summarized at the start of the section.

SEQUENCE OF STEPS

The next section summarizes specific steps required to achieve a goal. The starting point, steps, and options for a sequence of steps is summarized in a format similar to the following example:

Control Center Data Panel: [highlight file name]
F2 | ↵ Display Data

Here, the starting point is assumed to be the Data panel of the Control Center. The step [highlight file name] states that you next need to highlight a file name.

The next step actually refers to two alternative actions (separated by |), either of which produces the same result. In this example, **F2** | ↵ **Display Data** indicates that you can either press the F2 key, or press the ↵ key and select the Display Data option, to achieve the same result.

USAGE

The Usage section provides an in-depth discussion of the topic at hand, including how to use a dBASE IV feature, and any additional options that the topic offers.

SEE ALSO

This section directs you to related topics that provide additional information. For example, "Customizing Your Environment/Display Options (Chapter 11)" says that the detail section "Display Options," part of the broader topic "Customizing Your Environment" in Chapter 11, contains related information. To help you find any topic quickly, major headings such as "Customizing Your Environment" also appear next to the page number at the top of each page. A reference like "Chapter 11: Managing Your Workspace" tells you that the entire chapter is related to the topic at hand.

Tips for Tyros

Throughout this book, keypresses that require two or more keys are separated by a hyphen. For example, when you see a keypress named **Ctrl-Y**, that means "hold down the Ctrl key, tap the Y key, then release the Ctrl key."

Remember that, at any time in your work with dBASE IV, you can get immediate help by pressing the key labeled **F1** on your keyboard.

Also, remember that if, at any time, you accidentally select the wrong menu option and wind up in unfamiliar territory, you can simply press the **Esc** key to cancel the most recent menu selection and "back up" to more familiar territory. If necessary, you can keep pressing **Esc** to back up all the way to the Control Center.

CHAPTER 1

Starting and Using dBASE IV

This chapter is a reference for starting dBASE, using the Control Center and menus, and exiting dBASE. It assumes that dBASE is already installed on your computer.

Starting dBASE

When you first turn on your computer, DOS is in control. To use dBASE IV, you must tell DOS to locate and run the dBASE IV program.

SEQUENCE OF STEPS

From the DOS command prompt, enter:

DBASE ↵

USAGE

Turn on your computer, so that the DOS prompt (usually C:) appears on the screen. Note that, if you did not install dBASE so it can be activated from any directory, you must first log onto the directory that dBASE is stored on. Usually, this directory is named \DBASE. To log onto that directory, enter the command **CD\DBASE** and press ↵. Then type the command **DBASE** and press ↵.

The dBASE IV logo and copyright notice appear on the screen, along with the message *Press ↵ to assent to the License Agreement and begin dBASE IV.* Press ↵ to proceed; dBASE will then display the Control Center.

The Control Center

The Control Center has five major parts: the menu bar, the name of the current catalog, the work space, the name and description of the current file, and the navigation line (see Figure 1.1).

The Current Catalog

Centered beneath the title of the Control Center screen is the name of the current catalog. A *catalog* is a tool for grouping the names of related files, forms, and report formats in the

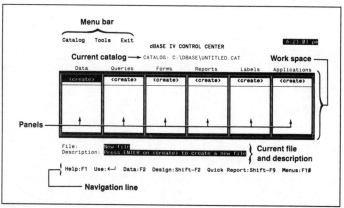

Figure 1.1: The dBASE IV Control Center

Control Center. You can use the Catalog menu on the Control Center menu bar to change catalogs or create a new catalog.

SEE ALSO

Managing Catalogs (Chapter 10)

The Work Space

The center of the screen shows the Control Center *work space*, which consists of six *panels*. Each panel holds the file names of various objects in the current catalog (though none is currently shown in Figure 1.1). An *object* is simply one piece of the overall collection of information. The leftmost panel, titled Data, holds the names of *database files* that store data. The panels labeled Forms, Reports, and Labels hold the names of *formats* used to display forms and to print reports and mailing labels. The panel labeled Queries holds the names of *queries* (or *views*) used to locate information in the database. The Applications panel holds the names of dBASE *applications*.

Creating New Objects

To create a new object in a panel, position the highlight to <create> in the appropriate panel and press ↵. Note that you must create a database file in the Data panel before you can create queries, forms, reports, labels, or applications for that database file (see Chapter 2).

Using Existing Objects

To use an object that is already listed in the Control Center, highlight its name and press ↵. If the Instruct mode is on, you will see a prompt box providing options to view the contents of the file, or to modify the underlying design of the file. As a shortcut to pressing ↵ and going through the prompt box, you can press F2 (Data) to see the contents of a file immediately, or press Shift-F2 (Design) to modify the underlying structure.

SEE ALSO

Chapter 5: Searching a Database; Chapter 6: Labels and Reports; Chapter 7: Custom Forms; Chapter 12: Developing Applications

The Current File Name and Description

The *current file* name and description section of the screen, beneath the work space, displays the name and description of the file that is currently highlighted in the panel. If <create> is highlighted instead of a file name, this area displays the messages *New file* and *Press ENTER on <create> to create a new file*.

SEE ALSO

Managing Files (Chapter 10)

The Navigation Line

The *navigation line* at the bottom of the screen lists some of the special keys that are currently available to you. Figure 1.2 shows how the key descriptions on the navigation line refer to options in the Control Center.

The Menu Bar and Pull-Down Menus

At the upper-left corner of the Control Center is the *menu bar*. At the Control Center, the menu-bar options are Catalog, Tools, and Exit. Each menu option has a *pull-down menu* associated with it. There are two ways you can access a pull-down menu and two ways you can select an option from one.

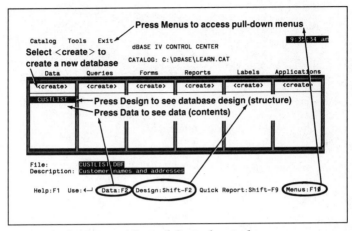

Figure 1.2: Summary of Control Center keystrokes

SEQUENCE OF STEPS

Keyboard: **F10** [highlight menu name] | **Alt**-*<first letter of menu name>*

Pull-down menu: [highlight option | type first letter] ↵

USAGE

You can access a pull-down menu by either pressing **F10** (Menu), or holding down the **Alt** key and typing the first letter of the menu you want. For example, if you type Alt-T (by holding down the Alt key, tapping the letter T, and then releasing the Alt key), the Tools pull-down menu appears.

Once any pull-down menu is displayed, you can move through menus and options using the keys listed in Table 1.1. You can also select an option from a pull-down menu simply by typing the first letter of the option. When you've selected an option by either method, confirm your selection by pressing ↵. Throughout this book, any instruction to "select" an option from a pull-down menu implicitly includes this ↵ keystroke, as shown in the accompanying

KEY	EFFECT
→	Moves to the pull-down menu on the right
←	Moves to the pull-down menu on the left
↓	Moves down to the next available (unshaded) menu option on the current pull-down menu
↑	Moves up to the next available (unshaded) menu option on the current pull-down menu
PgDn	Moves to the last available option on the current pull-down menu
End	Same as PgDn
PgUp	Moves to the first available option on the current pull-down menu
Home	Same as PgUp
↵	Selects the currently highlighted option
First letter	Selects the option on the current menu that begins with that letter
Esc	Backs up to the previous menu or to the Control Center

Table 1.1: Keys Used to Navigate the Pull-Down Menus

Sequence of Steps. If you select a menu option by accident, just press Esc to "back up" to the previous menu.

Shaded options are not available at the moment, usually because they make no sense in the current situation (see Figure 1.3). An option with an arrow at its left edge (a *bulleted* option) brings up a *submenu* containing more options. (Because most dBASE menus are actually submenus, this book often uses the term *menu* to refer to both pull-down menus and submenus.)

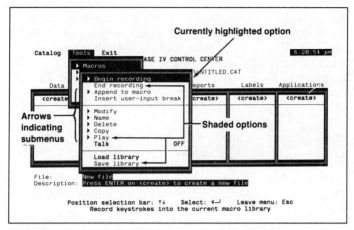

Figure 1.3: Submenu showing shaded and bulleted options

Some menu options have a variety of settings, such as Yes and No or On and Off. When you encounter such a menu option, you can press the Space bar to cycle through the optional settings. Pressing ↵ selects the currently displayed setting.

Another type of option is followed by curly brackets ({ }). These options require you to press ↵ to select the option, type some information in the brackets, then press ↵ again. Whatever you enter remains the default until you type in a new value.

You can leave a menu or submenu at any time by pressing **Esc**.

The Dot Prompt

The dot prompt is an alternative to the Control Center for using dBASE IV, where the screen displays only a dot (.) and blinking cursor. Instead of selecting options from menus, you instruct dBASE by entering commands at this prompt. To use this method efficiently, you need to be familiar with the dBASE command set. Since the Control Center's menu system offers the same capabilities and is much easier to use, this book assumes you will *not* work from the dot prompt. A companion volume, *dBASE IV Programmer's Instant References* (SYBEX, 1989), presents the full dBASE command set. If you inadvertently find yourself at the dot prompt, and wish to return to the Control Center, type the command **ASSIST** and press ↵.

The Help System

You can use the Help key at any time to get help with dBASE IV. The help screens are *context sensitive*, which means they provide help that is relevant to the operation you are currently performing.

SEQUENCE OF STEPS

Keyboard: **F1**

USAGE

Press **F1** (Help). You'll see a help screen (also called a help *window*) (see Figure 1.4). You can press **F4** to see the next screen or **F3** to see the previous screen. There are a few options—CONTENTS, RELATED TOPICS, BACKUP, and PRINT—displayed at the bottom of the help window (see Table 1.2). You can use the ← and → keys to move the highlight from one option to the next and press ↵ to select one. When you are finished with the help system, you can return to the Control Center by pressing **Esc**.

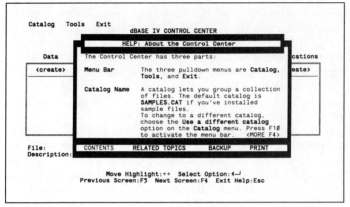

Figure 1.4: Help screen for the Control Center

OPTION	EFFECT
CONTENTS	Displays a table of contents for the current topic. When a table of contents is displayed, you can use the More General (F3) and More Specific (F4) keys to change to more general or more specific tables of contents.
RELATED TOPICS	Displays a list of topics that are related to the current topic.
BACKUP	Scrolls back to the previous screen. (This option appears only if there is a previous screen.)
PRINT	Prints a copy of the current help window.

Table 1.2: Help Window Options

The Instruct Mode

dBASE IV offers several modes of operation, which you control through the Settings menu. One setting, Instruct, tells dBASE whether to display prompt boxes and other aids to help you learn dBASE while using the Control Center. This book assumes that the Instruct setting is on, as it is by default. If another user has turned it off, the key sequences required for some operations will differ from those presented here, so you should turn it on again to follow these instructions. If you eventually decide you don't need the prompt boxes, the same keystrokes turn Instruct off. Chapter 11, "Managing Your Workspace," presents the entire Settings menu.

SEQUENCE OF STEPS

Control Center menu bar: **Tools**

Tools menu: **Settings** ↵

Settings menu: **Instruct** ↵

Instruct: **On** | **Off** [select with ↵]

Tools Exit menu: **Exit to Control Center** ↵

USAGE

Bring up the **Tools** menu in the Control Center menu bar, then select **Settings.** Highlight the **Instruct** option (or type the letter **I**). **Instruct** offers two choices: Off and On. The current setting is shown on the screen. Pressing ↵ turns on the opposite setting, an effect known as *toggling*. If **Instruct** is off, press ↵ now to turn it on. Set **Instruct** to **On.** Then, select the **Exit** option to return to the Control Center.

| SEE ALSO |

Customizing Your Environment/Environmental Settings
(Chapter 11)

Exiting dBASE

Whenever you finish a dBASE IV session, you should exit
(or quit) dBASE IV before you turn off your computer. If you
don't remember to do so, you may find that dBASE IV is not
saving your work, and you'll have to reenter all your data.

| SEQUENCE OF STEPS |

Control Center menu bar: **Exit**
Exit menu: **Quit to DOS** ↵

| USAGE |

Access the **Exit** pull-down menu, then select the **Quit to
DOS** option. You'll see the message *** *END RUN dBASE IV*
on your screen, followed by the DOS command prompt. You
can now safely turn off your computer or use another program.

| SEE ALSO |

Accessing DOS (Chapter 10)

CHAPTER 2

Creating a Database File

dBASE IV stores information in *database files* on a computer disk. Each database file consists of *records* (or *rows*) of information. Each record is divided into separate *fields* (or *columns*). Before you can store information in a database file, you need to *structure* an empty file that specifies the name and type of data to be stored in each field.

To ensure maximum flexibility in managing your data, store each unique item of information in its own field, regardless of how you want it to be printed later. Also, put different types of data, such as customer information and inventory information, into separate database files.

SEE ALSO ==================

Chapter 9: Managing Related Database Files

The Database Design Screen

The *database design screen* is where you define each field in your database structure (see Figure 2.1).

SEQUENCE OF STEPS ════════════

Control Center: [highlight **Data** panel]

Data panel: [highlight **<create>**] ↵ | [highlight file name]
Shift-F2

USAGE ════════════

To reach the database design screen from the Control Center
to create a new database, highlight **<create>** in the **Data**
panel and press ↵. To reach the database design screen from
the Control Center to change the structure of an existing
database file, highlight the name of the database file in the
Data panel and press **Shift-F2** (Design).

Like the Control Center, the database design screen includes pull-down menu options at the top of the screen. In
some situations, the Organize pull-down menu will appear
on the screen as soon as you enter the Database Design
screen. To remove the menu from the screen, press **Esc**.

The database design screen includes a table with six
columns labeled Num, Field Name, Field Type, Width, Dec
(for Decimal places) and Index. You define each field in your

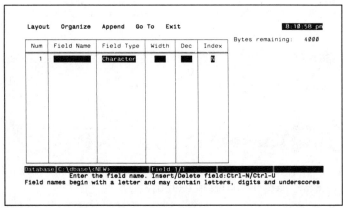

Figure 2.1: The database design screen

database structure within this table. (The Num column is defined by dBASE; it shows the position of the field in the database file structure.)

Field Names

Each field in the database file must have a unique name, which must conform to the following rules:

- The name can include no more than 10 characters.
- The first character must be a letter, but numbers can be used after the first letter.
- Blank spaces and punctuation marks are *not* allowed.
- The underscore character (_) is the only special symbol allowed.

SEQUENCE OF STEPS

Database design screen: [move cursor to **Field Name** column]

Field Name column: *<field name>* ⏎

USAGE

To enter a field name, first make sure that the blinking cursor is in the **Field Name** column in the screen. Type the field name and press ⏎. The cursor will jump to the Field Type column.

When you enter an invalid field name, dBASE will beep, and whatever you typed will not appear on the screen. Just type a different character, such as an underline instead of a space, or a letter instead of a number or punctuation mark.

Data Types

Each field in a database file must be categorized as a *data type* (or *field type*). dBASE offers six data types, listed in Table 2.1.

SEQUENCE OF STEPS

Database design screen: [move cursor to **Field Type** column]

Field Type column: [choose option with **Space** bar or type first letter] ↵

USAGE

While the blinking cursor is in the **Field Type** column, you can press the **Space** bar to scroll through the various data types before making a selection. Each time you press the Space bar, the name of a data type appears within the high-light, and a brief description of the data type appears at the bottom of the screen. To select the currently displayed data type, just press ↵. The cursor jumps to the Width column.

A shortcut for entering a data type is simply to type the first letter of its name. If you make a mistake, press ← or **Shift-Tab** to move back to the **Field Type** column. Then try again.

Field Widths

After you specify a data type, the next step is to specify a maximum width for the field.

SEQUENCE OF STEPS

Database design screen: [move cursor to **Width** column]

Width column: *<width>* ↵

DATA TYPE	DESCRIPTION	MAXIMUM WIDTH	EXAMPLES
Character	Any textual information that has no true numeric value and a maximum length of 254 characters.	254 characters	Jones Spark plug 123 Oak St.
Numeric	Any true numeric value on which you may want to perform arithmetic operations; best for most business applications, where numbers all have equal decimal places.	20 digits	10 −123.45 100 1234.567
Float	Best used for scientific applications that involve extremely large or small numbers with varying decimal places.	20 digits	10.0 −123.45 100.00 1234.567
Date	Any date stored in the format mm/dd/yy. Always use this option to store dates.	8 characters (cannot be changed)	1/1/89 12/31/89 6/12/90

Table 2.1: The dBASE IV Data Types and Field Widths

DATA TYPE	DESCRIPTION	MAXIMUM WIDTH	EXAMPLES
Logical	Contains either a true or false value and no other information.	1 character (cannot be changed)	.T. .F.
Memo	Very large volumes of text, perhaps including several paragraphs.	10 characters in design screen, but actual memo field can contain up to 64,000 characters.	Abstracts Resumes Lengthy documents

Table 2.1: The dBASE IV Data Types and Field Widths (continued)

Type the desired width in the **Width** column and press ↵.
Table 2.1 shows the maximum field widths for each data
type. The rule of thumb is to select a reasonable width with
frugality. The wider a field, the more disk space it consumes.

The cursor jumps to the Index column, unless you defined
the field as a numeric or float data type. In this case, the cursor jumps to the Dec column, where you specify the number
of decimal places the field requires.

Decimal Places

When you define a field as either the numeric or the float
data type, you need to specify both a width and a number of
decimal places for it.

Database design screen: [move cursor to **Dec** column]

Dec column: <*number*> ↵

Numeric and float fields can have up to 18 decimal places. If
you need only whole numbers, you can set the number of
decimal places to zero. For example, a numeric field with a
width of four characters and zero decimal places can handle
any number in the range –999 to 9999 (the minus sign requires a place in the width you specify).

When sizing numbers that require decimal places, remember that the decimal point takes up one digit in the width
you assign. Therefore, if you assign a width of nine characters and two decimal places to a field, the field can hold any
number in the range –99999.99 to 999999.99.

After you define the number of decimal places, the cursor
jumps to the Index column.

SEE ALSO ═══════════════

Formatting Fields (Chapter 6)

Indexes

An index provides rapid sorting and searching of a field in a database.

SEQUENCE OF STEPS ═══════════════

Database design screen: [move cursor to **Index** column]

Index column: <**Y** | **N**> ↵

USAGE ═══════════════

In the rightmost column, labeled **Index,** you can enter either **Y** (for yes), or **N** (for no) to indicate whether the field should be indexed. When designing a database structure, mark fields that are used regularly for sorting and searching as indexed (by pressing the Space bar to change the N to a Y). For example, in a mailing-list database, you might index the last-name and zip-code fields for indexing, so you can print names and addresses in alphabetical or zip-code order, and so you can locate a particular last name quickly.

Another method for creating an index is to use the **Create New Index** option on the **Organize** menu. This option enables you to create more complex indexes than the Index column allows.

At this point, the highlight jumps down to the next blank row, and you can enter the information for the next field. You can also move around the work area and make corrections or changes. By pressing ↵ again, you can choose to start entering data from the edit or browse screen.

SEE ALSO

Indexes/Activating an Index, Creating an Index (Chapter 4)

Database Descriptions

A *description* is simply a sentence that describes, in plain English, what is stored in the database. It is helpful not only for other people who might use your database, but for your own future reference as well.

SEQUENCE OF STEPS

Database design screen menu bar: **Layout**

Layout menu: **Edit Database Description** ↵

Highlighted bar: *<database description>* ↵

USAGE

Press **F10** and use the arrow keys (or type **Alt-L**) to access the **Layout** menu on the menu bar. Then select **Edit Database Description** from the pull-down menu. Press ↵ to select the menu option. The screen will display the message *Edit the description of this .dbf file* and present a highlighted bar for you to type in. (dBASE always adds the *extension* .DBF to a database file name, so the .dbf file that the message refers to is the database file you just created.) Type the description and press ↵.

Saving the Database Structure

Once you've finished entering the structure and description of a database file, you need to save your work.

SEQUENCE OF STEPS ═══════════

Database design screen menu bar: **Save This Database File Structure** on the **Layout** menu | **Save Changes and Exit** on the **Exit** menu ↵

Save as prompt: <*file name*> ↵

or

Keyboard: **Ctrl-End** | **Ctrl-W**

Save as prompt: <*file name*> ↵

USAGE ═══════════

dBASE offers several ways to save a database file. From the database design screen, press **F10** to make the pull-down menus available. Then, using the arrow keys or an Alt-combination, select either the **Layout** menu (**Alt-L**) and **Save This Database File Structure** or the **Exit** menu (**Alt-E**) and **Save Changes and Exit**. Or, from any point in dBASE, you can simply press **Ctrl-End** or **Ctrl-W**.

When you see the *Save as:* prompt, type in a file name and press ↵. Remember that the file name can contain no more than eight letters, may not contain spaces, and may not contain punctuation symbols other than the underline (_).

If you attempt to save a database file using a name that already exists, dBASE will beep and display the message *File already exists*. You are also given two options: Overwrite to replace the existing database with the new structure, and Cancel to stop and use a different file name.

If you use Ctrl-End to exit the database design screen after creating a new database structure, dBASE will display the prompt *Input data records now? (Y/N)*. You can type the letter **Y** to transfer to the browse or edit screen or type **N** to return to the Control Center.

Select **Save This Database File Structure** from the Layout pull-down menu, if you want dBASE to save the structure but not exit the database design screen. (You can press **Ctrl-End** to exit the design screen if you wish.)

To exit the database design screen without saving changes, Choose **Abandon Changes and Exit** from the **Exit** menu or press Esc. You will be asked to confirm that you want to abandon your work, then be returned to wherever you were previously.

From the database design screen, you can transfer to the edit or browse screen by pressing **F2** (Data). Or you can switch to the query design screen by pressing **Shift-F2**.

Modifying the Database Structure

You can change the structure of a database at any time, regardless of how many records are in the database. To do so, highlight the database name in the Control Center and press **Shift-F2** (Design). You'll see the database structure on the database design screen. There you can change field definitions, add fields, and delete fields.

As soon as you enter the database design screen, dBASE IV makes a temporary copy of the records in the current database. After you save your changes, dBASE attempts to copy records from the temporary database back into the original database. It will be successful at doing so only if you use a little caution while changing the database structure. (As an added precaution, make your own backup copy of the database first.)

If you delete a field from the database structure, keep in mind that you are also deleting all the data in that field. In other words, if you have a database with 10,000 names and addresses in it and you delete the City field from that database structure, you would lose all the cities that were in that field. To get them back, you would have to type each one in again by hand—not a pleasant task!

To change the position of a field in the database structure, first note the exact spelling of the field name, the data type, the width, and the number of decimal places. Then delete the field from its current position using the **Ctrl-U** key. Use **Ctrl-N** to insert a new blank field, or add the new field beneath the existing field names. Be sure to use the same spelling, data type, width, and number of decimal places. Do not perform any other operations at this time; save your changes and exit immediately. (Note, however, that the position of a field in a database structure does not in any way affect how you use the contents of the field.)

You can change the name of a field *only* if you do not add, change, move, or delete any fields during the same operation. If you change field names and rearrange fields in the same operation, dBASE will become confused, and there is no telling how things might be arranged after you save your changes.

The keys you use to change a database structure are described in Table 2.2. Note that they won't always work if you attempt to leave a row that has incomplete or invalid data. You may have to experiment with several keys or type **Ctrl-U** to completely delete an incomplete or invalid row to get the cursor moving in the direction you want.

Printing the Database Structure

You can easily print a copy of your database structure. This can be handy to keep available as an instant reference to the fields in a particular database. There is no convenient way to have the database structure visible on screen as you are entering data.

SEQUENCE OF STEPS

Control Center Data panel: [highlight database name] **Shift-F2**

Database design screen menu bar: **Layout**

Layout menu: **Print Database Structure** ↵

Print menu: **Begin Printing** ↵

Database design screen menu bar: **Exit**

Exit menu: **Abandon Changes and Exit** ↵

KEY	EFFECT
→	Moves cursor one character to the right
←	Moves cursor one character to the left
↓	Moves highlight down one row
↑	Moves highlight up one row
Tab	Moves cursor one column to the right (only if valid information is already in the present column)
Shift-Tab	Moves cursor one column to the left (only if valid information is already in the present column)
End	Moves cursor to the last column in the row
Home	Moves cursor to the first column in the row
↵	Completes an entry and moves to the next column or row
Backspace	Moves cursor back one character, erasing along the way
Ctrl-U	Deletes the entire current row (field)
Ctrl-N	Inserts a blank row between two existing rows
Ctrl-End	Saves changes and exits the database design screen
Ctrl-W	Same as Ctrl-End
Esc	Exits without saving changes and returns to previous screen
F1	Displays Help screen.
F2	Switch to browse or edit screen.
Shift-F2	Transfer to Query Design Screen

Table 2.2: Keys Used to Change a Database File Structure

USAGE

Highlight the database name in the Data panel and press the **Shift-F2** (Design). Select **Print Database Structure** from the **Layout** pull-down menu. Select **Begin Printing.**

If you need to eject the page from the printer, select **Print Database Structure** from the **Layout** menu again and **Eject Page Now** from the submenu. Then press **Esc.**

Select **Abandon Changes and Exit** from the **Exit** menu to return to the Control Center.

SEE ALSO

Printing Labels and Reports (Chapter 6)

CHAPTER 3

Adding, Editing, and Deleting Data

This chapter is a reference for adding, editing, and deleting your dBASE IV data. It also shows how to manage the edit and browse screens.

Accessing Your Data

Before you view, add, change, or delete information in a database file, you need to tell dBASE IV which file you want to use, and then bring up an *edit screen* or *browse screen* to work with the data.

SEQUENCE OF STEPS

Control Center panel: [highlight file name] **F2** | ↵ **Display Data** ↵

USAGE

To access the data in a database file, first use the arrow keys to highlight the name of the database or any query, form, report, or label associated with it. Then press **F2** (Data). If

Instruct mode is on, you can press ↵ rather than F2, then select **Display Data** from the prompt box.

Either the edit or the browse screen appears, depending on which you used most recently (except when you choose a form, which always brings up an edit screen). You can then switch between the two types of data-editing screens by pressing **F2** (Data) again.

The Data key also enables you to view data from any design screen associated with the database, without going back to the Control Center. This is especially useful when you design view queries.

SEE ALSO	

Managing Catalogs (Chapter 10); Chapter 5: Searching a Database

The Edit Screen

The edit screen looks like a blank form for a single record (see Figure 3.1). It is useful when you want to concentrate on one record at a time. The left column contains the field names you've assigned for the current database; use the right column to enter or change data for the current record. You can move from field to field using the navigation keys listed in Table 3.1.

At the upper-left corner is a menu bar containing the options Records, Go To, and Exit. At the upper right is a clock displaying the time.

dBASE also displays a highlighted *status bar* at the bottom of the edit screen (and most other dBASE screens) to help you with your work (see Figure 3.2). It shows the following information:

- Type of screen in use (such as edit or browse screen).
- Location and name of the database file currently in use.

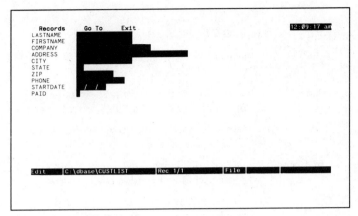

Figure 3.1: An edit screen

KEY	EFFECT
↓	Moves cursor down
↑	Moves cursor up
→	Moves cursor right one character
←	Moves cursor left one character
Del	Deletes character over cursor
Backspace	Moves left one character, erasing along the way
Ctrl-Y	Deletes all characters to right of cursor
Tab	Moves to next field, or indents paragraph in word-wrap editor
↵	Completes entry and moves to next field

Table 3.1: Navigation and Editing Keys for the Edit and Browse Screens

KEY	EFFECT
Shift-Tab	Moves to previous field, or outdents paragraph in word-wrap editor
Home	Moves to first field on browse screen or first character in current field on edit screen
End	Moves to last field on browse screen or end of current field on edit screen
Ctrl-Home	Moves from a memo-field marker into an editing window to add or change a memo.
Ditto	(Shift-F8) Carries data from same field in previous record to current record
PgDn	Moves down one record on edit screen or one screenful on browse screen
PgUp	Moves up one record on edit screen or one screenful on browse screen
Ins	Switches between Insert and Overwrite modes
F1	Displays help
F2	Toggles between browse and edit screens
F3	Scrolls back to previous field
F4	Scrolls to next field
F10	Accesses pull-down menus
Esc	Leaves current screen without saving changes to last-edited record.
Ctrl-End	Saves changes and exits to previously used screen

Table 3.1: Navigation and Editing Keys for the Edit and Browse Screens (continued)

- Current record in the database and total number of records. For example, the message *Rec 1/2* means that you are currently viewing record number 1 in a database containing two records.

- Source of the data currently on the screen.

- Settings of various toggle keys. For example, if *Num* appears, the NumLock key is on. If *Caps* appears, the CapsLock key is on. If *Ins* appears, you are in Insert mode, rather than Overwrite mode. Pressing the Num-Lock, CapsLock, or Ins key turns these settings (and the appropriate indicators) on and off.

To exit to the Control Center and save your work, highlight the **Exit** option on the menu bar, highlight **Exit,** and press ⌐. The Exit menu also enables you to return to a query or other design screen.

To switch to the previously used screen and save your changes, press **Ctrl-End.** To switch to the previously used screen without saving changes to the most recently modified record, press **Esc** when no pull-down menu is displayed. Before leaving the current screen, dBASE double-checks your intentions by displaying the message *Are you sure you want to abandon operation? Yes No.* If you have not made any changes to the current screen, answer **Yes** (either by highlighting the

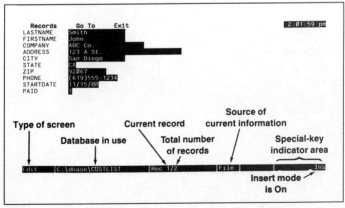

Figure 3.2: The status bar

word and pressing ↵ or by typing the letter **Y**). If you have made changes and want to save them, answer **No.** You can then save your changes and exit either by pressing **Ctrl-End** or by selecting an option from the **Exit** pull-down menu.

SEE ALSO

Chapter 7: Custom Forms; Searching for Specific Records (Chapter 5)

The Browse Screen

The browse screen enables you to see several records, though usually not all the fields from each record (see Figure 3.3). Each field has its own column with the field name at the top. You can move from field to field using the keys described in Table 3.1.

Like the edit screen, the browse screen has a menu bar at the upper left, which contains the options Records, Fields, Go To, and Exit. It has a clock at the upper right and a status

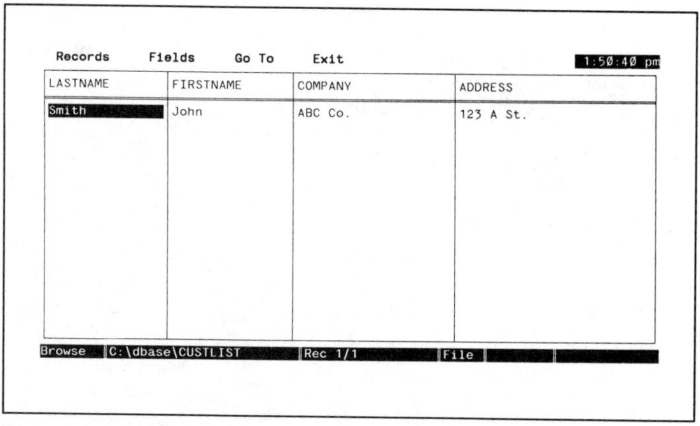

Records	Fields	Go To	Exit	1:50:40 pm
LASTNAME	FIRSTNAME	COMPANY	ADDRESS	
Smith	John	ABC Co.	123 A St.	

Browse   C:\dbase\CUSTLIST   Rec 1/1   File

Figure 3.3: A browse screen

line at the bottom (see the description of the status line on the edit screen).

To exit to the Control Center and save your work, highlight the **Exit** option on the menu bar, highlight **Exit,** and press ↵. The Exit menu also enables you to return to a query or other design screen.

To switch to the previously used screen and save your changes, press **Ctrl-End.** To switch to the previously used screen without saving changes to the most recently modified record, press **Esc** when no pull-down menu is displayed. When dBASE asks if you are sure you want to abandon the operation, select **Yes** if you have not changed the current screen. If you have made changes and want to save them, select **No.** You can then save your changes and exit by pressing **Ctrl-End** or by selecting an option from the **Exit** pull-down menu.

SEE ALSO

Searching for Specific Records (Chapter 5)

Customizing the Browse Screen

The Fields menu on the browse screen offers several features to help you edit a database that are particularly useful when you work with large databases: locking fields, freezing fields, and sizing columns.

Locking a Field

You can lock one or more fields at the left of the screen, so that they do not disappear when you scroll to the right.

SEQUENCE OF STEPS

Browse screen menu bar: **Fields**

Fields menu: **Lock Fields on Left** ↵

Lock Fields box: *<number>* ↵

USAGE

When you select **Lock Fields on Left** from the **Fields** menu, dBASE will ask how many fields you want to remain stationary. Enter a number and press ⏎.

Freezing a Field

This feature enables you to isolate a particular field on the browse screen.

SEQUENCE OF STEPS

Browse screen menu bar: **Fields**

Fields menu: **Freeze Field** ⏎

Freeze Field box: *<field name>* ⏎

USAGE

When you select the **Freeze Field** option, dBASE asks for the name of the field to freeze. Type the field name and press ⏎.

The highlight will move to the field you've named and cannot be moved out of that field. Pressing ← or → moves the highlight up or down, rather than across fields. To unfreeze the field, select **Freeze Field** again and press **Backspace** to remove the field name.

Sizing Columns

This feature enables you to change the size of a column on the browse screen.

SEQUENCE OF STEPS

Browse screen menu bar: **Fields**

Fields menu: **Size Field** ⏎

Keyboard: [change field width with ← or →] ⏎

USAGE

You can expand or contract the size of a column display on the browse screen by moving the highlight to the appropriate column and selecting **Size Field** from the **Fields** pull-down menu. After selecting the option, use ← or → to widen or narrow the field; then press ⏎.

Adding Records

You can add new records at any time from either the edit screen or the browse screen, or you can add groups of existing records using the database design screen.

Adding Records Using the Edit Screen

Place the highlight in the appropriate field before entering data.

SEQUENCE OF STEPS

Field: *<data>*

Next field: *<data>* ⏎

.

.

.

Last field: *<data>* ⏎

| USAGE | |

To add a new record using the edit screen, enter the data for each field, pressing ⏎ to record each line and move on to the next. When the entry completely fills the field, you need not press ⏎. dBASE beeps and automatically moves the cursor to the next field. (If you leave a logical field blank, dBASE interprets it as false.) When you finish entering a record, dBASE saves it and displays an edit screen for the next new record.

Once you have entered records in a database, you can add new ones either by selecting **Add New Records** from the **Records** pull-down menu or by pressing **PgDn** until you see the prompt = = = *Add new records? (Y/N)*. Then type **Y.**

Adding Records Using the Browse Screen

Place the highlight in the appropriate field before entering data.

| SEQUENCE OF STEPS | |

First column: <data> ⏎
Next column: <data> ⏎

.

.

.

Last column: <data> ⏎

| USAGE | |

Fill in the data for each field in the appropriate column, pressing ⏎ or the **Tab** key to move the highlight to the next column. When you are done adding the record, press ↓ to move to the next row. dBASE will save the record and display the prompt = = = *Add new records? (Y/N)*. Press **Y** to add another record. From this point on, you can commence adding new records; dBASE will not display the Add new records? prompt.

Once you have entered records in a database, you can add new ones either by selecting **Add New Records** from the **Records** pull-down menu or by pressing ↓ until you are prompted to add new records. Then type **Y**.

Adding Records Using the Database Design Screen

The Append menu on the database design screen enables you to copy groups of records from another file. Before doing this, you should save any changes you have made to the database.

SEQUENCE OF STEPS

Database design screen menu bar: **Append**

Append menu: **Append Records from dBASE File** ↵

File options menu: [highlight file name] ↵

USAGE

Pull down the **Append** menu from the menu bar and select **Append Records from dBASE File.** Choose the appropriate file name from the menu that appears. As dBASE copies the records, it will inform you of its progress in a message box, which disappears when the copying is done.

The Enter Records from Keyboard option on the Append menu simply brings up the edit screen, where you can enter records by hand as usual.

SEE ALSO

Importing and Exporting Data (Chapter 10)

Editing Data

You can change existing data from either the browse screen or the edit screen, using the keys described in Table 3.1.

There are two modes for entering text: *Insert* and *Overwrite*. In Insert mode, the characters you enter push existing characters to the right. In Overwrite mode, the characters you enter *replace* existing characters at the same position. You can easily switch between one mode and the other by pressing the **Ins** key. When Insert mode is on, *Ins* appears at the far right of the status line.

SEE ALSO

Adding Fields and Text/Memo Fields (Chapter 7)

Blanking a Field

Besides using the editing keys, you can use a menu option to blank an entire field.

SEQUENCE OF STEPS

Browse screen menu bar: **Fields**
Fields menu: **Blank Field** ↵

USAGE

To empty the contents of a field, move the cursor to the appropriate field and select **Blank Field** from the **Fields** pull-down menu.

Blanking a Record

You can use a menu option to blank an entire record.

SEQUENCE OF STEPS

Edit screen | browse screen menu bar: **Records**

Records menu: **Blank Record** ↵

USAGE

To empty all the fields in a record, select **Blank Record** from the **Records** pull-down menu and press ↵. The Blank Record option leaves an empty record in the database. It does not mark or delete the record.

Undoing an Edit

Once in a while, you'll probably make the common mistake of changing or erasing a field's contents without paying attention to what you are doing. Suddenly, you realize that you've changed the wrong information and do not remember what the old information was. Fortunately, you can easily undo accidental changes to a record.

SEQUENCE OF STEPS

Edit | browse screen menu bar: **Records**

Records menu: **Undo Change to Record** ↵

USAGE

Before you move to a new record (and save your changes), highlight the **Records** option on the menu bar. Then select **Undo Change to Record.** You'll see the record back on the screen, exactly as it was before you made your erroneous changes.

Preventing Automatic Re-sort

When you are using an index to maintain a sort order on the browse screen, changing values in the indexed field will cause the records to be re-sorted.

If you do not want the highlight to follow an edited record to its new position in the sort order, follow the steps below.

SEQUENCE OF STEPS

Browse screen menu bar: **Records**

Records: **Follow Record to New Position** ↵

Follow Record to New Position: **Yes** | **No** ↵

USAGE

To prevent automatic re-sort, select **Follow Record to New Position** from the **Records** pull-down menu and change its setting from Yes to **No.**

SEE ALSO

Indexes / Activating an Index (Chapter 4)

Locking Records

If you are using dBASE IV on a network, other users working on the same database may change information in the database while you are viewing it. You can prevent this by using the Lock Record option.

SEQUENCE OF STEPS

Edit | browse screen menu bar: **Records**

Records menu: **Lock Record** ↵

USAGE ═══════════════════

To prevent other users from changing the data in a record while you are viewing it, select **Lock Record** from the **Records** pull-down menu. The record will remain locked until you move the highlight to a different record.

Changing Several Records at Once

With dBASE IV's *global editing* capability, you have the power to replace a value in several records simultaneously. The tool for performing global editing is the *update query*.

SEQUENCE OF STEPS ═══════════════════

Control Center Queries panel: **<create>**

Query design screen: [filter field in file skeleton]

Filter field: *<filter condition>*

Keyboard: **F2** [to check selected records]

Keyboard: **Shift-F2** [to return to query design screen]

Database name field | **Specify Update Operation** ↵ on **Update** menu: **Replace** ↵

Confirmation message: **Proceed**

Update field: **With** *<new text>* ↵

Query design menu bar: **Update**

Update menu: **Perform the Update** ↵

Keyboard: **F2** [to check results]

USAGE ═══════════════════

When performing an update query, you use the usual query design screen and filter conditions, as discussed in Chapter 5, "Searching a Database." When performing update queries, it's a good idea to enter your filter condition first and test it by pressing the **F2** (Data) key. Scroll through the browse screen and make sure that only the records you want to change are displayed. If the appropriate records are not displayed, be sure to adjust the filter condition accordingly.

You must specify an update operator in the file skeleton. You can either type the update operator directly beneath the file name in the skeleton or choose it by selecting **Specify Update Operation** from the **Update** pull-down menu. The **Replace** update operator replaces the contents of fields that meet the filter condition with some new value.

If you are replacing text in the same field as the filter condition, you must put the original text and the replacement text in the same field and type a comma before the **With** keyword.

Unlike other queries, where you press **F2** (Data) to see the results, update queries require you to select **Perform the Update** from the **Update** pull-down menu on the query design screen. You can save the query and exit from the **Exit** pull-down menu.

SEE ALSO

Chapter 5: Searching a Database

Adding and Editing Memo Fields

A memo field marker appears as a highlight with the word *memo* on the edit and browse screens. This marker reminds you that the field can actually contain a much larger memo. When the memo field contains information, the marker is shown in uppercase letters.

You must open the marker before you can enter and edit text in the memo by positioning the cursor in the field and pressing Ctrl-Home.

SEQUENCE OF STEPS

Browse or Edit Screen: Move cursor to Memo field

Press **Ctrl-Home**

After adding or editing: press **Ctrl-End.**

USAGE ======================

To open the memo marker, you can move the cursor to it and press **Ctrl-Home** or **F9** (Zoom). If the cursor is in the field directly above the memo field, pressing **F4** (Next) moves the cursor into the memo field, automatically preparing the screen for data to be added or modified. If the cursor is in the field beneath the memo field, pressing **F3** (Previous) automatically takes you to the memo-field editor.

The top of the editor screen displays a menu bar and a ruler. Within the ruler, the left bracket ([) shows the left margin, and the right bracket (]) shows the right margin. By default, the left margin is set at 0 and the right margin is set at 65; this is just about the right width for printing on 8 1/2-x-11-inch paper with proper margins. The triangles show tab stops, which are used for indenting and outdenting memo-field paragraphs.

The memo-field editor is virtually identical to the word-wrap editor discussed in Chapter 6. The basic editing keys (listed in Table 3.1) work in much the same manner in the word-wrap and memo-field editors as they do elsewhere. Note, however, the special features of the Tab and Shift-Tab keys in these editors.

Like a word processor, the memo-field editor automatically word wraps long sentences into paragraphs, so that if you change something in a paragraph, the entire paragraph is reformatted automatically. You need not enter ↵ at the end of a line, only at the end of a paragraph.

After you've finished entering or editing your memo field, you can save your work and return to the form or edit screen by selecting **Save Changes and Exit** from the **Exit** pull-down menu or by typing **Ctrl-End**.

SEE ALSO

Adding Fields and Text/Memo Fields (Chapter 7)

Deleting Records

There are two phases to deleting database records. The first is to *mark* a record for deletion. This does not actually remove the record from the database, but instead allows you to hide or temporarily delete the record. You can bring marked records out of hiding and unmark them at any time.

The second method for deleting records is often called *packing*. Packing a database permanently removes all records currently marked for deletion. Any records beneath a deleted one move up a notch to fill the void left by the deleted record (hence the term *packing*). There is no way to recover deleted records once you've packed the database.

Marking Records for Deletion

You can mark individual records for deletion using the edit or browse screen, or delete all the records that meet some condition using a database query.

Deleting Records One at a Time

First select the record to be marked on the edit or browse screen.

SEQUENCE OF STEPS

Edit screen | browse screen menu bar: **Records**
Records menu: **Mark Record for Deletion** ↵

or

Keyboard: **Ctrl-U**

USAGE ═══════════════════

First, use the usual arrow, **PgUp,** and **PgDn** keys to move the cursor to the record you want to mark. Then mark the record either by selecting **Mark Record for Deletion** from the **Records** pull-down menu or by pressing **Ctrl-U.** The only indication that the record has been marked is the word *Del* in the status bar at the bottom of the screen (see Figure 3.4).

Marking Groups of Records

dBASE's global editing capability enables you to quickly delete all records that meet a specified condition.

SEQUENCE OF STEPS ═══════════════

Control Center Queries panel: <**create**>

Query design screen: [filter field in file skeleton]

Filter field: <filter condition>

Keyboard: **F2** [to check selected records]

Keyboard: **Shift-F2** [to return to query design screen]

Records	Fields	Go To	Exit		2:21:22 pm

LASTNAME	FIRSTNAME	COMPANY	ADDRESS
Smith	John	ABC Co.	123 A St.
Adams	Annie		3456 Ocean St.
Watson	Wilbur	HiTech Co.	P.O. Box 987
Mahoney	Mary		211 Seahawk St.
Newell	John	LoTech Co.	734 Rainbow Dr.
Beach	Sandy	American Widget	11 Elm St.
Kenney	Ralph		1101 Rainbow Ct.
Schumack	Susita	SMS Software	47 Broad St.
Smith	Anita	Zeerocks, Inc.	2001 Engine Dr.
Jones	Fred	American Sneaker	P.O. Box 3381

Current record is
marked for deletion
↓

Browse	C:\dbase\CUSTLIST	Rec 3/10	File	Del

Figure 3.4: A record marked for deletion

Database name field | **Specify Update Operation** ↵ on **Update** menu: select **Mark** ↵

Confirmation message: **Proceed**

Query design menu bar: **Update**

Update menu: **Perform the Update** ↵

Keyboard: **F2** [to check results]

USAGE ══════════════════

To mark for deletion all records that meet some filter condition, enter the appropriate filter condition on the query design screen and test it. Then return to the query design screen. Enter the update operator **Mark** under the field name in the file skeleton or select **Mark Records for Deletion** from the **Specify Update Operation** menu. **Mark** deletes all records that meet the filter condition. Select **Perform the Update** from the **Update** pull-down menu and press **F2** to view the data. All the records will be marked for deletion (unless Deleted is On, in which case they will be hidden).

SEE ALSO ══════════════════

Chapter 5: Searching a Database

Hiding Deleted Records

You can hide marked records without permanently deleting them. At the Control Center, follow the steps described below.

SEQUENCE OF STEPS ══════════════════

Control Center menu bar: **Tools**

Tools menu: **Settings** ↵

Settings menu: **Deleted** [use **Space** bar | ⏎ to change option to **On**]

Tools Exit menu: **Exit to Control Center** ⏎

USAGE

Highlight **Tools** on the Control Center menu bar. Select **Settings.** Highlight the **Deleted** option and press the **Space** bar or ⏎ to change the option from Off to **On**. Then select **Exit to Control Center** from the **Exit** pull-down menu.

If you now view the records in your database, you'll see that the hidden records no longer appear, but that the records shown have not been renumbered. The hidden records still exist; they're just hidden for the time being.

To bring marked records out of hiding, return to the Control Center and follow the same steps that you followed to hide the records, but change the **Deleted** setting from On back to **Off**. The records will be displayed but still marked for deletion.

When the Deleted option is On, marked records are excluded from *all* dBASE operations, as though the records do not exist. Always remember to set Deleted to Off when you no longer need to hide marked records.

SEE ALSO

Customizing Your Environment/Environmental Settings (Chapter 11)

Unmarking Deleted Records

You can unmark records one at a time using either a menu option or the keyboard. You can unmark multiple records by using either a menu option or a database query.

Unmarking Records One at a Time

To remove the mark for deletion from a record, first make sure that the Deleted option is set to Off (otherwise, you won't be able to see the marked record that you are trying to unmark). Then move the cursor to the record that you want to unmark and use one of the following two techniques.

SEQUENCE OF STEPS ═══════════════

Edit | browse screen menu bar: **Records**

Records menu: **Clear Deletion Mark** ⏎

or

Keyboard: **Ctrl-U**

USAGE ═══════════════════════

Select the record for unmarking and then either select **Clear Deletion Mark** from the **Records** pull-down menu or press **Ctrl-U.**

The Clear Deletion Mark option appears on the Records pull-down menu *only* if the current record is already marked for deletion. Otherwise, the option reads Mark Record for Deletion.

Ctrl-U acts as a toggle. That is, each time you press it, the current record's status changes from marked to unmarked or vice-versa. You'll see the *Del* indicator in the status bar appear or disappear each time you press Ctrl-U.

Unmarking Multiple Records

You can unmark multiple records that meet some filter condition using a query, and unmark all the deleted records in a database by using either a query or a menu option.

SEQUENCE OF STEPS ══════════════

Control Center Queries panel: <**create**>

Query design screen: [filter field in file skeleton]

Filter field: <filter condition>

Keyboard: **F2** [to check selected records]

Keyboard: **Shift-F2** [to return to query design screen]

Database name field | **Specify Update Operation** ⅃ on **Update** menu: **Unmark**⅃

Confirmation message: **Proceed**

Query design menu bar: **Update**

Update menu: **Perform the Update** ⅃

Keyboard: **F2** [to check results]

or

Database design screen: **Organize**

Organize menu: **Unmark All Records** ⅃

USAGE ══════════════

To unmark records that meet some filter condition, use the **Unmark** operator in the file skeleton or choose it from the **Specify Update Operation** menu. Select **Perform the Update** from the **Update** pull-down menu.

To unmark all the records in a database, you can either use the **Unmark** operator in a query with no filter conditions or select **Unmark All Records in <filename>** from the **Organize** menu on the database design screen. If you use the latter method, the **Deleted** setting should be **Off.**

SEE ALSO ══════════════

Chapter 5: Searching a Database

Removing Deleted Records

Because packing the database permanently removes all marked records, use this option with caution. A good approach is to isolate all marked records and look at them on the browse screen before you pack the database.

Checking Deleted Records

Although it's not essential, it's a good idea to create a query that checks which records are marked for deletion.

SEQUENCE OF STEPS ================================

Control Center Queries panel: **<create>**

Queries design screen menu bar: **Condition**

Condition menu: **Add Condition Box** ⏎

Condition box: **DELETED()** ⏎

Keyboard: **F2** [to view results]

USAGE ==

To isolate the records that are marked for deletion, you use a query, but place the filter condition in the *condition box* rather than in a specific field. (The condition box is like any other box on the query design screen, except that it takes into consideration the record as a whole, rather than a specific field.) Then place the dBASE function **DELETED()** in the condition box. Press ⏎, then **F2** (Data) to see only records that are marked for deletion.

Use **Ctrl-U** or the **Clear Deletion Mark** option to unmark any records that you do not want permanently removed; *then* pack the database.

SEE ALSO

The Query Design Screen/The File Skeleton/The Condition Box (Chapter 5)

Packing the Database

To permanently erase all marked records from the database, you need to return to the database design screen and select Erase Marked Records.

SEQUENCE OF STEPS

Control Center Data panel: **Shift-F2**

Database design screen: **Organize**

Organize menu: **Erase Marked Records** ↵

Confirmation prompt: **Y**

Exit menu: **Save Changes and Exit** ↵ | **Ctrl-End**

USAGE

Highlight the database name in the Data panel and press **Shift-F2** (Design). Select **Erase Marked Records** from the **Organize** pull-down menu. When dBASE asks *Are you sure you want to erase all marked records?*, select **Yes.** When the job is complete, you'll see an indicator after the marked records that were erased. Select **Save Changes and Exit** or press **Ctrl-End** to return to the Control Center.

CHAPTER 4

Sorting a Database

Typically, you enter information into a database as it becomes available to you. Very often, you need to rearrange, or *sort*, that information into a more useful order, such as alphabetical order by name, or zip-code order for bulk mailing.

dBASE IV offers two ways to sort database files. By far the fastest and most efficient method is *indexing*. A second, slower, and less efficient way is making a *sorted copy* of a database file. This chapter discusses both methods.

Indexes

A dBASE IV index is a sorted list of items in a database file. The purpose of the index is twofold, and dBASE uses it in two different ways.

First, when you activate the index, dBASE automatically *displays* the records in the sort order specified by the index. Note that the actual records in the database are still in their original order; the index just "tells" dBASE the order in which to display information on the screen (or printer), but it does this so quickly that it *appears* as though the database has actually been sorted.

Second, dBASE can use the index to locate an item of information in the database quickly, just as you would use the index at the back of a book.

Creating an Index

You can create or modify an index from the database design screen at any time—it doesn't matter if the database contains no records or thousands of records. You can create up to 47 indexes for any given database. However, indexes do take up disk space and some time (for dBASE) to manage, so you should create indexes only on fields you use often for sorting or for certain types of searches.

Once you create an index for a particular sort order, you need not recreate it in the future. dBASE IV stores all the indexes for a given database in a file with the same name as the database, but with the extension .MDX. When you add, change, or delete database records, dBASE updates the indexes in the .MDX file automatically.

SEQUENCE OF STEPS ════════════════════

Database design screen menu bar: **Organize**

Organize menu: **Create New Index** ↵

Create New Index menu: **Name of Index** ↵

Name of Index option: *<index name>* ↵

Create New Index menu: **Index Expression** ↵

Index Expression option: *<index expression>* ↵

Create New Index menu: **Order of Index** ↵

Order of Index option: **Ascending** | **Descending**
[select with **Space** bar] ↵

Create New Index menu: **Display First Duplicate Key
Only** ↵

Display First Duplicate Key Only option: **Yes** | **No**
[select with **Space** bar] ↵

Keyboard: **Ctrl-End** [to save changes]

or

Database design screen: **Index column**

Index column: **Y**

USAGE

You begin creating an index by highlighting the database name in the Data panel of the Control Center and then pressing **Shift-F2** to invoke the database design screen. Select **Create New Index** from the **Organize** pull-down menu and press ↵ (see Figure 4.1). A submenu appears, asking for information about the index (see Figure 4.2).

Press ↵ to select **Name of Index**. Type the index name (also called the *tag*) and press ↵.

You can assign any name you wish to the index, following the same basic guidelines as for creating field names (the name can have up to 10 characters, must start with a letter, and contain no spaces or punctuation). But to help keep track of your indexes, it's best to use the field name itself as the index name.

Now select the **Index Expression** option. Type the *index expression* and press ↵. The index expression is a single field name for a simple index, but you cannot index on logical fields (unless they are converted with the IIF function) or memo fields.

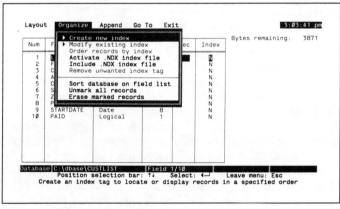

Figure 4.1: The Organize menu

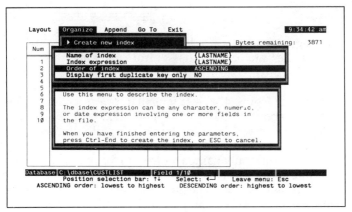

Figure 4.2: The Create New Index menu

Next select the **Order of Index** option. You can choose either **Ascending** or **Descending** by pressing the **Space** bar. Ascending orders items from lowest to highest (that is, A to Z, smallest number to largest number, or earliest date to latest date). Descending orders records in the opposite order.

One indexing feature that you may find useful is hiding duplicate records. For example, if you have an employee database you might want to send only one copy of a memo to a given department, even if several employees work in it. To ensure that the database displays only one record for each value (such as DEPARTMENT) in the index expression, set the **First Duplicate Key Only** option to **Yes.**

After you have filled out or accepted values for all the options on the Create New Index menu, press **Ctrl-End** to save your work. dBASE IV will create the index and show its progress on the screen briefly. When it is done, the database design screen reappears. Note that the option in the Index column for the indexed field is changed from N (for no) to Y (for yes).

You can also create an index while you are creating or modifying a database structure simply by changing the **Index** option in the rightmost column of the database design screen to **Y**. dBASE will assign the name of the field as the name of the index and actually create the index when you save the database structure.

Sorts within Sorts

Sometimes sorting a database on a single field is not sufficient. For example, in a large name-and-address database you might want to sort records into last-name order, then into first-name order within identical last names—a sort within a sort. To sort database records into this kind of order, you use an index expression that lists the fields to sort on, with the fields listed in priority order and a plus sign between each field name.

SEQUENCE OF STEPS

Organize pull-down menu: **Create New Index**

Create New Index menu: **Index Expression** ↵

Keyboard: **Shift-F1** [to bring up Expression Builder menu]

Expression Builder menu: [highlight Fieldname panel]

Fieldname panel: [highlight fieldname to index on] ↵

Expression Builder menu: [highlight Operator panel]

Operator panel: [highlight + operator] ↵

Keyboard: **Shift-F1** [to bring up Expression Builder menu]

Expression Builder menu: [highlight Fieldname panel]

Fieldname panel: [highlight fieldname to index on] ↵

Keyboard: **Ctrl-End** [to save changes]

USAGE

When you create an index for a sort within a sort, you follow the steps described in "Creating an Index" for naming the index, specifying its order, specifying an expression, and saving the index. However, the expression is slightly more complicated than for a simple index.

The first field in the expression is the primary sort field, the second is the secondary sort field, and so on. For example, to sort records by last name, then first name within last name, you might use the expression LASTNAME + FIRSTNAME. (You can only use the + operator to join fields of the character data type, but you can convert other types to character data, as described below in "Refining Sort Orders."

When you create an index expression, or for that matter any dBASE expression, you have the option of using the Expression Builder menu instead of typing in the expression (see Figure 4.3). This menu is most useful when you are creating an index expression that is more complex than a single field name. The Expression Builder has three columns from which you can select field names to index on, operators, and dBASE functions. Move the highlight to the appropriate panel and use **PgUp** and **PgDn** to scroll through the options. To select an option, highlight it using the arrow keys and press ⏎.

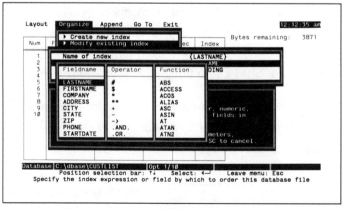

Figure 4.3: The Expression Builder menu

If you do enter a long index expression manually instead of using the Expression Builder, you may run out of typing room. Just press **F9** (Zoom) to produce an edit box.

Note that when a field name is part of an index expression, rather than the sole field for the index, the Index column on the database design screen does not mark the field as Y.

You view the sorted records the same way as for a simple index (see "Activating an Index").

SEE ALSO

The Database Design Screen/Data Types (Chapter 2)

Refining Sort Orders

Using dBASE *functions*, you can mix data types in sorts within sorts, mix ascending and descending sort orders, and sort by the results of calculations. There is also a function you can use to perform *dictionary sorts*.

A function is a predefined procedure that performs an immediate operation on one data item. All functions use the same syntax: a word or abbreviation followed by a pair of parentheses (for example, the DATE() function). Some dBASE functions require one or more *arguments*, data to operate on, which are enclosed in the parentheses. All functions *return* a value; for example, the DATE function returns the current date.

Mixing Data Types   Although you can use the + operator only to join fields of the character data type, you can use *conversion functions* to change date, numeric, and float data to character data. You enter a conversion function as part of the index expression, not in the actual database. Place the function before the name of the field to be converted and enclose the field name in parentheses. For example, to sort records in a database by last name and by date within each last name, you could use the index expression LASTNAME + DTOS(STARTDATE).

The DTOS() (date-to-string) function converts the date data type to the character data type, in the format *yyyymmdd* (for example, it converts 12/31/89 to 19891231).

The STR() function converts numeric and float data to character strings. Within the STR function, define the width and number of decimal places for the number. (If you do not define these, dBASE assumes a width of 10, with no decimal places.) Your best bet is to use the same width and number of decimal places defined in the database structure.

If you are combining dates and numbers in an index expression, convert both to the character data type. If you want to combine numbers to obtain a sort within a sort, convert both numeric fields to the character data type. Otherwise, the index will contain the sum of two numeric fields—that is, the result of a calculation—rather than a combination of the two fields.

Just as with numeric and date fields, you can index on a logical field by converting it to the character data type (that is, convert ".T." to "T" and ".F." to "F"). The function you use is IIF () (an abbreviation for immediate IF). This function makes a spur-of-the-moment decision about which of two alternative actions to take. The plain English syntax for this function is

IIF(*this-is-true,do-this,otherwise-do-this*)

The first argument must be either the name of a Logical field (which is always either true or false) or an expression with a true or false result. The other two arguments (both are required) can be any expression.

Here is an example that describes how to use IIF to index on logical fields. Suppose you have a customer database with the fields LASTNAME, FIRSTNAME, and the logical field PAID. You want to sort this database into customers who have paid and customers who have not, and then display the names in each group in alphabetical order. You would use the usual techniques to create an index, using the index expression

IIF(PAID,"T","F")+LASTNAME + FIRSTNAME.

After you select Order Records by Index to activate the new index and press **F2** (Data) to view your data, you'll see all customers who have not paid listed before all those who have paid (because the letter F is "less than" the letter T).

If you want to place the trues before the falses in the sort order, use a "lower" letter for the trues. For example, the index expression

IIF(Paid,"A","Z") + LASTNAME + FIRSTNAME

would place all those who have paid before those who have not. (Remember, though, that if you wanted to search the PAID field using an index search, you would need to search for the letter A to find a .T. value, and the letter Z to search for an .F. value.)

For more information, see Data Types (Chapter 2) and Chapter 8: Performing Calculations.

Mixing Ascending and Descending Orders   Whenever you create an index, dBASE gives you the opportunity to specify the entire sort in either ascending or descending order. In some situations, you might want to combine ascending and descending sort orders. For example, in a database containing records of parts ordered, you might want to display the records in ascending part-number order, but in descending quantity order within each part number.

To do this, you would index on the *inverse* of the second field (quantity) by subtracting each quantity from the largest possible quantity. For example, if the quantity field had a width of 3, with no decimal places, the largest possible number would be 999. Because the result has to be converted to character data, the appropriate index expression would be <*part_number_field*> + STR(999 −<*quantity_field*>,3). You would still use Ascending as the overall sort order, to make sure the part numbers are in ascending order.

An inverted numeric field is always displayed in the opposite order of the overall index. If the overall sort order for the example above were descending, the quantity field would be displayed in ascending order.

You can reverse the order of dates within an ascending index by subtracting each date from the latest possible date within the field. Again, you need to use the STR function to convert the numeric result of subtracting two dates to the character data type. Like an inverted numeric field, an inverted date field is displayed in the opposite order of the overall index.

There is no reliable technique for inverting character data. To display records in descending order in a character field, you must select Descending as the overall sort order for the index. But you can still invert a date or numeric field to present their sort orders in the opposite direction.

For more information, see Data Types (Chapter 2) and Chapter 8: Performing Calculations.

Sorting by the Results of Calculations   You can index on a calculated field, such as extended price. Using the example of a database of parts ordered, to display records in extended-price order from smallest to largest total sale, you would use the index expression *<quantity field>* * *<unit price field>* and specify ascending as the overall sort order. To display records in order from largest to smallest extended price, you would use the same index expression, but specify descending as the overall sort order. (To see the results of this index, you would need to use a query or report format that includes a calculated field to display the extended price.)

If you wanted to display records sorted by part number and by extended price within each part number, you would need to convert the results of the calculation to the character data type. To ensure an adequate width in the character field, use the sum of the two field widths within the STR function.

For more information, see Calculated Fields (Chapter 8).

Dictionary Sorts via Index   When you make a sorted copy of a database, you can use either ASCII or dictionary order (see "Making a Sorted Copy of a Database," below). Indexes use the ASCII method, in which all uppercase letters are considered to be "larger than" all lowercase letters.

To get around this limitation, you use the UPPER() function in the index expression to convert all values in a character field to uppercase. For example, you might use the expression UPPER(LASTNAME) or UPPER(LASTNAME + FIRSTNAME). Remember that only the index contains words converted to uppercase; the names in the actual database are still in their original format.

Activating an Index

After you create an index, you need to tell dBASE to use it, so that you can view database records in the sorted order.

SEQUENCE OF STEPS

Database design screen: **Organize**

Organize menu: **Order Records by Index** ↵

Index options menu: [highlight index name] ↵

Keyboard: **F2** [to view data in sorted order]

USAGE

From the database design screen, select the **Organize** pull-down menu. Highlight the **Order Records by Index** option; then press ↵. A submenu with a list of existing index options appears on the screen. Highlight the desired option and press ↵.

To view the data in sorted order, press **F2** (Data). The sort order is best viewed on the browse screen. If the edit screen appears instead, press **F2** to switch to the browse screen. If necessary, press **PgUp** to scroll to the first record.

SEE ALSO

Searching for Information/Index Searches (Chapter 5)

Modifying an Index

You can modify an index from the database design screen at any time you wish.

SEQUENCE OF STEPS

Database design screen menu bar: **Organize**
Organize menu: **Modify Existing Index** ↵
Index options menu: [highlight index name] ↵
Create New Index menu: [make changes]
Keyboard: **Ctrl-End** [to save changes]

USAGE

Pull down the **Organize** menu and select **Modify Existing Index.** From the list of options that appears, select the name of the index you want to modify. Now you have available the same menu of options as when you create a new index. Make your changes, then press **Ctrl-End** to save them.

Deleting an Index

As mentioned earlier, index management takes up some of dBASE's time. You can reduce the amount of time by removing indexes you don't need any more (and remember they're easy to recreate, if necessary).

SEQUENCE OF STEPS

Database design screen: **Organize**
Organize menu: **Remove Unwanted Index Tag** ↵
Index options menu: [highlight index name] ↵

USAGE

Pull down the **Organize** menu and select **Remove Un-wanted Index Tag.** Highlight the index tag (name) on the list that appears and press ↲.

Using Indexes from Earlier Versions of dBASE

Unlike dBASE IV, earlier versions of dBASE stored each index in a separate file, with the extension .NDX, which was not maintained automatically. You can use these earlier indexes with dBASE IV, but you can't use dBASE IV's .MDX index files with earlier versions of dBASE. If you are using dBASE IV databases with earlier software, you might want to maintain some old index files. You must update .NDX files manually, before you make any changes to the database.

SEQUENCE OF STEPS

Database design screen menu bar: **Organize**

Organize menu: **Activate .NDX Index File** ↲

Index options menu: [highlight index name] ↲

USAGE

From the **Organize** menu, select **Activate .NDX Index File.** dBASE will display a list of .NDX files that belong to the current database and are in the current catalog. Choose an index to activate and press ↲. Now the index will reflect any changes you make to the database.

You can add .NDX files from different catalogs to the list shown by Activate .NDX Index File. Select **Include .NDX Index File** from the **Organize** menu. dBASE displays a list of all the .NDX files for the current database that are in the current directory. Choose an index to include and press ↲. dBASE includes the index and activates it at the same time.

You can have a total of 10 .NDX and .MDX index files open at once.

Making a Sorted Copy of a Database

dBASE IV offers sorting as an alternative to indexing a database file to display data in sorted order. However, sorting is generally slower and less efficient than indexing.

When sorting, dBASE always makes a copy of the original database with a new file name that you provide. The original database remains unsorted, and the new database contains the same information in the sort order you specify.

SEQUENCE OF STEPS

Database design screen: **Organize**

Organize menu: **Sort Database on Field List** ↵

Keyboard: <*field name*> | **Shift-F1** [highlight field name] ↵

Field Order column: [highlight field name] ↵

Type of Sort column: **Ascending** | **Descending** | **Ascending Dictionary** | **Descending Dictionary** [highlight option with **Space** bar] ↵

Keyboard: **Ctrl-End** [to save changes]

File name prompt: <*file name*> ↵

USAGE

Press **Shift-F2** (Design) to display the database design screen. From the **Organize** pull-down menu, select **Sort Database on Field List**. Type in a field name or press **Shift-F1** to see a list of valid field names. Highlight the desired field name, press ↵ to select it, and then press ↵ a second time to complete the entry.

The cursor jumps to the **Type of Sort** column, where you can select from four different sorting techniques, listed in Table 4.1. Press the Space bar till the desired sort order appears; then press ↵.

Note that the basic difference between the dictionary technique and the ASCII technique is that ASCII considers uppercase letters "smaller than" lowercase letters and hence will place Zeppo before aardvark in an ascending sort.

ORDER	EXAMPLE SORT
Ascending ASCII (0..9, A..Z, a...)	123 999 Albert Zeppo van der Pool
Descending ASCII (z..a, Z..A, 9..0)	van der Pool Zeppo Albert 999 123
Ascending Dictionary (0..9, Aa..Zz)	123 999 Albert van der Pool Zeppo
Descending Dictionary (Zz..Aa, 9..0)	Zeppo van der Pool Albert 999 123

Table 4.1: Options for Sorting a Database

Both ASCII and dictionary sorts consider numeric characters to be "smaller than" alphabetic characters. Hence, if you sort a list of addresses in ascending order, all addresses beginning with numbers (for example, 123 A St. or 999 Z St.) will be listed before addresses beginning with letters (for example, P.O. Box 2802).

If you are sorting a character field that does not use consistent capitalization, you'll want to use the dictionary technique. If you are sorting any other data type, you can use the ASCII technique instead.

Once you choose a sort order, the highlight moves down to let you put more fields into the sort order. These are sortwithin-a-sort fields, as discussed under indexing.

When you are done adding fields to the sort list, press **Ctrl-End** to finish your work. When dBASE presents the prompt *Enter name of sorted file:* you can enter any valid file name (eight characters maximum length, with no spaces or punctuation). Then press ↵.

To view the data in the sorted database, you can't just press F2, because the sorted records are in the new database file. You must return to the Control Center and browse the new database.

As mentioned earlier, whenever you create an index, dBASE automatically manages it for you, updating it when you add, change, or delete information. This is not the case for sorted copies of files. Any changes you make to the old database have no effect on the new one (and vice versa). Because of this, it is not a good idea to keep sorted copies of database files because you might accidentally use the wrong file, and your work could quickly become confused.

CHAPTER 5

Searching a Database

Regardless of the contents or size of your database, dBASE can always help you find the information you need. In some cases, you may simply want to look up a piece of information, such as a person's address and phone number. In other cases, your search might be more complex, such as for "all customers who live on the West Coast, subscribed before January 1, and still have not paid." This chapter is a reference for the wide range of dBASE's search features.

Searching for Specific Records

Both the browse screen and the edit-screen menu bars include the Go To menu, which provides options for simple, basic searches (see Figure 5.1).

The first four options on the Go To menu (summarized in Table 5.1) let you position the edit- or browse-screen highlight on a particular record, based on the record's position in the database file. They are of limited value, because they assume you know the location of the record you want to access, and because they do little more than mimic the action of the navigation keys.

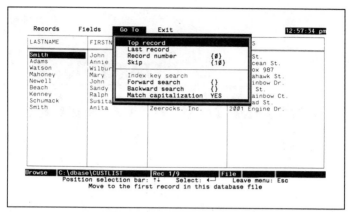

Figure 5.1: The Go To menu

COMMAND	ACTION	SEQUENCE OF STEPS
Top Record	Moves the edit screen or browse highlight to the first record in the database	Highlight **Top Record** Press ↵
Last Record	Moves the edit screen or browse highlight to the last record in the database	Highlight **Last Record** Press ↵
Record Number	Moves the edit screen or browse highlight to a particular record based on its position in the database	Highlight **Record Number** Press ↵ Type *<number>* Press ↵

Table 5.1: Simple Searches Using the Go To Menu

COMMAND	ACTION	SEQUENCE OF STEPS
Skip	Moves the edit screen or browse highlight a certain number of records from its current position. To move backward, use negative number	Highlight **Skip** Press ⏎ Type <*number*> Press ⏎

Table 5.1: Simple Searches Using the Go To Menu (continued)

Searching for Information

In most cases, you do not simply want to go to a particular record in a database. Instead, you want to find information, such as a person's address or phone number. The bottom half of the Go To menu displays options for locating information.

Forward and Backward Searches

The Forward Search option enables you to search forward in the database for specified information. The Backward Search option enables you to search backward. It can be handy for double-checking newly entered records.

SEQUENCE OF STEPS

Edit | browse screen: [highlight field to search on]

Edit | browse screen menu bar: **Go To**

Go To menu: **Forward Search** | **Backward Search** ⏎

Prompt message: <*search string*> ⏎

First bring up the browse or edit screen, get to the position in the database you want to search from (for example, select Top Record from the Go To menu to go to the beginning of the database), and move the highlight to the field you want to search.

Call up the **Go To** menu and select **Forward Search** (or **Backward Search**). When dBASE displays the prompt *Enter search string*, type the *string* (any text and/or numbers) you want to search for and press ↵.

Ordinarily, dBASE will search for information that exactly matches your request, without accounting for variations in capitalization or spelling. You can use the **Match Capitalization** option on the **Go To** menu to control case sensitivity.

Before selecting Forward Search or Backward Search, move the highlight to **Match Capitalization**. Press the **Space** bar to change the option setting from Yes to **No**. When the setting is Yes, a forward or backward search is case sensitive; the upper- and lowercase letters in the search string must match those in the database. When the setting is No, upper- and lowercase designations do not matter.

You can use wildcard characters to locate items that match a pattern rather than an exact value. Use the wildcard character ? to match a single character, and the wildcard character * to match any group of characters.

dBASE highlights (or brings up on the edit screen) the first record that matches your search requirement. It also records the string you searched for as the current default for both **Forward Search** and **Backward Search**. You can then use **Shift-F4** (Find Next) or **Shift-F3** (Find Previous) to search forward or backward for other matching records.

If no match is found, dBASE displays the message ***Not Found*** and waits for you to press any key to resume your work. After this message is displayed, dBASE may erase the value specified for Forward Search and Backward Search. Before using the Find Next and Find Previous keys again, look at the Go To pull-down menu to see if any string is specified.

Index Searches

When you work with large databases, you may find the Forward Search and Backward Search options to be quite slow. As an alternative, you can use the Index Key Search option on the Go To pull-down menu. This option searches the database index, not the database file, and can usually find information in any size database in less than a second.

There are two stages of an index key search. First, using the database design screen, you activate the index that contains the field you want to search. Then, using the browse or edit screen, you perform the search.

SEQUENCE OF STEPS

Database Design screen: **Organize**

Organize menu: **Order Records by Index** ↵

Index options menu: *<index name>* ↵

Keyboard: **F2** [to display the edit or browse screen]

Edit | browse screen menu bar: **Go To**

Go To menu: **Index Key Search** ↵

Prompt message: *<search string>* ↵

USAGE

Highlight the database name in the Data panel of the Control Center and press **Shift-F2** (Design). From the **Organize** pull-down menu, select **Order Records by Index**. From the submenu, select the desired index. The field you search must be either the sole field indexed on, or the first field in the index expression. (If an appropriate index does not exist, you can, of course, create one.)

Now that the index is activated, you can go straight to the browse or edit screen to conduct your search. To do so, press **F2** (Data).

Move to the **Go To** menu option. Select **Index Key Search;** dBASE presents the prompt *Enter search string for <field name>*. This is the expression for the current index; dBASE displays this to tell you what field you currently can search.

Type the value to search on (using the correct upper- and lowercase letters) and press ↵. dBASE will immediately locate and display the first record that matches your search string. You *cannot* use the Find Next or Find Previous key with an index search to find more records that contain the same string. However, because the records are presented in alphabetical order, you can use ↓ and ↑ (on the browse screen) or **PgDn** and **PgUp** (on the edit screen) to scroll through them.

Although index key searches are very fast, they are not as flexible as the forward and backward searches. First, an index search works only when upper- and lowercase letters match exactly, even when the Match Capitalization option is off. Second, you cannot use wildcard characters with index searches. (However, because dBASE looks for a match between the search value and the leftmost characters in the database field, you can scroll through records containing strings similar to your search string.)

Third, if you used any functions in creating the index, you must use these same functions in your search string. For example, suppose you used the index expression STR({12/31/1999} – DATE) + PARTNO to organize records into descending date order and ascending part-number order within each date. If you want to search this index for a particular date, you must convert that date the same way you converted the dates in the index. That is, to search for the first record with 06/01/89 in the field, you would need to enter STR({12/31/1999} – {06/01/89}) as the Index Key Search value.

| SEE ALSO | |

Creating an Index (Chapter 4)

Isolating or Filtering Records

In some situations, you may want to *isolate* or *filter* some type of information. For example, if you want to send a form letter to all California residents in your customer database, you will want to isolate records that have CA in the state field, filtering out all other records. You can use filtered databases to print mailing labels and form letters, perform calculations, make copies of database files, simplify editing, and facilitate other tasks. These kinds of searches are called *queries*, because you query (ask) dBASE for some information, and dBASE answers by displaying only records that meet your requirements. Queries are not handled through the Go To pull-down menu. Instead, they are handled via the *query design screen*.

The technique that you use to construct queries is called *query by example*, often abbreviated as QBE. dBASE IV presents a skeleton of the database file in use, and you give examples of the kinds of information you want dBASE to display.

The Query Design Screen

Before you can query a database, you must make sure that the database file is open at the moment. Then you need to get to the query design screen. To do so, follow the steps below.

| SEQUENCE OF STEPS | |

Control Center Queries panel: **<create>** ↵

or

Edit | browse screen menu bar: **Transfer to Query Design** option on **Exit** menu

---

USAGE

To design a query for the currently open database, use the arrow keys to highlight **<create>** in the Queries panel and press ⏎. After you've viewed or worked with the results of a query, you can return to the query design screen by selecting **Transfer to Query Design** from the **Exit** pull-down menu.

The query design screen (or *surface,* as it is sometimes called) is shown in Figure 5.2. Like other dBASE work areas, the query design screen includes a menu bar at the top of the screen and a status bar and navigation line at the bottom. The menu bar contains the Layout, Fields, Condition, Update, and Exit menus.

The query screen also includes a *file skeleton* and a *view skeleton.* The file skeleton displays the names of all fields in your database; you will use it to specify search criteria. The view skeleton shows the names of the fields that your query will display. If you create calculated fields for the current view, these are shown in a *calculated field skeleton.* The query design screen may also contain an optional *condition box.* The

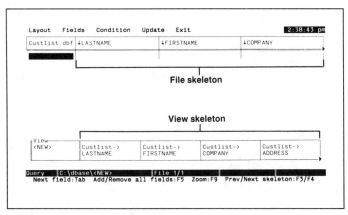

Figure 5.2: The query design screen

following sections show how to use these screen components to design queries.

SEE ALSO ═══════════════════

Using Queries to Perform Calculations (Chapter 8)

The File Skeleton

The file skeleton is near the top of the screen. In the leftmost column is the name of the database file that the skeleton represents. Each field name in the database is listed in boxes to the right of the database name. You can use the Home, End, Tab, and Shift-Tab keys to scroll left and right through these field names and to view those that are off the right edge of the screen (see Table 5.2).

Although the query design screen initially contains only one file skeleton, you can add as many as seven more, enabling you to construct complex queries involving several databases. To add more file skeletons, go to the Layout menu and select Add File to Query, then choose a database name from the list that appears.

SEQUENCE OF STEPS ═══════════════

Query design screen file skeleton: [highlight field]

Field box: <*filter condition*> ↵

Keyboard: **F2** [to view query results]

USAGE ═══════════════════════

To specify the records you want a query to display, you enter *filter conditions* in the file skeleton. You put the filter condition under the appropriate box and then press **F2** (Data) to see the results. If the edit screen appears after you press F2, press **F2** again to switch to the browse screen.

KEY	EFFECT
→	Moves cursor one character to the right in the file or view skeleton
←	Moves cursor one character to the left in the file or view skeleton
Tab	Moves cursor one field to the right in the file or view skeleton
Shift-Tab	Moves cursor one field to the left in the file or view skeleton
Home	Moves cursor to the first field in the file or view skeleton
End	Moves cursor to the last field in the file or view skeleton
F6	Highlights a group of adjacent fields in the view skeleton
Enter	Completes an entry in the file or view skeleton
↓	Moves highlight down one row in the file skeleton
↑	Moves highlight up one row in the file skeleton
Ctrl-N	Inserts a blank row between two existing rows in the file skeleton
Ctrl-PgDn	Moves to the bottom of the file skeleton column
Ctrl-PgUp	Moves to the top of the file skeleton column
PgDn	Moves to the next page of file skeletons

Table 5.2: Keys Used to Design a Database Query

KEY	EFFECT
PgUp	Moves to the previous page of file skeletons
F9	Expands and shrinks skeleton columns and condition boxes
Del	Deletes the character the cursor is on, in the file or view skeleton
Backspace	Moves cursor one space back, erasing along the way, in the file or view skeleton
Ctrl-U	Deletes the entire current row in the file skeleton or condition box
Ctrl-Y	Deletes the entire current row in the view skeleton
F5	Deletes or reinserts all fields in the view skeleton
F7	Moves selected text to a new location in the view skeleton
F4	Moves forward to the next skeleton
F3	Moves back to the previous skeleton
Ctrl-End	Saves changes and exits the query design screen
Ctrl-W	Has the same effect as Ctrl-End
Esc	Exits without saving changes and returns to the previously used screen
Shift-F2	Brings up a query design screen for the selected database

Table 5.2: Keys Used to Design a Database Query (continued)

You can remove filter conditions using the file skeleton's navigation and editing keys. Note that if you forget to remove the previous filter condition from the query design screen before entering a new one, the old filter condition will affect the new query.

The Condition Box

The condition box is an optional area you can call up for entering a filter condition that applies to the whole query. The condition box is required for querying memo fields. Each line in the condition box must be a valid dBASE expression. You can use only one condition box per query.

SEQUENCE OF STEPS

Query design screen menu bar: **Condition**

Condition menu: **Add Condition Box** ↵

Condition box: <*filter condition*> ↵

USAGE

Highlight the **Condition** option on the menu bar, highlight **Add Condition Box**, and press ↵. The condition box will appear in the lower-right area of the screen. You then type in your filter condition(s). You must name each field you want to filter and spell out any AND and OR operators, using .AND. and .OR.. You may find the Expression Builder helpful when you use the condition box (press Shift-F1 to bring it up).

Figure 5.3 shows a sample condition box containing a filter condition to isolate records that have the words *dBASE IV* in a Memo field named Abstract.

If you need more room to work with the condition box, you can use **F9** (Zoom) to expand the box to screen size. You can display or hide the condition box using the **Show Condition Box** option on the **Condition** menu. A hidden box shrinks to a small marker that you can expand by pressing **F3, F4, F9**, or selecting **Show Condition Box** again.

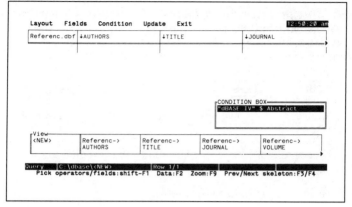

Figure 5.3: The condition box

When you are done working with the condition box you can delete it using **Delete Condition Box** on the **Condition** menu.

SEE ALSO

Entering Filter Conditions in Dialog Boxes (Chapter 12)

The View Skeleton

The view skeleton, near the bottom of the screen, shows the names of the fields that will be displayed by the query. You can move to the view skeleton by pressing F4 and move back to the file skeleton by pressing F3. Note the changes in the navigation key options at the bottom of the screen.

The file skeleton and the view skeleton work somewhat independently of one another in that you can place a filter condition in any field in the file skeleton, regardless of whether the view skeleton includes that field. Initially, the query feature assumes that you want to display all fields, so all fields are included in the view skeleton.

Adding and Removing Fields There are several techniques you can use to move fields into and out of the view
skeleton.

SEQUENCE OF STEPS

To delete all database fields from the view skeleton or restore
them

File skeleton: [highlight file name] **F5** [toggles addi-
tion/deletion of all fields]

To add a single field to the view skeleton

File skeleton: [highlight field name] **F5** | **Fields** menu
option **Add Field to View** ↵

To delete a single field from the view skeleton

File | view skeleton: [highlight field name] **F5** | **Fields**
menu option **Remove Field from View** ↵

USAGE

You can remove all the field names or put them back in by
positioning the highlight beneath the file name in the file
skeleton and pressing **F5** (Field). (This key acts as a toggle.)
You can also add a field to the view skeleton by highlighting
it in the file skeleton, then either pressing **F5** or selecting
Add Field to View from the **Fields** pull-down menu.

   You can work directly with the view skeleton by pressing
F4 (Next). Once you highlight a field in the view skeleton
you can edit it using the keys described in Table 5.2. You can
also delete a field by highlighting it in either the file or view
skeleton, then pressing **F5** or selecting **Remove Field from
View** from the **Fields** menu.

Moving Fields You can move fields in the view skeleton,
rearranging the order in which they are displayed.

SEQUENCE OF STEPS

View skeleton: [highlight field to move] **F7**

View skeleton: [highlight new position] ↵

USAGE

First make sure that the highlight is in the view skeleton. Then use the **Tab** or **Shift-Tab** key to highlight the field that you want to move. Finally, press **F7** (Move).

dBASE will highlight the frame around the field and present the instructions *TAB or BACKTAB to move fields. <Return> to end.* This means that dBASE wants you to use the **Tab** or **Shift-Tab** key to move the highlighted box to the new location for the field. When the field is in its new location, press ↵.

Working with Groups of Fields While at the view skeleton, you can use the Select key (F6) to highlight a group of adjacent fields to work with.

SEQUENCE OF STEPS

View skeleton: [highlight leftmost | rightmost field] **F6**

Leftmost | rightmost field: [extend highlight] ↵

USAGE

To use Select (F6), move the highlight to the leftmost or rightmost field in the group you want to select. Press **F6**, and then press **Tab** or **Shift-Tab** to extend the highlight to the right or left respectively, as instructed on the screen (but don't highlight all the fields, or you won't be able to move them). Press ↵ after highlighting a group of fields.

Once you have highlighted a group of fields, pressing **F5** removes the entire group from the view; pressing **F7** allows you to move that group to a new location. After you complete your job, the highlighting disappears.

Searching for a Value

You need to use different syntaxes for querying number/float, character, date, logical, and memo fields. The steps for entering each kind of data in the file skeleton are shown below.

SEQUENCE OF STEPS

To query a number, character, date, or logical field

Query design screen file skeleton: [highlight field]

Field box: *<number field>* |*"<character field>"* | {*<date field>*} | .*<logical field>*. ⏎

Keyboard: **F2** [to view query results]

To query a memo field

Query design screen menu bar: **Condition**

Condition menu: **Add Condition Box** ⏎

Condition box: *<string>* $ *<memo field name>*⏎

Keyboard: **F2** [to view query results]

USAGE

You must put quotation marks around the filter condition in a character field search. If you forget to do this, dBASE will still accept the value and execute the query. However, the results of the query will probably be inaccurate.

When querying a field of the date data type, you must enclose the date you are searching for in curly braces. For example, you might search for a STARTDATE value of {12/15/89}.

When you query a field the logical data type, you must enclose the logical operator in periods so that dBASE can distinguish it from regular characters. In Logical fields you can use .T., .t., .Y., or .y. for true, and .F., .f., .N., or .n. for false—where Y and N stand for yes and no. Numeric and float fields do not require delimiters.

Memo fields must be searched via a condition box and typically use the $ operator. The value being searched for must be enclosed in quotation marks. For example, to search a Memo field named Abstract for the words *dBASE IV*, the condition box would contain the filter expression **"dBASE IV" $ Abstract** as shown in Figure 5.3.

SEE ALSO ════════════════════════════

The Database Design Screen/Data Types (Chapter 2)

Searching with Relational Operators

dBASE IV includes many *relational operators* that you can use to refine your queries (see Table 5.3). If you don't use an operator, equals (=) is assumed. That is, putting "CA" in the STATE field tells dBASE that you want to see records where STATE equals "CA."

You can use the =, >, <, >=, <=, <>, and # operators with the numeric, float, date, and character data types. For example, the query condition <= {12/31/89} will display records that contain dates that are less (earlier) than or equal to December 31, 1989. The query condition >= "M" will display records in a character field that begin with the letters M through Z. The query condition >0 displays records in a numeric (or float) field with values that are greater than zero.

The $ operator can be used only with the character and memo field data types. The Like and Sounds Like operators can be used only with the character data type.

To use an operator in a query, precede the value that you are searching for with the appropriate operator.

OPERATOR	MEANING
=	Equals
>	Greater than
<	Less than
>=	Greater than or equal to
<=	Less than or equal to
<> or #	Not equal to
$	Contains
Like	Pattern match using wildcard characters
Sounds like	Soundex search for words that sound alike

Table 5.3: The dBASE IV Relational Operators

SEQUENCE OF STEPS

Query design screen file skeleton: [highlight field]

Field box: *<operator> <value>* ⏎

Keyboard: **F2** [to view query results]

USAGE

In the field box in the file skeleton, type a filter condition composed of the operator and the value in that order. The value must have the appropriate syntax. For example, you might search only for records with last names beginning with the letters A through M by placing the filter condition <= "N" in the LASTNAME field.

While building a query, you can select operators from the Expression Builder by pressing **Shift-F1**. Move the highlight to the Operator panel and use **PgUp** and **PgDn** to scroll through the operators. To select an operator, highlight it using the arrow keys and press ↵.

Searching for Similar Spellings

The Sounds Like operator uses a technique called *soundex* to locate words that sound alike, regardless of their spelling. For example, you might want to use this operator when trying to locate a last name that could be Kinny or Kenney.

SEQUENCE OF STEPS

Query design screen file skeleton: [highlight field]

Field box: **Sounds like** "*<text>*" ↵

Keyboard: **F2** [to view query results]

USAGE

In the field box, enter the filter condition **Sounds Like** "*<text>*" and then press ↵. You must use quotation marks. Press **F2** (Data) to execute the query.

Pattern-Matching Searches

You can use the wildcard characters ? (to stand for any single character) and * (to stand for a group of characters) with queries, provided you use the Like operator first.

SEQUENCE OF STEPS

Query design screen file skeleton: [highlight field]

Field box: **Like** *<data including wild card>* ↵

Keyboard: **F2** [to view query results]

In the field box, place the filter condition **Like**, followed by the data to search for, including appropriate wild cards. For example, you could search for all zip codes that begin with 92 with the filter condition Like "92*" (assuming that zip codes are stored as the character data type). Press **F2** (Data) to see the results of the query.

Searching for Embedded Text

You can use the $ operator to search for text embedded within a character or memo field.

Query design screen file skeleton: [highlight field]
Field box: **$** "*<text>*" ↵
Keyboard: **F2** [to view query results]

In the field box, place the filter condition **$**, followed by the character string to search for. For example, you could search for all records that contain the word Rainbow in the street address by typing $ "Rainbow." Press **F2** (Data) to see the results of the query.

The $ operator is especially useful for isolating records that have a particular word or group of words in a memo field. Remember that you must use a condition box to query memo fields (see Figure 5.3).

Creating Memo-Field Windows (Chapter 7)

Searching for Exceptions

You can use the # or <> operator interchangably to execute a query that shows all records *except* those that meet some condition.

SEQUENCE OF STEPS

Query design screen file skeleton: [highlight field]

Field box: **#** | **<>** *<data>* ↵

Keyboard: **F2** [to view query results]

USAGE

In the field box, place the filter condition # or <>, followed by the data to search for. For example, you could search for all records except those with CA in the STATE field with the filter condition # "CA". Press **F2** (Data) to see the results of the query.

Searching Multiple Fields

As you develop larger databases, you may want to use more sophisticated queries. For example, you might want to ask dBASE to display records for customers who live in California *and* began subscribing in 1988 *and* have not yet paid. You might also want to create a query that says "Show me all the customers that live in Washington *or* Oregon *or* California."

You can create such complex queries using AND logic, OR logic, and combined AND and OR logic. dBASE imposes no limitations on the complexity of your queries, as long as they make sense.

AND Logic

There is a simple rule of thumb for creating AND queries: You put all of the filter conditions for the query on the same row in the query design screen. For example, to search for

Anita Smith you would put "Smith" in the LASTNAME field and "Anita" in the FIRSTNAME field (see Figure 5.4).

SEQUENCE OF STEPS

Query design screen file skeleton: [highlight field]

Field box: *<condition>* ⏎

Query design screen file skeleton: [highlight next field]

Field box: *<next condition>* ⏎

.

.

.

Query design screen file skeleton: [highlight last field]

Field box: *<last condition>* ⏎

Keyboard: **F2** [to view query results]

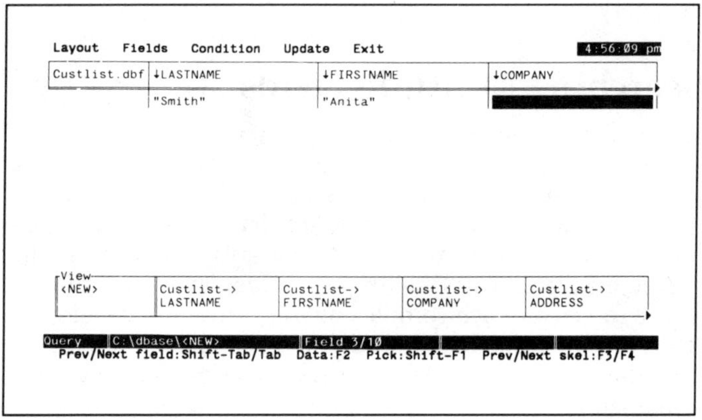

Figure 5.4: A query using AND logic

USAGE

Move through the file skeleton, highlighting the fields to search and entering the appropriate filter conditions. You use the same syntax for searching character, date, and logic fields as for a simple query. Likewise, you can use the relational operators the same way you'd use them in a simple query. Check the filter conditions to make sure they are all entered correctly and press **F2** to view your data.

Range Searches   You often need to search for data that falls within some range of values, such as zip codes in the range 92000 to 92555 or names in the alphabetical range A through J. Range searches can be particularly useful in numeric fields.

SEQUENCE OF STEPS

Query design screen file skeleton: [highlight field]

Field box: **>=** <*low value*>,**<=** <*high value*>⏎

Keyboard: **F2** [to view query results]

USAGE

To perform a range search, use an AND query within a single field. Use the >= operator before the low end of the range and the <= operator before the high end of the range; separate the two with a comma. For example, the filter condition >="A",<="J" translates, in English, to "greater than or equal to A AND less than or equal to J"—in other words, "between A and J."

SEE ALSO

Chapter 8: Performing Calculations

OR Logic

To design an OR query, you need to stagger the values that
you are searching for on separate rows within the query
design screen (see Figure 5.5). You may search for different
values in the same field (for example, records that have *either*
CA or WA in the STATE field) or different values in multiple
fields (for example, records that have an area code of 717 in
the PHONE field *or* CA in the STATE field). You use the same
field syntax and relational operators as for a simple query.

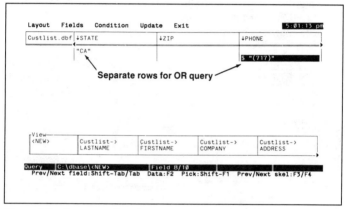

Figure 5.5: A query using OR logic

SEQUENCE OF STEPS

First row in file skeleton: [highlight field]
Field box: *<condition>* ↓
Next row in file skeleton: [highlight next field]
Field box: *<next condition>* ↓
.
.
.

Last row in file skeleton: [highlight last field]

Field box: *<last condition>* ↵

Keyboard: **F2** [to view query results]

USAGE

Initially, dBASE IV displays only a single row for entering information into a query form. However, you can easily create as many more rows as you wish by pressing ↓. (You can move back to previous rows to edit or delete them by pressing ↑.) Press **F2** (Data) to view your data.

Combining AND and OR Logic

You may sometimes need to combine AND and OR logic in a dBASE IV query. To state such a query correctly, you need to repeat the AND information for each OR condition (see Figure 5.6).

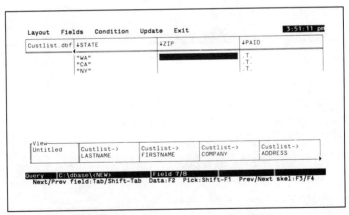

Figure 5.6: A query that combines AND and OR logic

First row in file skeleton: [highlight OR field]
Field box: *<first OR condition>*
First row in file skeleton: [highlight AND field]
Field box: *<AND condition>* ↓
Next row in file skeleton: [highlight next OR field]
Field box: *<next OR condition>*
Next row in file skeleton: [highlight AND field]
Field box: *<AND condition>* ↓

.

.

.

Last row in file skeleton: [highlight last OR field]
Field box: *<last OR condition>*
Last row in file skeleton: [highlight AND field]
Field box: *<AND condition>* ↵
Keyboard: **F2** [to view query results]

or

File skeleton: [enter all OR conditions]
Query design screen menu bar: **Condition**
Condition menu: **Add Condition Box** ↵
Condition box: *<and condition>* ↵
Keyboard: **F2** [to view query results]

Suppose you want to see records for all the customers in the states of California, New York, and Washington who have paid. You cannot simply enter a .T. AND condition for the first OR condition ("CA"), because this query will locate not only all customers in California who have paid, but *all* customers in Washington and New York, regardless of whether they have paid. To locate the correct records, you must enter three separate "AND" queries, each which specifies a State to search for and a value in Paid to search for (as in Figure 5.6).

If you find AND and OR combinations confusing, remember that dBASE considers each row in the query design screen to be a separate "question", and only records that meet the requirements of any one of those questions will be included in the results of the query. Hence, the query in Figure 5.6 asks these three questions of each record in the database file, and displays only records that can answer "Yes" to one of these questions:

Does this record have CA in STATE and .T. in PAID?

Does this record have WA in STATE and .T. in PAID?

Does this record have NY in STATE and .T. in PAID?

Omitting Duplicate Records

The query design screen provides a way to filter out identical records in a view. This feature is useful for such purposes as bulk mailing—you probably want to avoid the expense of sending duplicate mail to the same person or company.

SEQUENCE OF STEPS

Query design screen file skeleton: [enter filter conditions]

Database file name: **Unique** ⏎

Keyboard: **F2** [to view query results]

USAGE

To use a query to omit duplicate records, you enter the filter conditions in the query as usual. Then you enter the word

Unique beneath the database file name in the file skeleton (or one of them, if you are using multiple databases). When you press **F2** (Data) to execute the query, only one of several duplicate records will be displayed.

SEE ALSO

Chapter 9: Managing Related Database Files

Finding a Record

You can use a query simply to *find* a particular record in the database, without filtering out any other records. It's a valuable alternative to the Forward Search option on the Go To menu, because it allows you to search multiple fields, using all of the capabilities of the query design screen.

SEQUENCE OF STEPS

Query design screen file skeleton: [enter filter conditions]

Database file name: **Find** ↵

Keyboard: **F2** [to view query results]

USAGE

To use a query to locate a particular record, you enter the filter conditions in the query, as usual. Then you enter the word **Find** beneath the database file name in the file skeleton. When you press **F2** (Data) to execute the query, the highlight will be positioned on the first record that meets the filter conditions. All other database records are still accessible, with the usual arrow, PgUp and PgDn keys.

Sorting Query Displays

There may be times when you want the results of your queries to be sorted. For example, you might want to send form letters to California residents and to print them in zip-code order for bulk mailing. Hence, you need a *query* to isolate records with CA in the state field and a *sort order* to arrange the records into zip code order.

SEQUENCE OF STEPS

Query design screen: [highlight field to sort on]

Query design screen menu bar: **Fields**

Fields menu: **Sort on This Field** ↵

Sorting options menu: **Ascending ASCII | Descending ASCII | Ascending Dictionary | Descending Dictionary** ↵

Query design screen: [enter filter conditions]

Keyboard: **F2** [to view query results]

USAGE

If the filter conditions are not entered in a field to be sorted on, they may be entered either before or after choosing a sort field and sort order. To sort the results of a query, use the **Sort This Field** option from the **Fields** pull-down menu on the query design screen. A submenu of sorting options will appear. Select one. dBASE inserts a label in the sort field, such as *AscDict1*, to indicate the sort type and sort order. Press **F2** (Data) to execute the query.

A query sort actually creates a separate, sorted database file, which can be seen on the browse (or edit) screen when you press F2. This is a *read-only* file, as indicated by the message in the status bar. If you attempt to change the data in this file, dBASE will beep and reject your keystrokes. This protects you from inadvertently making changes on the sorted copy of the database, rather than on the original database.

SEE ALSO

Chapter 4: Sorting a Database

Sorting Multiple Fields

You can perform sorts within sorts in a query form simply by selecting fields to sort on in most-important to least-important order. For example, if you wanted to sort the results of a query alphabetically by last name and then by first name within last names, you would move the highlight to the LASTNAME field, select Sort This Field, move the highlight to the FIRSTNAME field, and select Sort This Field again. The sorted result is the same as when you use LASTNAME + FIRSTNAME in an index.

SEQUENCE OF STEPS

Query design screen: [highlight first field to sort on]

Query design screen menu bar: **Fields**

Fields menu: **Sort on This Field** ⏎

Sorting options menu: **Ascending ASCII | Descending ASCII | Ascending Dictionary | Descending Dictionary** ⏎

Query design screen: [highlight second field to sort on]

Query design screen menu bar: **Fields**

Fields menu: **Sort on This Field** ⏎

Sorting options menu: **Ascending ASCII | Descending ASCII | Ascending Dictionary | Descending Dictionary** ⏎

Query design screen: [enter filter conditions]

Keyboard: **F2** [to view query results]

USAGE

dBASE indicates the field's position in the sort order with a number. For example, your primary sort might be labeled *AscDict1*, and your secondary sort might be labeled *Asc-Dict2*. dBASE continues to add 1 to the symbol each time you select **Sort on This Field** from the **Fields** menu, as long as you are still in the same query session. (A query session ends when you exit the query design screen and return to the Control Center.)

SEE ALSO

Creating an Index/Sorts Within Sorts (Chapter 4)

Combining Filter and Sort Conditions

Any field on the query design screen can contain both a filter condition and a sort condition.

SEQUENCE OF STEPS

Query design screen: [enter filter conditions]

Query design screen: [highlight field to sort on]

Query design screen menu bar: **Fields**

Fields menu: **Sort on This Field** ↵

Sorting options menu: **Ascending ASCII | Descending ASCII | Ascending Dictionary | Descending Dictionary** ↵

Keyboard: **F2** [to view query results]

USAGE

First put in all of your filter conditions; then select fields to sort on. dBASE will automatically place the sort condition, preceded by a comma, after the filter condition (see Figure 5.7).

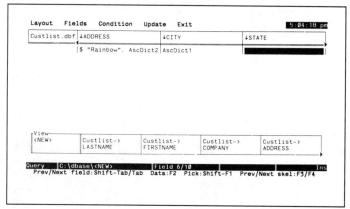

Figure 5.7: Combined filter and sort conditions

Using Indexes to Sort Query Results

When you work with large databases, you may find using an index to sort query results to be quicker than using the sorting method described above. You'll also be able to make changes in the resulting browse (or edit) screen.

SEQUENCE OF STEPS

Query design screen menu bar: **Fields**

Fields menu: **Include Indexes** ⏎

Query design screen: [enter filter conditions]

Query design screen: [highlight indexed field to be sorted on]

Query design screen menu bar: **Fields**

Fields menu: **Sort on This Field** ⏎

Sorting options menu: **Ascending ASCII** | **Descending ASCII** | **Ascending Dictionary** | **Descending Dictionary** ⏎

Keyboard: **F2** [to view query results]

USAGE ═══════════════════

These instructions assume you have already created the index to include in your query. You can use either a simple or a complex index.

Bring up the **Fields** menu and select the **Include Indexes** option (at first, nothing appears to happen). Enter your filter conditions. Now highlight the indexed field to be sorted on. Notice that a pound sign (**#**) appears next to the field name to indicate that this is an index field.

Select **Sort on This Field** from the **Fields** pull-down menu. Then select a sort order from the submenu. The sort operator appears in the sorted field. Although this is the same sort operator you would use if no index file were involved, dBASE automatically uses the index to speed the sort because it now "knows" that this is an index field.

SEE ALSO ═══════════════════

Creating an Index, Activating an Index (Chapter 4)

Saving a Query for Future Use

You can save any query that you create, then reuse it at any time without reentering all the keystrokes for filter conditions and so forth.

SEQUENCE OF STEPS

Query design screen: [create query]

Keyboard: **F2** [to test query]

Query design screen menu bar: **Layout**

Layout menu: **Edit Description of Query** ⏎

Prompt box: *<query description>* ⏎

Query design screen menu bar: **Layout | Exit**

Layout | Exit menu: **Save This Query | Save Changes and Exit** ⏎

Prompt box: *<query file name>* ⏎

USAGE

At the query design screen, compose your query as usual. Press **F2** (Data) to make sure the query works correctly. Now go back to the query design screen.

First you provide a description for the query, then save it as a DOS file. To provide the description, highlight the **Layout** option in the menu bar and select **Edit Description of Query**. When prompted, type a description, such as California phone numbers. Press ⏎.

To save the query and its description, select **Save This Query** from the **Layout** menu or **Save Changes and Exit** from the **Exit** menu. When dBASE displays the prompt *Save as:* enter a valid DOS file name and press ⏎. The file name must be eight letters maximum and contain no spaces or punctuation. dBASE will automatically add the extension .QBE to the file name you provide.

In dBASE IV, a saved query is also referred to as a *view*. This is because a query provides a particular way of viewing the data in a database. Unlike a database file, a query does not actually contain data. Instead, it contains instructions that dBASE IV reads to see how you want to view the data in a database. Therefore, any changes you make to the original database will be reflected in the view. Incidentally, views are a two-way street; if you change any data displayed by the view, that change actually occurs in the database.

Activating a Saved Query

When you activate a saved query, you can either use it immediately to view data in the selected database or simply make it active.

SEQUENCE OF STEPS

Control Center Queries panel: [highlight query name] **F2**

USAGE

To view database data through a saved query, highlight the name of the query in the Queries panel and press **F2** (Data). Or, if Instruct mode is on, highlight the name and press ↵. If the query is not already active, the three options you see will be Use View, Modify Query, and Display Data. Selecting **Display Data** activates the view and takes you to the edit or browse screen (as though you had pressed the Data key). Selecting **Use View** puts the view name above the line in the queries panel.

When you've finished looking at (or editing) the data through the view, select **Exit** from the **Exit** pull-down menu to return to the Control Center. At the Control Center, you'll notice that the view name is above the line in the Queries panel, indicating that it is still active. (As long as the view is in use, you can access only the associated database through this view.)

Changing a Query

You can modify a saved query at any time you wish.

SEQUENCE OF STEPS

Control Center Queries panel: [highlight query name]
Shift-F2 | ↵ ~ **Modify Query** ↵

USAGE

If you want to change a query, highlight its name in the Queries panel and press **Shift-F2** (Design). Or, if Instruct mode is on, highlight the name and press ↵. You'll be taken to the query design screen where you can make any changes you wish to the query.

While you are in the query design screen, you can modify the query using the same techniques used to create queries. You can also see the results of the query by pressing **F2** (Data). To return to the query design screen, press **Shift-F2** (Design).

When you have finished making changes to the query, select **Save Changes and Exit** from the **Exit** pull-down menu to return to the Control Center. The name of the query will still be accessible in the Control Center, and any changes you've made will be included the next time you activate the query.

Deactivating a Query

You must deactivate a query to remove its effect on your view of the associated database.

SEQUENCE OF STEPS

Control Center Data panel: [highlight database name]
F2

or

Control Center Queries panel: ⏎ **Close View** ⏎

USAGE

When you want to stop using a query and regain access to all the records and fields in your database file, simply opening the database file deactivates the query. Highlight the database name in the Data panel and press **F2** (Data). You'll be sent to the edit or browse screen, where you will see the entire database. To leave the edit or browse screen and return to the Control Center, select **Exit** from the **Exit** pull-down menu. When you get back to the Control Center, the database name will be above the line in the Data panel, indicating that the database is open and ready for use. The query name will be below the line in the Queries panel, indicating that the query is no longer active.

There is another way to deactivate a query. If the Instruct mode is on, and the highlighted query is active when you press ⏎, the prompt box will display the **Close View** option. Selecting **Close View** deactivates the query, putting its name below the line.

CHAPTER **6**

Labels and Reports

This chapter presents techniques for using your printer and formatting your dBASE IV information into a variety of useful *reports*, such as customer lists, mailing labels, and form letters.

Printing a Quick Report

The quickest and easiest way to get a printed copy of your information is to use the Quick Report option (Shift-F9) from the Control Center. This technique simply dumps data from your database onto the printer without much regard for formatting (see Figure 6.1).

```
Page No.    1
06/30/89

LASTNAME        FIRSTNAME       PHONE

Smith           John            (619)555-1234
Adams           Annie           (714)555-0123
Kenney          Ralph           (213)555-9988
Smith           Anita           (415)555-9854
```

Figure 6.1: A Quick Report

SEQUENCE OF STEPS ≡≡≡≡≡≡≡≡

Control Center Data | Queries panel: [highlight file name] **Shift-F9**

Print menu: **Begin Printing** ⏎

USAGE ≡≡≡≡≡≡≡≡

To use Quick Report, you highlight the name of the database file or query that you want to print from and press **Shift-F9** (Quick Report). The report is arranged in a column layout (identical to the quick column layout available with formatted reports). It prints every field in the database file or view, using field names for column headings, and shows a sum for every numeric field.

In some situations, dBASE may not be sure if you want to print data directly from a database file or from a query (for example, if a database file is in use, but a query is highlighted in the Control Center). In these cases dBASE displays options that let you clarify the source of the report (see Figure 6.2). You can select an option using the usual technique of highlighting and pressing ⏎. Selecting a database (.DBF) file always prints the entire contents of the database file.

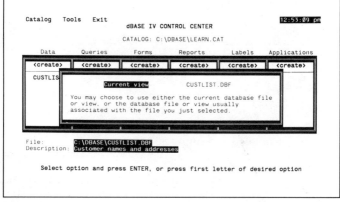

Figure 6.2: Prompt for source of data

Selecting a .QBE query, or view, prints only the fields and records that are specified in the query.

After you've told dBASE what to print, select **Begin Printing** from the **Print** menu that appears. Before printing starts, dBASE IV generates a program that it uses to print the report. This task may take a few seconds. As dBASE prints the report, you'll see another submenu that allows you to cancel or pause printing. Don't do anything; the submenu will disappear when printing is complete.

Designing Labels

Before you print labels, you need to design their appearance, or *format*. Note that dBASE IV uses the term *labels* rather loosely. Not only can you use the labels design screen to print any type of mailing label, but you can also use it to print envelopes, Rolodex-like cards, and general-purpose labels such as identification stickers.

The Labels Design Screen

You design a label format using the *labels design screen* (or *labels design work surface*).

SEQUENCE OF STEPS	

Control Center Data | Queries panel: [highlight file name] ↵

Prompt box: **Use File** ↵

Control Center Labels panel: **<create>** ↵

USAGE	

Before you begin to design a label format, you need to make sure the appropriate database file (or query) is open. Then highlight the **<create>** option in the Labels panel and press ⏎. You'll see the labels design screen, as shown in Figure 6.3.

The labels design screen has the same components as most other dBASE screens: a menu bar at the top and a status bar and navigation line at the bottom. The menu bar contains the Layout, Dimensions, Fields, Words, GoTo, Print, and Exit menus. The box in the center of the screen represents a blank label; this is where you design your label format. The ruler above the box shows you the width of the label (in inches).

Choosing a Label Size

The window at the center of the labels design screen is sized to show the space available on the printed label. Before you actually design the label format, you should select your label size.

SEQUENCE OF STEPS ═══════════════════════════

Labels design screen menu bar: **Dimensions**

Dimensions menu: **Predefined Size** ⏎ [select standard size from submenu]

or

Dimensions menu: [highlight option] ⏎

Prompt box: *<dimension>* ⏎

Keyboard: **Ctrl-End** [to record changes]

USAGE ═══════════════════════════════════════

Pull down the **Dimensions** menu from the menu bar (see Figure 6.4). This menu enables you to select one of dBASE IV's predefined label sizes or to select individual options from the bottom half of the menu to specify your own label size.

If you select **Predefined Size,** you'll see a submenu of common label sizes (see Figure 6.5). The label sizes are described using the height and width in inches and the number

of labels printed across each page. For example, the option
$15/16 \times 3\frac{1}{2} \times 3$ prints labels that are $15/16$ (or about 1) inch tall,
$3\frac{1}{2}$ inches wide, and printed three across a page (like many
photocopy-machine labels). Select any option you wish by
highlighting it and pressing ⏎.

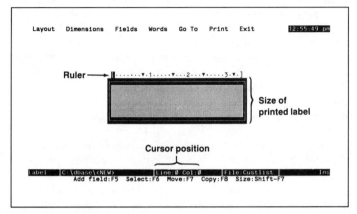

Figure 6.3: The labels design screen

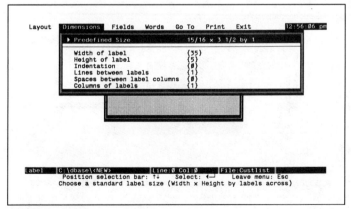

Figure 6.4: The Dimensions menu

If the label size you want is not available from the predefined sizes, select individual options for the label format from the bottom half of the **Dimensions** pull-down menu. These options are Width of Label, Height of Label, Indentation, Lines between Labels, **and** Columns of Labels.

The **Width of Label** option specifies line length. It assumes that your printer is using the standard print size of 10 characters per inch (*pica* type). The **Height of Label** option specifies the number of lines allowed on a label. It assumes the common print size of 6 lines per inch. If your printer uses different print sizes, you may have to adjust these settings accordingly, which might require a little experimentation.

The **Indentation** option specifies the number of blank spaces printed before the first column of labels; that is, the left margin. The **Lines between Labels** option enables you to specify the number of lines (up to 16) to print between labels. The **Spaces between Label Columns** and **Columns of Labels** options enable you to adjust the column spacing.

See the section titled Saving Report and Label Formats later in this chapter for information on saving a label format. For printing labels, see the sections titled Printing Labels and Reports near the end of this chapter.

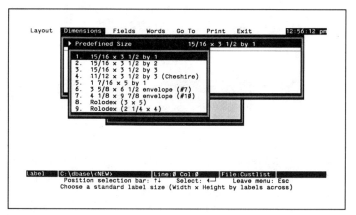

Figure 6.5: Predefined label sizes

Designing Reports

Just as the labels design screen lets you specify how data from the database should be displayed on a label, the reports design screen lets you specify how data should be printed on a full page. Unlike labels, full printed pages might consist of many different sections of text, such as page headings, page numbers, totals sections, subtotals sections, and other types of information.

The Reports Design Screen

To access the reports design screen, open the database file that contains the data that you want to print; then select <create> from the Reports panel.

SEQUENCE OF STEPS

Control Center Data panel: [highlight database name] ↵
[Select Use File]
Control Center Reports panel: **<create>** ↵

USAGE

If the database is not currently in use, highlight its name in the **Data** panel, press ↵, and select **Use File**. Highlight **<create>** in the **Reports** panel and press ↵. You'll see the reports design screen, partially obscured by the **Layout** menu. Press **Esc** if you want to remove the Layout menu. Your screen should look like Figure 6.6.

As you can see, the reports design screen has many of the same characteristics as other design screens. The menu bar at the top of the screen has pull-down menus associated with it, which you open, as usual, by pressing F10 or by typing Alt followed by the first letter of the menu name. The ruler just beneath the menu bar shows margins and tab stops. At the

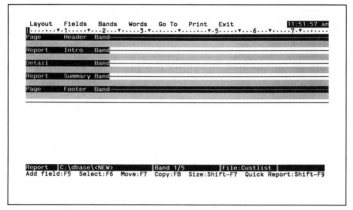

Figure 6.6: The reports design screen

bottom of the screen, the navigation line displays special keys that you can use to format your report.

The center of the screen, where you design the format of the report, is currently divided into five *bands*. Each band corresponds to a section of the printed report. Anything that you place within a band is printed only in the corresponding section of the report. For example, any text that you place in the Page Header band is printed at the top of each printed page.

Designing a Report Format

When you design a report format you must select a general layout, specify margins, then edit the field templates and text to your satisfaction.

General Layouts

dBASE IV lets you select from three general layouts for printing your report: the column layout, the form layout, and the mailmerge layout. You can use a general layout as the starting point for designing your own report.

SEQUENCE OF STEPS

Reports design screen menu bar: **Layout**

Layout menu: **Quick Layouts** ⏎

Quick Layouts menu: **Column Layout** | **Form Layout** | **Mailmerge Layout** ⏎

USAGE

Highlight **Layout** on the menu bar. Select **Quick Layouts.** Then select one of the three layout options. dBASE arranges the database fields in the general report format you selected.

The *column layout* prints the data in even-sized columns and shows totals for all numeric fields. A report that presents data as a list, or that includes totals or subtotals, would likely use a column layout (see Figure 6.7). The *form layout* does not present data in even columns, but instead stacks or arranges it in some other free-form format.

The *mailmerge layout* is usually used to combine (merge) a large body of text with information from a database. This is the layout you use to create form letters (mail). You add name and address field templates from the database, then type the body of the letter in the report's detail band.

SEE ALSO

Chapter 7: Custom Forms

Margins

After you have selected a general format for your report, it's a good idea to select margins. Selecting margins before modifying the layout helps you center titles or other information in your report. When printing on 8½ × 11-inch paper, a right margin setting of about 64 will provide adequate left and right margins on the printed page.

SEQUENCE OF STEPS ══════════════

Reports design screen menu bar: **Words**

Words menu: **Modify Ruler** ↵

Reports design screen: [move to right margin position] **]**

Keyboard: **Ctrl-End** [to record changes]

USAGE ══════════════

Pull down the **Words** menu from the menu bar. Select **Modify Ruler** (the cursor will move to the ruler). Press **Tab** or → to move to the left-margin column, then type **[** to mark the left-margin position. Then, use → or **Tab** to position the cursor to the right-column margin, and type **]** to mark the right margin. Press **Ctrl-End** to finish modifying the ruler.

Note that you can also adjust printed margins on the Print menu (see the section titled Managing the Printer later in this chapter).

Report Bands

When you bring up the reports design screen, it displays the five bands shown in Figure 6.6: Page Header, Report Intro, Detail, Report Summary, and Page Footer. Each report band corresponds to a section of the printed report (see Figure 6.7 and Table 6.1).

SEQUENCE OF STEPS ══════════════

Reports design screen: [move cursor to band border] ↵

Reports design screen: [move cursor into band]

Reports design screen: [edit fields and text]

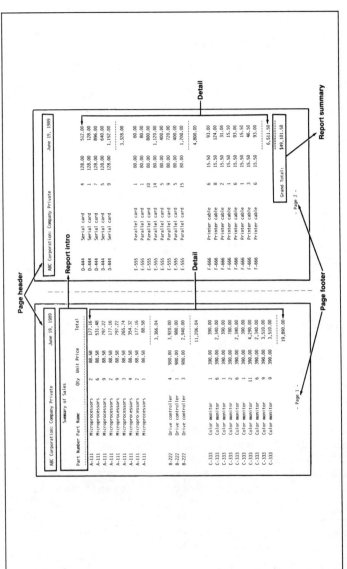

Figure 6.7: Sections of a typical report

REPORT BAND	CONTENTS
Page header	Printed once at the top of each page.
Report intro	Printed once at the beginning of the report.
Detail	The body of the report. Typically, this section displays records from a database file.
Report summary	Printed once at the end of the report. It can be used to display totals or closing information about the report.
Page footer	Printed once at the bottom of each page. It can be used to display page numbers or other useful information.

Table 6.1: The Report Bands

USAGE

The first step in working with a band is to move the cursor to the band border (which contains the band name). If the band is closed (no blank space appears beneath the border), you need to *open* the band by pressing ⏎. Move the cursor into the band. Now you can enter and edit text, move fields around, and modify the contents of the band using **F5** to place fields in the band as well as the general editing techniques listed in Table 6.3, later in this chapter.

As you add new bands to your report format (see below), your screen may become cluttered and difficult to read. You can close a band that you are not using at the moment by moving the cursor to the band border and pressing ⏎. Just remember to reopen the band before you print the report, because closed bands do not print.

To open a closed band, move the cursor to the band border and press ↵ again. You can also select **Open All Bands** from the **Bands** pull-down menu to open all closed bands.

Formatting Individual Bands You can specify the pitch, quality, and spacing of lines for an individual band by moving the cursor to the band border and selecting an appropriate option from the Bands menu.

SEQUENCE OF STEPS

Reports design screen: [move cursor to band border]

Reports design screen menu bar: **Bands**

Bands menu: **Text Pitch for Band** | **Quality Print for Band** | **Spacing of Lines for Band** [press **Space** bar or ↵ to scroll through options]

Keyboard: **Ctrl-End** [to record changes]

USAGE

The **Bands** menu makes the following print options available for individual bands: **Text Pitch for Band, Quality Print for Band,** and **Spacing of Lines for Band**. The settings for these options are the same as for printing an entire report, but they affect only the current band when selected from this menu. Use the **Space** bar to scroll through the settings. When they are to your liking, press **Ctrl-End** to finish making changes.

Group Bands You can add *group bands* to your report format to group similar records on a report. For example, in a database recording parts ordered, you might want to group records by part number or order date (see Figure 6.8).

```
07/08/89                                        Page No.   1


Part                                 Unit       Extended
Number    Part Name      Date   Qty  Price      Price


A·111     Astro Buddies  06/01/89   2   50.00      100.00
A·111     Astro Buddies  06/02/89   3   50.00      150.00
A·111     Astro Buddies  06/05/89   4   50.00      200.00
                                 - - - - -      - - - - - - - - - -
                         Subtotal   9              450.00

B·222     Banana Man     06/01/89   2  100.00      200.00
B·222     Banana Man     06/01/89   1  100.00      100.00
B·222     Banana Man     06/15/89   1  100.00      100.00
                                 - - - - -      - - - - - - - - - -
                         Subtotal   4              400.00

C·333     Cosmic Critters 06/01/89  1  500.00      500.00
C·333     Cosmic Critters 06/15/89  2  500.00     1000.00
C·333     Cosmic Critters 06/15/89  1  500.00      500.00
C·333     Cosmic Critters 07/01/89  2  500.00     1000.00
                                 - - - - -      - - - - - - - - - -
                         Subtotal   6             3000.00
                                 = = = = =      = = = = = = = = = =
                         Total     19             3850.00
```

Figure 6.8: A report using group bands

SEQUENCE OF STEPS

Reports design screen: [move cursor out of Detail band]

Reports design screen menu bar: **Bands**

Bands menu: **Add a Group Band** ↵

Grouping options menu: **Field Value | Expression Value | Record Count** [enter value in curly brackets] ↵

Reports design screen: [move cursor to group summary band] **F5**

Field options menu: [select summary function] ↵

Summary field menu: **Name** *<summary field name>*

Summary field menu: **Description** *<summary field description>*

Summary field menu: **Field to Summarize On** *<field>*

Summary field menu: **Reset Every** *<value>*

Summary field menu: **Template** *<template>* ↵
Keyboard: **Ctrl-End** [to record changes]

USAGE

A group band actually consists of two parts: a Group Intro
band and a Group Summary band. Information in the Group
Intro band is displayed once at the top of each group. For example, a report grouped by part number might display the
group headings "Part number: A-111" for one group and
"Part number: B-222" for the next. The Group Summary
band displays its contents once at the bottom of each group.
This is where you would place summary fields to display
subtotals.

To add a group band, move the cursor to where you want
its top border (the bottom border of the band above). Pull
down the **Bands** menu and select **Add a Group Band.** You
will be presented with a menu of grouping options: Field
Value Expression Value, and Record Count.

Selecting **Field Value** lets you specify a particular field to
group by. The **Expression Value** option lets you group by an
expression rather than a field. The expression you enter can
be a combination of character fields joined with a plus sign,
or an expression that contains a function. (A few functions
that are especially useful for report groupings are summarized in Table 6.2. Note that the LEFT function requires
you to specify both the field name and the number of characters.) The **Record Count** option simply prints rows of
records in equal-sized blocks.

Because the report format tells dBASE how to *display* the
groups, but not how to *create* the groups, you must choose a
field on which the database is indexed (or sorted). The index
must be activated before you print the report.

You'll see the new group band appear in the report format.
While the cursor is still on the group band, the message
Group by <field> appears centered at the bottom of the screen.
However, the Group Summary band is still empty.

FUNCTION AND RETURN VALUE	USED WITH DATA TYPE	EXAMPLE
CMONTH() The month of a date	Date	CMONTH(DATE)
YEAR() The year of a date	Date	YEAR(DATE)
CDOW() The day of the week	Date	CDOW(DATE)
LEFT() Leftmost characters	Character	LEFT(LASTNAME,1)

Table 6.2: Functions Used in Grouping

To tell dBASE what to put in the Group Summary band, first move the cursor to its bottom border. Then press **F5** (Field) and select a summary function from the list in the Summary column. This brings up a submenu requesting several types of information about the Group Summary.

Select **Name** and enter a name for the summary field (such as "SUBQTY"). Then select **Description** and enter a field description (such as "Subtotal of QTY field"). Select **Field to Summarize On** and enter the appropriate field (such as "QTY"). Use the **Reset Every** option to tell dBASE where to reset subtotals as it prints the report. The **Template** option lets you edit the template in the curly brackets, so it matches the template used for the field being summarized. When you finish specifying all these details, press **Ctrl-End.**

To display repetitious data only once in a group, move the appropriate templates into the Group Intro band. To repeat the Group Intro if a particular group continues onto a new page, change the **Group Intro on Each Page** option on the **Bands** menu from No (the default) to **Yes.**

You can *nest* group bands inside each other to produce groups within groups. For instance, suppose you place a group band for PARTNO in the format of a report and then a group band based on the DATE field within that group. You could then print a report that subtotals sales for a particular product and, for each product, subtotals sales by date. Although you cannot index on PARTNO + DATE, you can use a function within your index expression, PARTNO + DTOS(DATE), to create the index that the report grouping requires. There is no limit to the number of group bands that you can nest, so long as you create the appropriate index expression to print the report.

To change the field that a group band is based on, move the cursor to the group band border and select **Modify Group** from the **Bands** menu.

To remove a group band from a report format permanently, place the cursor in the band's border and press **Del** or select **Remove Group** from the **Bands** pull-down menu.

SEE ALSO

Creating an Index (Chapter 4), Performing Calculations in Reports (Chapter 8)

Editing Label and Report Formats

A report band can be modified using either of two editors: the layout editor or the word-wrap editor. The *layout editor* enables you to place fields on the band; move them around; and add fields, boxes, and lines to the report. The *word-wrap editor* works more like a word processor. It is not available in the labels design screen.

Most bands, except the detail band in a mailmerge layout, initially use the layout editor. You can switch to the word-wrap editor by pressing ↵ to change the setting of the **Word Wrap Band** option on the **Bands** menu from No to **Yes.**

The Layout Editor

Table 6.3 lists the keys you can use to change a report or label format. As you can see, many of the keys are similar to those used in the edit and browse screens.

KEY	EFFECT
→	Moves right one character or to end of field template
←	Moves left one character or to beginning of field template
End	Moves to end of line
Home	Moves to beginning of line
↓	Moves down one row
↑	Moves up one row
↵	If Insert mode is off, moves down one row; if Insert mode is on, inserts a new line
Ctrl-N	Inserts a new line
PgDn	Moves to bottom of screen
PgUp	Moves to top of screen
F5	Adds a new field template or changes the currently highlighted one
F6	Selects field template or block
F7	Moves field or block selected with F6
F8	Copies field or block selected with F6
Shift-F7	Changes size of currently selected field template

Table 6.3: Keys for Editing Label and Report Formats

KEY	EFFECT
Backspace	Erases character to the left
Del	Deletes character, field template, or block selected with F6
Ctrl-T	Removes word or field to right
Ctrl-Y	Removes entire line
Tab	Moves to next tab setting (reformats paragraph in word-wrap editor)
Shift-Tab	Moves to previous tab setting (reformats paragraph in word-wrap editor)
Ins	Toggles Insert mode on/off
F1	Provides help
Esc	Abandons current format without saving changes

Table 6.3: Keys for Editing Label and Report Formats (continued)

Adding Fields

You can add a new field to a label or report format at any time. You do this by placing *field templates* that show dBASE where to print the information from the field (see Figure 6.9).

SEQUENCE OF STEPS

Labels | reports design screen: [put cursor at leftmost character of location] **F5** | **Add Field** option on **Fields** menu [highlight field] ↵

Fields menu: [highlight field to add] ↵

Keyboard: **Ctrl-End** [to record changes]

126 Labels and Reports

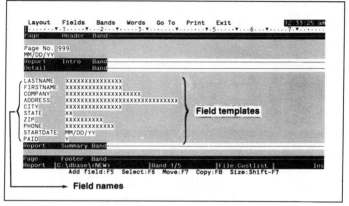

Figure 6.9: Report format showing field templates

First position the cursor where you want the leftmost character of the field template to appear. The status line tells you the line and column position of the cursor.

Then either press **F5** (Field) or select **Add Field** from the **Fields** pull-down menu. You'll see a submenu of possible fields to add to the format, including *database, calculated,* and *predefined* fields. When designing report formats, you'll also see a panel of *summary* fields (see Figure 6.10).

Database fields are simply those fields available from the current database file (or query). Calculated fields display the results of dBASE calculations. Summary fields summarize the information in a group of records. Predefined fields are those that dBASE IV provides and handles automatically. dBASE provides four predefined fields:

Date	The date that the report or labels were printed
Time	The time that the report or labels were printed
Recno	The record number (position) of the record
Pageno	The page number

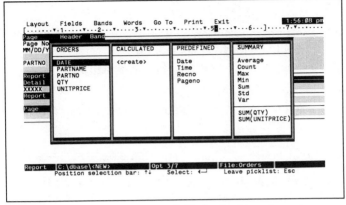

Figure 6.10: Options for placing fields in the report format

Select a field using the usual technique (move the highlight to the option you want and press ↵). You'll be given an
opportunity to change the Template and Picture Function
options assigned to the field. Press **Ctrl-End** to place the field
and return to the design screen.

A series of X's (or H's or V's) fills in a portion of the screen.
These X's are the field template. They show the maximum
amount of space that information in the database will oc-
cupy on the printed page.

To guarantee that a space separates two fields on a printed
label or report, press the **Space** bar when the cursor is at the
place where you want the space to appear.

SEE ALSO

Performing Calculations in Reports (Chapter 8)

Moving and Copying Fields

To move or copy any part of a report or label format, follow
the basic steps below.

SEQUENCE OF STEPS ═══════════════

Labels | reports design screen: [move cursor to corner of area to be moved | copied] **F6**

Design screen: ⏎ | [highlight larger area] ⏎

Keyboard: **F7** | **F8**

Design screen: [move cursor to new location] ⏎

USAGE ══════════════════════

Place the cursor in a corner of the area you want to move and press **F6** (Select). If you are moving only a field template, press ⏎. If you are moving more than a single template, use the arrow keys to highlight the entire area that you want to move or copy and then press ⏎.

Press either **F7** (Move) or **F8** (Copy), depending on the operation you want to perform. Move the highlight to the new location and press ⏎. (You can also press Move or Copy after moving the cursor to the destination.)

If you attempt to move or copy selected text to a place where it overlaps existing text or templates, dBASE will present the message *Delete covered text and fields? (Y/N)*. If you select **Yes,** any covered text or field template will be deleted. If you select **No,** nothing will be deleted. You can then press **Esc** to stop copying or moving, or move to another location. Note that if you press Select and then make a mistake while highlighting, you can just press **Esc** to cancel the selection.

Deleting Fields

You can delete either a single field, or an entire line of fields and text.

SEQUENCE OF STEPS

Labels | reports design screen: [move cursor to field template] **Del** | **Remove Field** on **Fields** menu [highlight field name] ↵

or

Design screen: [move cursor to line] **Ctrl-Y**

USAGE

To delete a field from the format, move the cursor to the field template and either press **Del** or select **Remove Field** from the **Fields** menu. Any field template that is only partially contained in a highlighted (selected) area will not be deleted.

To delete an entire line, including all fields and text, move the cursor to the appropriate line and press **Ctrl-Y.**

Adding and Deleting Text

You can place text, such as words, punctuation marks, and blank spaces, anywhere in a report or label format.

SEQUENCE OF STEPS

Labels | reports design screen: [position cursor]
Design screen: [type new text] | **Del**

USAGE

To *insert* text into an existing format, position the cursor where you want the new text to appear. Make sure that Insert mode is on and then type your text. To *change* existing text, position the cursor on the text to be changed and activate Overwrite mode (press **Ins** until the *Ins* indicator disappears). When you type your changes, the new characters will overwrite (replace) existing characters.

To delete text from the format, position the cursor on the character you want to delete and press **Del**. You can delete an entire section of text and fields by using the Select key (**F6**) to highlight the area you want to delete. After pressing ↵ to complete the selection, press **Del** to delete the entire highlighted block.

Adding and Deleting Lines

You can add and delete lines in a report format, using the following steps.

SEQUENCE OF STEPS =====================

Labels | reports design screen: [place cursor at location of new line] **Ctrl-N** | **Add Line** option on **Words** menu ↵ | [press ↵ if Insert mode is on]

or

Design screen: [move cursor to line] **Ctrl-Y** | **Remove Line** option on **Words** menu ↵

USAGE ==========================

To insert a new line on a report format, first position the cursor where you want the new line to appear. Then use any one of three methods to add the new line: press **Ctrl-N**, select **Add Line** from the **Words** pull-down menu, or press ↵ while you are in Insert mode.

To delete a line from a report format, move the cursor to the appropriate line and either press **Ctrl-Y** or select **Remove Line** from the **Words** menu.

Note that any blank lines in a report band appear as blank lines in the printed report. Include blank lines in your report formats to make your reports easier to read.

Formatting Fields

dBASE IV automatically assigns certain display attributes to field templates used in label and report formats. Sometimes these automatic attributes may not quite fit your needs, and you may want to change them.

Picture Functions

A *picture function* is a code that tells dBASE how to display a piece of information. dBASE offers many different picture functions.

SEQUENCE OF STEPS

Labels | reports design screen: [move cursor to field template]

F5 | **Modify Field** on **Fields** menu [highlight field name] ⏎

Display Attributes menu: **Picture Functions** ⏎

Picture functions menu: [highlight option and use **Space** bar or ⏎ to scroll through settings]

Keyboard: **Ctrl-End** [to record changes]

USAGE

You can change the display attribute of a field template in a label or report format by moving the cursor to the template on the design screen and accessing the **Display Attributes** menu. To do this, either press **F5** (Field) or select **Modify Field** from the **Fields** pull-down menu. Either technique displays a submenu that describes the field and presents the **Picture Functions** options (see Figure 6.11).

The dBASE picture functions relevant to label and report formats are summarized in Table 6.4. You can turn any available option on or off by highlighting that option and pressing

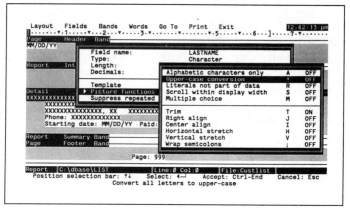

Figure 6.11: Picture Functions options for Character Fields

PICTURE FUNCTION	ACTION	EFFECT
!	Uppercase conversion	Displays all letters (a–z) in uppercase (A–Z)
T	Trim	Removes leading and trailing blanks
J	Right align	Right-aligns text within the space allotted for the field
I	Center align	Centers text within the space provided
H	Horizontal stretch	Adjusts template width to width of data
V	Vertical stretch	Wraps text onto several lines within the allotted width

Table 6.4: Common Picture Functions for Reports and Labels

the **Space** bar. Press **Ctrl-End** when you are finished making changes.

Many of the picture functions affect how data is displayed within the width provided by the field template, as the next section explains.

SEE ALSO

Making Your Form More Attractive/Boxes and Lines (Chapter 7), Controlling Input/Picture Functions/Numeric Picture Functions (Chapter 7)

Field Widths

You can control the width of a field on the printed report by changing the size of the field template (except for date fields). By default, dBASE assigns a width that matches the field's width in the database.

SEQUENCE OF STEPS

Labels | reports design screen: [move cursor to field template] **Shift-F7**

Design screen: [use → and ← to change field size] ↵

or

Design screen: [move cursor to field template] **F5** | **Modify Field** on **Fields** menu ↵

Display Attributes menu: **Template** ↵

Template option: **Del** | **Backspace**

Keyboard: **Ctrl-End** [to record changes]

USAGE

You can change the display attributes of a field template in a label or report format by moving the cursor to the template on the design screen and accessing the **Display Attributes** menu. To do this, either press **F5** (Field) or select **Modify Field** from the **Fields** pull-down menu. Either technique displays a submenu that describes the field and presents the **Template** option.

To widen or narrow a field, you can use either of two techniques. The first technique is to move the cursor to the field template, press **Shift-F7** (Size), and use → and ← to widen or narrow the field. Then press ↵.

The second technique is to move the cursor to the field template, press **F5**, and select **Template.** Press **Backspace** or **Del** to narrow the template, or type characters to widen the template. (Note that if you use this latter technique, dBASE will display a submenu of *character input symbols.* These are more relevant to custom forms than they are to reports.)

Three picture functions determine how dBASE fits data from the database into the space allotted by the field template on the report: Trim, Horizontal Stretch, and Vertical Stretch. For example, suppose your database contains a field named ADDRESS that is 30 characters wide, but on your report, you narrow the template to 15 characters. How would dBASE display a longer address?

If you assign the **Trim** picture function to the ADDRESS field, dBASE will *truncate* the data to fit within the template. That is, only the first 15 characters will be displayed. When you assign the Trim picture function to a field, the template appears as X's.

If you assign the **Vertical Stretch** picture function to the ADDRESS field, dBASE will word-wrap the address within the width allotted. With Vertical Stretch, the template appears as V's rather than X's. When either V's or X's appear, you can use **Shift-F7** to size the template. The Vertical Stretch picture function is automatically assigned to memo fields and in these fields cannot be changed to another picture function.

If you assign the **Horizontal Stretch** picture function, dBASE will automatically adjust the size of the template to fit the data being displayed. Hence, regardless of the size of the template, the Horizontal Stretch picture function always displays the full address. It also trims off any leading or trailing blanks when it prints data. When you assign the Horizontal Stretch picture function to a field, the template appears as H's, and you cannot resize the field.

The Center and Right Align picture functions also let you determine how data is displayed within the width provided by the field template. If you assign the **Center** picture function, text will be centered within the width. If you assign the **Right Align** attribute to the field, text will be right aligned within the width allotted by the field template.

SEE ALSO

Chapter 7: Custom Forms

The Word-Wrap Editor

The dBASE word-wrap editor is especially useful for composing the body of a form letter, and is thus the default for the Detail band of the mailmerge layout. It works much like a conventional word processor, in that it wraps text, so you don't have to press the ↵ key at the end of each line. Once you indicate the end of a paragraph by pressing ↵, you have a block of text that can be reformatted using the keys available with the layout editor. You can also use any special key listed in the navigation line.

SEE ALSO

Creating Memo-Field Windows (Chapter 7)

Working with Text Blocks

You can mark blocks of text to copy, move, or delete.

Labels | reports design screen: [move cursor to leftmost characters] **F6**

Design screen: [move cursor to rightmost characters] ↵

Keyboard: **Del** | **F7** | **F8**

Use the arrow keys to move the cursor to the left edge of the text to be selected and press **F6** (Select). Press → until the highlight covers the whole selection. Then press ↵ to complete the selection (or highlighting).

Press **Del**, **F7**, or **F8** to delete, move, or copy the highlighted text. Instantly, dBASE performs the edit and automatically reformats the entire paragraph, so that it still fits perfectly within the margins. You can indent a paragraph by simply pressing **Tab** before the first word, or remove the indent by pressing **Shift-Tab.**

Finding Text on the Design Screens

The Go To pull-down menu provides search and replace options for specific text on the reports and labels design screens. These options can be handy for making corrections in a report format.

Labels | reports design screen menu bar: **Go To**

Go To menu: [highlight option] ↵ *<search string>* ↵

To find a word or phrase in a report, pull down the **Go To** menu from the menu bar, highlight a search option, and type a search or search-and-replace string in the curly brackets. Select **No** or **Yes** for the **Match Capitalization** option, using the **Space** bar or ⏎, depending on what you want dBASE to search for.

Go To Line Number searches for the specified line. **Forward Search** and **Backward Search** look for the first occurrence of a string in the specified direction. When you choose **Replace** and specify a replacement string, dBASE will search for the first occurrence of the search string, highlight it, and display these options:

Replace/Skip/All/Quit (R/S/A/Esc)

You can select any single option. Selecting Replace (by typing **R**) replaces the current string and moves on to the next occurrence of it. Selecting Skip (by typing **S**) skips the current string without replacing it and moves on to the next occurrence. Selecting All (by typing **A**) replaces all remaining occurrences of the search string with the replacement string without asking for permission. Pressing **Esc** cancels the search-and-replace operation.

SEE ALSO

Searching for Specific Records (Chapter 5)

Saving Label and Report Formats

Once you have gone to the trouble of creating a custom format, you will want to save it for repeated use.

SEQUENCE OF STEPS

Labels | reports design screen menu bar: **Layout**

Layout menu: **Edit Description of Label Design | Report** ⏎

Prompt box: *<description>* ↵

Labels | reports design screen menu bar: **Save This Report** on **Layout** menu | **Save Changes and Exit** on **Exit** menu ↵

Save as: prompt: *<file name>* ↵

USAGE ════════════════

Highlight **Layout** on the menu bar and select **Edit Description of Label Design** or **Edit Description of Report.** Type a description, such as "2-across mailing labels" or "List of customer names and addresses." Press ↵.

Now you must actually save the report format and description. Pull down either the **Layout** or the **Exit** menu and select **Save This Report** or **Save Changes and Exit,** respectively. When dBASE presents the prompt *Save as:,* type a valid DOS file name (eight characters maximum, no spaces or punctuation) and press ↵.

dBASE will take some time to write a program for itself to print the report later. When that is done, it will return you to the Control Center. You'll see the new label or report name in the appropriate panel.

Modifying Label and Report Formats

If you save a format, print some labels or a report, and then decide to make some changes, it's easy to return to the design screen to do so.

SEQUENCE OF STEPS ════════════

Control Center Labels | Reports panel: [highlight format name] **Shift-F2** | ↵ **Modify Layout** ↵

Labels | reports design screen: [make changes]

Design screen menu bar: **Exit**

Exit menu: **Save Changes and Exit** ⏎

USAGE ═══════════════════════

Just highlight the name of the format in the Labels or Reports panel of the Control Center and press **Shift-F2** (Design). You can also press ⏎ and then select **Modify Layout** from the submenu that appears. You'll be returned to the appropriate design screen.

Although the design screen shows only templates (X's) of where data will be printed on the label, you can easily determine which database field is associated with each template. Just use the arrow keys to move the cursor into the template of interest and look at the bottom of the screen. The line indicates the database and field used as well as the data type, width, and number of decimal places, as defined in the database structure.

After you've modified your format, don't forget to save your work by selecting **Save Changes and Exit** from the **Exit** pull-down menu. If you do *not* want to save your changes, select **Abandon Changes** and **Exit** instead. You'll be returned to the Control Center.

If you want to save your modified format as a new file (leaving the original, unmodified format intact) select **Save This Report** from the **Layout** pull-down menu and provide a new file name. Then select **Abandon Changes and Exit** from the **Exit** pull-down menu.

Printing Labels and Reports

This section first describes the basic label- and report-printing procedures, then goes on to discuss printing options in detail.

The Basic Procedure

After you have designed a label or report format, you can use that format to print the data from your database.

SEQUENCE OF STEPS

Control Center Labels | Reports panel: [highlight label or report format name] ↵

Prompt box: **Print Label | Report** ↵

Print menu: **Begin Printing** ↵ | **View Labels | Report on Screen** ↵ [press **Space** bar to scroll through display]

USAGE

Make sure the label or report format name is highlighted in the appropriate panel of the Control Center. Press ↵. From the options that appear, select **Print Label** or **Print Report.** From the **Print** menu that appears next, select either **View Labels/Report on Screen** (to see a screen display only) or **Begin Printing** (to actually print the text). The Print menu is shown in Figure 6.12.

If you select **Begin Printing,** your printer begins printing immediately. While dBASE IV is printing, it displays the following instructions:

Cancel printing: ESC

Pause printing: CTRL-S

Resume printing with any key

Note that printing might not stop or pause immediately if your printer has a buffer

You can cancel printing altogether by pressing the **Esc** key. To pause printing temporarily, press **Ctrl-S** and then press any key later to resume printing.

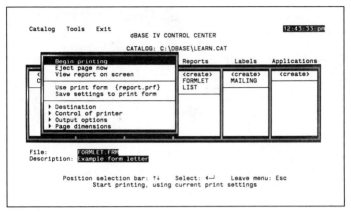

Figure 6.12: The Print menu

When you select **View Labels/Report on Screen,** you'll
see the text go by on your screen. dBASE will pause after each
screenful and display a prompt at the bottom of the screen indicating that you should press the Space bar to scroll to the
next screenful. Do so at your leisure until you get back to the
Control Center, or press **Esc** to cancel the display.

You can preview or print labels or a report during the design process. Select either **Begin Printing** or **View Labels/
Report on Screen** from the **Print** pull-down menu on the
design screen.

SEE ALSO

Importing and Exporting Data/Exporting Printed Reports
(Chapter 10), Printing the Database Structure (Chapter 2)

Managing the Printer

Whether you are printing labels, reports, or form letters,
you'll always see the Print menu before printing starts. The
printing options on it include Eject Page Now, Control of

Printer, Output Options, Page Dimensions, and Save Settings to Print From.

Starting with a Clean Sheet

If you are using a laser printer, you may need to eject the pages from the printer. If you are using a tractor-feed printer, you may want to ensure that printing starts at the top of a new page.

SEQUENCE OF STEPS ════════════════════════

Print menu: **Eject Page Now** ↵

Keyboard: **Esc** [to return to Control Center]

Control Center Reports panel: [highlight label | report format name] ↵

Prompt box: **Print Label | Report** ↵

Print menu: **Begin Printing** ↵

USAGE ═════════════════════════════════

If you are using a tractor-feed printer, make sure that a page perforation is aligned just above the print head before you turn on the printer. **Eject Page Now** works only if the paper is aligned in your printer. If you select **Eject Page Now**, and the paper does not move to the top of a page, turn off your printer, hand crank the paper to the top of a new page, and turn the printer on again. As long as you do not hand crank the paper in the printer again, the pages will stay aligned.

Aligning Mailing Labels

You may need to experiment a bit to get the data properly aligned on mailing labels. To help you, dBASE offers the **Generate Sample Labels option.**

SEQUENCE OF STEPS

Print menu: **Generate Sample Labels** ↵

Prompt box: **Y** | **N**

USAGE

When you select the option **Generate Sample Labels** from the **Print** menu, dBASE prints a row of sample labels as X's and displays the message, *Do you want more samples? (Y/N)*. You can realign the labels in the printer and select yes (by typing **Y**) until your labels are lined up properly. Then answer no (**N**) to the query, and dBASE will print your labels.

Controlling Print Size

Some printers allow you to print in large or small letters. If you have such a printer, you can select the Control of Printer option from the Print menu to choose a print size.

SEQUENCE OF STEPS

Control Center Reports or Labels panel: [highlight label | report format name] ↵

Prompt box: **Print Label** | **Report** ↵

Print menu: **Control of Printer** ↵

Control of Printer menu: **Text Pitch**

Text pitch options: **Pica** | **Elite** | **Condensed** | **Default** [use **Space** bar or ↵ to scroll through options] **Ctrl-End** | ←

Print menu: **Begin Printing** ↵

Select **Control of Printer** from the **Print** menu. Highlight the **Text Pitch** option on the submenu that appears. Press the **Space** bar to scroll through the options, listed here:

Pica	Prints 10 characters per inch
Elite	Prints 12 characters per inch
Condensed	Prints very small letters (their exact size is determined by your printer)
Default	Uses whatever size the printer is set to

After selecting a print size, press ← or **Ctrl-End** to return to the **Print** menu.

Controlling Print Quality

Some printers offer two or more options for print quality: *draft quality* (for faster printing) and *near letter quality* (for neater, though slower, printing). If your printer supports these features, you can specify a print quality by selecting Control of Printer from the Print submenu.

SEQUENCE OF STEPS

Control Center Reports panel: [highlight label | report format name] ↵

Prompt box: **Print Label | Report** ↵

Print menu: **Control of Printer** ↵

Control of Printer menu: **Quality Print**

Quality print options: **Yes | No| Default** [use **Space** bar or ↵ to scroll through options] **Ctrl-End** | ←

Print menu: **Begin Printing** ↵

USAGE

Highlight **Quality Print** on the **Control of Printer** menu and press the **Space** bar or ↵ to scroll through the options. Select **Yes** to use the best-quality print, select **No** to use the draft-quality print, and select **Default** to use whatever quality the printer itself is currently set for. Then press **Ctrl-End** or ← to return to the **Print** menu.

Printing Single Sheets

When you need to hand-feed individual sheets into the printer, you can have dBASE pause between each printed page.

SEQUENCE OF STEPS

Control Center Reports panel: [highlight label | report format name] ↵

Prompt box: **Print Label | Report** ↵

Print menu: **Control of Printer** ↵

Control of Printer menu: **Wait Between Pages**

Wait between Pages options: **Yes | No** [use **Space** bar or ↵ to scroll through options] **Ctrl-End** | ←

Print menu: **Begin Printing** ↵

USAGE

Select **Control of Printer** from the **Print** menu, highlight **Wait between Pages** on the submenu that appears, and press the **Space** bar or ↵ until the option reads **Yes**. Then press ← or **Ctrl-End** to return to the **Print** menu.

Controlling Extra Pages

You can specify when dBASE ejects the page currently in the printer: before printing a report, after printing a report, both before and after printing a report, or not at all (no blank or incomplete pages are ejected).

SEQUENCE OF STEPS ═══════════════

Control Center Reports panel: [highlight label | report format name] ↵

Prompt box: **Print Label | Report** ↵

Print menu: **Control of Printer** ↵

Control of Printer menu: **New Page**

New Page options: **Before | After | Both | None** [use **Space** bar or ↵ to scroll through options] **Ctrl-End** | ←

Print menu: **Begin Printing** ↵

USAGE ═══════════════

Select **Control of Printer** from the **Print** menu and highlight **New Page** on the submenu that appears. Then press the **Space** bar or ↵ until the option you want is displayed. Press ← or **Ctrl-End** to return to the **Print** menu.

Controlling Page Numbers

Suppose you notice an error on page 39 of a long printed report. After correcting the error with dBASE, you need not reprint the entire report.

SEQUENCE OF STEPS ═══════════════

Control Center Reports panel: [highlight label | report format name] ↵

Prompt box: **Print Label | Report** ↵

Print menu: **Output Options** ↵

Output options menu: [highlight option] ↵

Prompt box: *<number>* ↵
Keyboard: **Ctrl-End** | ← [to return to Print menu]
Print menu: **Begin Printing** ↵

USAGE

Select **Output Options** from the **Print** menu; then set the **Begin on Page** and **End after Page** options to print only those pages that need reprinting. For example, if you set Begin on Page to 39 and End after Page to 39, only page 39 will be printed.

The **First Page Number** option on this submenu lets you choose the starting page number for the entire report. This option prints every page in the report, but starts numbering pages at the value you set. For example, if you set this value to 100, the first page of the report will be numbered as page 100, and the remaining pages will be numbered 101, 102, and so forth. This feature is useful when you want to combine several reports in a single document and want the pages to be numbered consecutively.

Printing Multiple Copies

dBASE enables you to print multiple copies of a report without reissuing the Print command.

SEQUENCE OF STEPS

Control Center Reports panel: [highlight label | report format name] ↵

Prompt box: **Print Label | Report** ↵

Print menu: **Output Options** ↵

Output options menu: **Number of Copies** ↵

Prompt box: *<number>* ↵

Keyboard: **Ctrl-End** | ← [to return to Print menu]
Print menu: **Begin Printing** ↵

USAGE

If you want to print multiple copies of a report, select **Output Options** from the **Print** menu and **Number of Copies** from the next submenu. Enter the number of copies that you want to print and press ↵. Press ← or **Ctrl-End** to return to the Print menu.

Controlling Page Length and Margins

When you select Page Dimensions from the Print menu, dBASE gives you three options for formatting the printed page: Length of Page, Offset from Left, and Spacing of Lines.

SEQUENCE OF STEPS

Control Center Reports panel: [highlight label | report format name] ↵

Prompt box: **Print Label | Report** ↵

Print menu: **Page Dimensions** ↵

Page Dimensions menu: [highlight option] ↵

Prompt box: *<number>* ↵

Keyboard: **Ctrl-End** | ← [to return to Print menu]

Print menu: **Begin Printing** ↵

USAGE

Length of Page is preset to 66 lines (for 6 lines to the inch on an 11-inch sheet of paper). You can change this number to print a different page length.

If you want to use an unusual size of page, and you cannot set your printer to the new page height, select the **Control of**

Printer option from the **Print** menu and the **Advance Page Using** option from the next submenu that appears. Change the setting from Form Feed to **Line Feed** by pressing the **Space** bar. dBASE will calculate the number of lines required to get to the top of the next page based upon the Length of Page option.

The **Offset from Left** option on the **Page Dimensions** menu lets you decide how many blank spaces are printed at the left of each page. The larger this number, the wider the left margin will be on the printed page. The **Spacing of Lines** option lets you choose among single, double, and triple spacing options for the printed report by scrolling through them with the Space bar.

Saving Printer Settings

If you find that you use the same printer settings for many different reports and labels, you might want to save these settings for future use.

SEQUENCE OF STEPS

Control Center Reports panel: [highlight label | report format name] ↵

Prompt box: **Print Label | Report** ↵

Print menu: **Save Settings to Print Form** ↵

Prompt box: *<file name>* ↵

Print menu: **Begin Printing** ↵

USAGE

To save printer settings, select **Save Settings to Print Form** from the **Print** menu. If you've already saved the report or label format, dBASE will suggest using that same name, with the extension .PRF. Press ↵ if you wish to use the suggested file name. If dBASE does not suggest a name, enter any valid DOS file name.

When you later want to reuse your print settings, select **Use Print Form** from the **Print** menu and select the appropriate file name from the submenu that appears on the screen.

Sorting Labels and Reports for Printing

To print reports or mailing labels in sorted order, activate the appropriate index and then print the report or labels.

SEQUENCE OF STEPS

Control Center Data panel: [highlight database name] **Shift-F2**

Database design screen menu bar: **Organize**

Organize menu: **Order Records by Index** ↵

Index options menu: [highlight index name] ↵

Database design screen menu bar: **Exit**

Exit menu: **Save Changes and Exit** ↵

Control Center Labels | Reports panel: [highlight label | report format name] ↵

Prompt box: **Print Label | Report** ↵

Print menu: **Begin Printing | View Label | Report on Screen** ↵

USAGE

From the Control Center, highlight the database name in the Data panel and press **Shift-F2** (Design) to get to the database design screen. Select **Order Records by Index** from the **Organize** menu. Select the desired index. Then select **Save Changes and Exit** from the **Exit** pull-down menu.

In the Labels or Reports panel, highlight the file name and press ↵. Select **Print Report.** Then select either **Begin Printing** or **View Report on Screen,** whichever you prefer. The printed data will be sorted in the order you wanted.

SEE ALSO

Chapter 4: Sorting a Database

Using Queries to Print Labels and Reports

You can use any existing query to filter records that are printed in a report or as labels. The only requirement is that the view skeleton in the query must include all the fields that the form or report displays.

SEQUENCE OF STEPS

Control Center Queries panel: [highlight query name] ↵

Prompt box: **Use View** ↵

Control Center Labels | Reports panel: [highlight label | report format name] ↵

Prompt box: **Print Label | Report** ↵

Prompt box: **Current View** ↵

Print menu: **Begin Printing | View Label | Report on Screen** ↵

USAGE

If necessary, open the database file. Highlight the name of a report or label format in the **Labels** or **Reports** panel and then press ↵. Select **Print Label** or **Print Report.** When dBASE double-checks your intentions, select **Current View.**

Then select **Begin Printing** or **View Label I Report on Screen,** whichever you prefer.

The query will stay in effect for any other reports that you print, until you deactivate it either by opening another query or database file, or by selecting the current query name from the Queries panel and choosing Close View.

SEE ALSO

Chapter 5: Searching a Database

CHAPTER 7

Custom Forms

This chapter discusses techniques for creating custom forms for entering and editing data. Custom forms look better than the standard edit screen and can provide useful information to inexperienced dBASE users (see Figure 7.1 for an example). They can also do some of the work involved in entering data as well as trap and correct errors before they are stored in the database.

```
 Records    Go To    Exit                                    9:34:33 am
 ┌─────────────────────────────────────────────────────────────────────┐
 │    Enter/Edit Customer Information                                    │
 └─────────────────────────────────────────────────────────────────────┘

   First Name John            Last Name Smith

     Company ABC Co.            Address 123 A St.

        City San Diego     State CA   Zip 92067

       Phone (619)555-1234    Paid? (Y/N) Y  Start Date 11/15/88

 ┌────────────────────────┬──────────────────────────┬──────────────────┐
 │ ↑ previous field       │ PgDn  next record        │ F1    help       │
 │ ↓ next field           │ PgUp  previous record    │ F2    browse     │
 │ → cursor right         │ Ins   insert mode on/off │ F10   menu       │
 │ ← cursor left          │ Del   delete character   │ ↑F8   ditto      │
 └────────────────────────┴──────────────────────────┴──────────────────┘


 Edit    C:\dbase\CUSTLIST        Rec 8/9          File
```

Figure 7.1: A custom form

The Forms Design Screen

The dBASE IV forms design screen lets you be as creative as you wish when developing custom forms for your database files.

SEQUENCE OF STEPS

> Control Center Data panel: [highlight database name] ⏎
> Prompt box: **Use File** ⏎
> Control Center Forms panel: **<create>** ⏎

USAGE

To create a custom form, you first open the database file for which you want to design the form and select **<create>** from the Forms panel of the Control Center. You'll be taken to the forms design screen, with the Layout menu already displayed.

The forms design screen is similar to the reports design screen, except that the word *Form* appears in the lower-left corner of the screen and there are no bands. The menu bar consists of the Layout, Fields, Words, GoTo, and Exit menus. The ruler just beneath the menu bar shows margins (marked with square brackets) and tab stops (marked with triangles). The navigation line at the bottom of the screen shows special keys you can use to design your form.

The current row and column position of the cursor is displayed in the center of the status bar near the bottom of the screen. A custom form can be as wide as the screen (from column 0 to column 79).

When you use the form later to enter or change data, the top row of the screen (row 0 on the form) will display the menu bar and rows 22, 23, and 24 at the bottom of the screen will display the status bar and other messages. Therefore, when designing a form, try to use only rows 1 through 21.

The Edit Screen (Chapter 3)

Creating a Quick Layout

The easiest way to create a form is first to allow dBASE to create a simple form similar to the standard edit screen on the forms design screen. You can use this initial form as the starting point for designing your custom form.

Forms design screen: **Layout**

Layout menu: **Quick Layout** ↵

Select **Quick Layout** from the **Layout** pull-down menu. Figure 7.2 shows a quick layout.

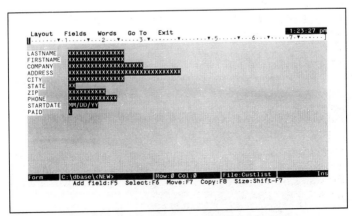

Figure 7.2: Quick layout of a form on the forms design screen

Adding Fields and Text

The basic editing keys for rearranging and designing a custom form are the same as those used for report and label design. See Table 7.1 for quick reference.

The text search and replace options available for the reports and labels design screens can also be used with the forms design screen. They are on the Go To pull-down menu, and are described in detail in Chapter 5.

SEE ALSO

Editing Label and Report Formats (Chapter 6), Searching for Information (Chapter 5)

KEYS	ACTION
→	Moves cursor right one character or to end of field template
←	Moves cursor left one character or to beginning of field template
Ctrl-→	Moves cursor to beginning of next word
Ctrl-←	Moves cursor to beginning of previous word
Tab	Moves cursor to next tab stop
End	Moves cursor to end of line
Home	Moves cursor to beginning of line
↓	Moves cursor down one line
↑	Moves cursor up one line

Table 7.1: Keys for Editing Custom Forms

KEYS	ACTION
F5	Adds a new field template or changes the currently highlighted one
F6	Selects field template or block
F7	Moves field or block selected with F6
F8	Copies field or block selected with F6
Shift-F7	Changes size of currently selected field template
Del	Deletes character at cursor or field, template, or block selected with F6
Backspace	Moves cursor left one character and erases along the way
Ctrl-T	Deletes word or field to the right of the cursor
Ctrl-Y	Deletes entire line
↵	Adds a new blank line if Insert mode is on or moves down one line if Insert mode is off
Ctrl-N	Inserts a blank line, regardless of whether Insert mode is on
PgDn	Scrolls down one screen or to bottom of existing text on the current page
PgUp	Scrolls up one screen or to top of existing text on the current page
Ins	Toggles between Insert and Overwrite modes
F1	Provides help
Ctrl-End	Saves changes and exits
Escape	Abandons changes and exits

Table 7.1: Keys for Editing Custom Forms (continued)

Making Your Form More Attractive

You can improve the appearance (and usability) of a custom form by adding boxes, lines, graphics characters, and color.

Boxes and Lines

Options for drawing boxes and lines are on the Layout pull-down menu.

SEQUENCE OF STEPS

Forms design screen: [move cursor to upper-left corner of box | left edge of line]

Forms design screen menu bar: **Layout**

Layout menu: **Box | Line** ⏎

Line options menu: **Single Line | Double Line** ⏎

Keyboard: ⏎ [to mark starting point of box | line]

Forms design screen: [use arrow keys to draw box | line]

Keyboard: ⏎ [to mark ending point of box | line]

USAGE

The **Box** option is always used to draw an even, rectangular box. While the **Line** option is generally used to draw straight lines, it can also be used to draw any shape, even a single-line special graphics character.

Box drawing and line drawing use the same basic techniques. That is, you first select either **Box** or **Line** from the **Layout** pull-down menu, and then select a style either single line or double line. You then mark the starting point for the box or line by pressing ⏎, draw the box or line using the arrow keys. When the entire box or line is drawn, press ⏎ again to complete your drawing. The bottom of the screen provides instructions to help you as you work.

Notice that while the cursor is within the box, the box frame is highlighted. As long as the frame is highlighted, you can manipulate the box. For example, you can use **F6** to select the box and then press **F7** or **F8** to move or copy the box. You can press **Del** to delete the box or **Shift-F7** to resize the box, using the usual arrow keys.

Special Graphics Characters

The Using Specified Character option allows you to use characters other than the single- and double-line characters to draw boxes. This option can also be used to place special graphics characters individually on the screen.

SEQUENCE OF STEPS

Forms design screen: [move cursor to upper-left corner of box | left edge of line]

Forms design screen menu bar: **Layout**

Layout menu: **Box | Line** ↵

Line options menu: **Using Specified Character** ↵

Character options menu: [highlight character] ↵

Keyboard: ↵ [to mark starting point of box | line]

Forms design screen: [press an arrow key once to place character]

Keyboard: ↵ [to mark ending point of box | line]

USAGE

When you select **Using Specified Character,** you'll see a submenu of graphics characters and ASCII numbers assigned to those characters. Use the arrow, **PgDn,** and **PgUp** keys to scroll through the menu. When the character you want is highlighted, press ↵ to select it.

Colors

You can select a box frame, field template, or any other area of a custom form on the forms design screen and color it by selecting Display from the Words pull-down menu.

SEQUENCE OF STEPS

Forms design screen: [highlight area to color] **Words**

Words menu: **Display** ⏎

Monochrome | color options menu: [cycle through **On** | **Off** options with ⏎ or select colors]

Keyboard: **Ctrl-End** [to record changes]

Keyboard: **F6 Esc** [to see results]

USAGE

The display options differ depending on whether you are using a monochrome or a color monitor. If you are using a monochrome monitor, you'll be given the options **Intensity** (to display letters in a bright boldface), **Underline** (to underline words), **Reverse Video** (to reverse the light and dark shades used for letters and their background), and **Blink** (to cause letters to blink on and off).

If you are using a color monitor, you will see the dBASE IV *electronic palette* for selecting a foreground and background color combination as well as an option for blinking.

Note that after you select a display attribute or color combination and return to the forms design screen, the selected area that you colored will still be highlighted, so your selection might not be readily apparent. To unselect the area and see the effects of your selection, press **F6** (Select) and then **Esc**.

SEE ALSO

Customizing Your Environment/Display Options (Chapter 11)

Creating Memo-Field Windows

Memo windows are very handy because they let you see at least a portion of a memo field while still viewing other fields in the database (see Figure 7.3).

Initially, the memo field will be displayed as a marker on the custom form. If you want to change the marker to a memo window, first rearrange all other fields on the form, leaving enough space to accommodate the memo window.

SEQUENCE OF STEPS

Forms design screen [move cursor to inside memo field template] **F5** | **Modify Field** on **Fields** menu

Field options menu: **Display As** [press **Space** bar to change setting to **Window**]

Field options menu: **Border Lines** ↵

Border options menu: [select border type]

Keyboard: **Ctrl-End** [to record changes]

Forms design screen: [move cursor into window, then use keys to size window]

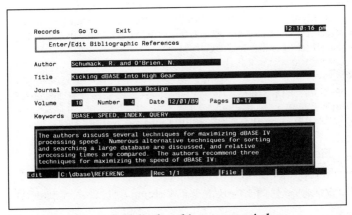

Figure 7.3: A memo field displayed in a memo window

To create a memo window, you first change the memo-field display format from Marker to **Window** and select a border for the window. When you return to the design screen, a large memo field window filled with X's will appear.

Now you need to size and position the window, using **Shift-F7** (Size) and **F7** (Move).

Controlling Input

There are three ways that you can control what is actually entered into a field on the form, so you can trap errors as they occur, before they are actually stored in the database. The same techniques can also ensure that data in a field is consistent: for example, that all phone numbers are entered with an area code, in the format (999)999-9999. You can control input using *template characters, picture functions,* and *edit options.*

Template Characters

A field template marks the place where actual database data will appear. Initially, character fields use templates such as XXXXXXXXXXXX, date fields use MM/DD/YY, and logical fields use the template L. You can also use other template characters to control what users enter in the field (see Table 7.2).

| SEQUENCE OF STEPS |

Forms design screen: [highlight field template] **F5** | **Modify Field** on **Fields** menu

Field options menu: **Template** ↵

Template option: [edit template]

Keyboard: **Ctrl-End** [to save changes]

USAGE

The basic steps in editing a template are to highlight that template on the forms design screen, then bring up the field options menu by pressing **F5** (Field) or selecting **Modify Field** from the **Fields** menu. Then select **Template** from the list of field options that appears, make your changes, and press **Ctrl-End**. Make sure that Insert mode is off, so you don't change the size of the template.

Besides the special characters in Table 7.2, you can insert *literal characters*, which become part of the data stored in the field. For example, the phone number template

SYMBOL	DESCRIPTION
A	Accepts only alphabetic characters A-Z and a-z (no numbers, spaces, or punctuation)
N	Accepts alphabetic and numeric characters, A-Z, a-z, 0-9, and the underscore, but no spaces or other punctuation
Y	Accepts either Y or N
#	Accepts numbers 0-9, spaces, periods (.), and plus (+) and minus (-) signs
L	Accepts T, F, Y, and N
X	Accepts any character
!	Accepts any character and converts letters to uppercase
9	Accepts real numbers only, including plus and minus signs
Other	Any other characters are *literal* characters and are actually stored in the database

Table 7.2: Characters Used in Field Templates

(999)999-9999 accepts any 10 numeric digits, 0-9, and automatically adds parentheses and hyphens. Hence, entering "2139876543" produces (213)987-6543.

Numeric Templates

When you place a numeric field in a report or form design, you'll see a template that reflects the width and decimal places assigned to the number in the database. For example, if a number is assigned a width of eight characters and two decimal places, the template for that field will automatically be 99999.99.

Unlike character data, numeric data is never truncated to fit within the space provided by a template. When a number is too large for the space allotted, dBASE displays only asterisks. For example, the template 999 displays only numbers with three or fewer digits. It displays any larger number, such as 1,000, as asterisks (***). Therefore, if you change a template on a form or report format, be sure to specify enough digits to accommodate the largest possible number for the field or calculation.

To specify how many decimal places to display in printed numbers, insert a decimal point in the appropriate position in the template. dBASE will round the number to fit the template. For example, the template 99999 displays the value 12345.678 as 12346 (no decimal places displayed). The template 99999.99 displays the same value as 12345.68. The template 99999.9999 displays the value as 12345.6780.

To display numbers with embedded commas, such as 12,345 (rather than 12345), insert commas into the template wherever you want them to appear in the printed number. If you use the template 999,999.99 to display extended prices, then the value 3850.00 will be displayed as 3,850.00.

For more information, see Chapter 8: Performing Calculations.

Picture Functions

Whereas template characters control the individual characters that are typed into a field, picture functions affect the entire field. Picture functions are available for two data types: character and numeric.

SEQUENCE OF STEPS

Forms design screen: [highlight field template] **F5** | **Modify Field** on **Fields** menu

Field options menu: **Picture Functions** ↵

Picture functions menu: [highlight option and press **Space** bar | ↵ to turn it **On** | **Off**]

Keyboard: **Ctrl-End** [to leave submenu]

Keyboard: **Ctrl-End** [to save changes]

USAGE

Picture functions operate on data as it is entered into or changed in a custom form. To assign picture functions to a field template in the forms design screen, you move the cursor to the appropriate field template and press **F5** (Field), or select **Modify Field** from the **Fields** menu. The **Picture Functions** option on the menu that appears will display the currently assigned picture functions (if any) between curly braces. To add or change picture functions, highlight **Picture Functions** and press ↵.

You will see a menu of picture-function options that are available for the current data type. Each option can be turned on or off by highlighting the option and pressing the **Space** bar. You won't notice any change on the design screen, because picture functions do not appear in the field template.

Character Picture Functions

The picture-function options you can assign to character types include Alphabetic Characters Only, Uppercase Conversion, Literals Not Part of Data, Scroll within Display Width, and Multiple Choice (see Table 7.3).

Alphabetic Characters Only If you assign the Alphabetic Characters Only picture function to a field template, the field will accept only letters (A to Z and a to z) later when you use the completed form. Note that even blank spaces are unacceptable. Thus, a field template that has this picture function turned on could not accept "Pulver-Smith," or "Pulver Smith" as an entry.

Uppercase Conversion The Uppercase Conversion picture function converts all lowercase letters entered in the field to uppercase. For example, if you assign it to a database field named PARTCODE, dBASE will convert an entry such as Ak7-7jl to AK7-7JL.

SYMBOL	EFFECT
A	Accepts alphabetical characters only (entire field)
!	Accepts any data, but converts all letters to uppercase
R	Removes literal characters from entry before storing them on the database
S	Allows long text to be entered into short field displays
M	Allows multiple-choice options to be displayed in a form and selected by pressing ↵

Table 7.3: Character Picture Functions for Custom Forms

Literals Not Part of Data   The Literals Not Part of Data
picture function removes all literals from data typed in a form
before storing the data in the database. For example, suppose
you specify the field template (999)999-9999 for entering data
into a field named PHONE. When you type a phone number
into the field, dBASE will fill in the literals (the parentheses
and hyphen) and store your entry in the database with these
characters included. But if you turn on the Literals Not Part
of Data picture function for the PHONE field, dBASE will
remove the literals after you enter a phone number. That is,
the form will still *display* the phone number with the parentheses and hyphen inserted, but dBASE will *store* only the
numbers in the database. Hence, if you enter (213)555-1212 as
the phone number, the actual database record will contain
2135551212.

Using the Literals Not Part of Data picture function saves
a little disk space by not storing the repetitive parentheses
and hyphen. However, when designing report formats, you
would always need to be certain to include the (999)999-9999
template to display data from the PHONE field; otherwise,
phone numbers would be printed without the parentheses
and hyphen.

Scroll within Display Width   This picture function enables you to enter data into a field that is wider than the
standard screen width. Although you can define a field
width of up to 254 characters for the character data type
when you create a database, a standard screen is only 80
characters wide. Now suppose you created a database with
a character field named REMARKS, which has a width of
100 characters. How would you place such a field in a custom form? Your best bet would be to modify the field
template to whatever size best fits on your custom form.
You could use the full 80-character width of the screen or
any smaller width.

Let's assume that you use a field template that consists of
40 X's to display the REMARKS field on your custom form.
To ensure access to the full 100 characters that the
REMARKS field offers, you would need to turn on the Scroll

within Display Width picture function. Later, when you use the completed custom form, it will display a highlight that is 40 characters wide for entering data into the REMARKS field. But when the cursor gets to that field in the form, you can still type up to 100 characters into the field. As you type beyond the fortieth character, the text in the field will scroll to the left to make more room.

When viewing existing data through the completed form, the form will initially display only the first 40 characters stored in the REMARKS field. But once the cursor gets to the REMARKS field, you'll be able to use ← and → to scroll to the left and right within the field and thereby view all 100 characters.

Multiple Choice   The Multiple Choice picture function allows you to create a multiple-choice field on your custom form. Such fields allow only certain entries. For example, suppose you create a database of members in a club, and that database includes a character field named STATUS. Any given member can have a status of Regular, Officer, Honorary, or Expired. Because only these four options are acceptable entries for the field, there is no need to allow the field to accept other data.

When typing in the multiple-choice entries, separate each option with a comma. For example, the string *Regular, Officer, Honorary, Expired* provides four multiple-choice options. Never use double quotation marks (") when listing options for a multiple-choice field; these are reserved for use with the dBASE programming language.

When you use a completed custom form that contains a multiple-choice field, the form initially displays one of the acceptable values in the field. When the cursor gets to that field on the form, you can press ↵ to use the displayed value or the Space bar to view other possible options. When the option you want to enter is displayed, press the ↵ key to accept it.

Numeric Picture Functions

Numeric picture functions let you further refine the format of printed numbers. Whenever you add or modify a field template and select Picture Functions from the Display Attributes menu, you'll see the options shown in Figure 7.4. You can move the highlight to any option and press the **Space** bar or ↵ to turn it on or off.

Table 7.4 shows picture functions that you can assign to numeric fields and calculations, as well as examples of how those functions affect the numbers 0, –123, and 98765.43. Each example assumes that the current template is 999,999.99.

You can combine numeric picture functions. For example, combining C and X places CR after positive numbers and DB after negative numbers. Combining Z and the left parenthesis character prints positive numbers normally, negative numbers in parentheses, and zeros as blank spaces (rather than as 0 or 0.00).

For more information, see Chapter 8: Performing Calculations.

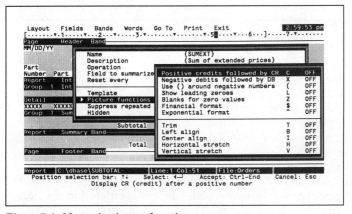

Figure 7.4: Numeric picture-functions menu

PICTURE FUNCTION	ACTION	EXAMPLES
C	Follows positive numbers (credits) by CR	0.00 CR −123.00 98,765.43 CR
X	Follows negative numbers (debits) by DB	0.00 123.00 DB 98,765.43
(	Uses () Around negative numbers	0.00 (123.00) 98,765.43
L	Shows leading zeroes	000000.00 000−123.00 098,765.43
Z	Uses blanks for zero values	 −123.00 98,765.43
$	Financial format	$0.00 $−123.00 $98,765.43
^	Exponential format	.00000000000E+−.123 .123000000000000E+3 .987654300000000E+5

Table 7.4: Numeric Picture Functions for Custom Forms

Edit Options

Another way you can control what is entered into a field is through edit options. These options are summarized in Table 7.5.

EDIT OPTION	EFFECT
Editing Allowed	If Yes, field contents can be changed; if No, field contents can be viewed, but not changed.
Permit Edit If	Allows you to enter a logical formula to determine when a field can be changed.
Message	Lets you enter a message that is displayed at the bottom of the screen when the field is highlighted.
Carry Forward	If Yes, data entered into one record is automatically carried over to the next record when you add new records (only data for the current field is carried forward).
Default Value	Lets you automatically place a suggested value into a field, which can be accepted or changed when you actually enter data.
Smallest Allowed Value	Specifies the smallest allowable value for the field.
Largest Allowed Value	Specifies the largest allowable value for the field.
Accept Value When	Lets you define a logical formula that determines whether a value can be entered into a field.
Unaccepted Message	Lets you define a message that is displayed on the screen if an unacceptable value is entered into a field.

Table 7.5: Edit Options for Custom Forms

Forms design screen: [highlight field template] **F5** | **Modify Field** on **Fields** menu

Field options menu: **Edit Options** ↵

Edit options menu: [highlight option] ↵

Option: *<text>* | [select **Yes** | **No** with **Space** bar | ↵] ↵

Keyboard: **Ctrl-End** [to leave submenu]

Keyboard: **Ctrl-End** [to save changes]

The general technique for assigning or changing an edit option for a field is similar to that for changing templates and picture functions. You need to get to the forms design screen and move the cursor inside the appropriate field template. Then you press **F5** (Field) (or select **Modify Field** from the **Fields** menu) and select **Edit Options** from the menu that appears. The **Edit Options** submenu will appear on the screen, where you can highlight and press ↵ to select any option. Note that you will not see any immediate effects on the form while you are designing it, only when you use the completed form.

Editing Allowed

The Editing Allowed option lets you determine whether a particular field can be edited. By default, all fields on a custom form can be changed when the completed form is used. If you change the Editing Allowed option to No, the form will display the contents of a field, but you will not be able to change them.

Permit Edit If

The Permit Edit If option lets you enter an expression that defines when a field can be edited. The expression you enter can take the form of any filter condition that you would use in a query, except that it must be a *complete expression*. For example, in the query design screen, you can place the *incomplete expression* "CA" in the STATE box to limit the display to California residents. But when creating an expression for the Permit Edit If edit option, you need to use the complete expression, STATE = "CA".

Use the Permit Edit If option when you want your custom form to permit a field to be edited only when the field's (or some other field's) contents meet a particular condition. For example, suppose you have a database with two character fields named PARTCODE and PARTNAME. To ensure that a part is assigned a part code before the part name is entered onto the custom form, you could use the Permit Edit If expression PARTCODE <> " " (part code does not equal blank) in the PARTNAME field. Table 7.6 shows examples of expressions that you could use in the Permit Edit If (or Accept Value When) edit option.

Remember that when you use your custom form in the future, dBASE will always move the cursor from field to field, from left to right, and from top to bottom. Therefore, when placing a field on your custom form, place any field that depends on the contents of another field below or to the right of the field that it depends on. This placement allows the independent field to be filled before the dependent field decides whether to permit editing.

For more information, see About Expressions (Chapter 8).

Message

The Message option lets you create a custom message that appears centered at the bottom of the screen when the cursor is in the appropriate field. You can create a separate and unique message for each field in your custom form. The message can be no more than 79 characters wide and cannot contain double quotation marks (").

Carry Forward

Normally when you enter records into a database, each new record is displayed with empty fields (except those that use a default value). Alternatively, you can use the Carry Forward option to tell dBASE to carry the value entered into a particular field in a new record to the next new record. In the next new record, you can accept the value carried forward by pressing ↵ when the cursor gets to that field, or you can type a new value.

Suppose you have a name-and-address database with a STATE field, and you set the Carry Forward option to Yes.

EXPRESSION	MEANING
LASTNAME <> " "	True when the first character in a character field named LASTNAME is not a blank space
STARTDATE <= DATE()+30	True when the date field named STARTDATE contains a date that is no more than 30 days beyond the current date
"-" $ PARTCODE	True when the character field named PARTCODE has a hyphen (-) embedded in it
PAID	True when the logical field named PAID contains .T.
.NOT. PAID	True when the Logical field named PAID contains .F.

Table 7.6: Examples of Valid Expressions

The first value entered for that field (for example, CA) will be carried forward to the STATE field of the next new record and to all subsequent records until a different value is entered. Then that value will be carried forward.

Default Value

You can use the Default Value option to specify a value, such as the current date, to be displayed as a suggestion when you add new records to the database. You can either accept the suggested value as is (by pressing ↵ when the cursor is in the field) or type a new value.

You can enter any value as a default value, as long as you use the correct data type. For example, if most of the records in a name-and-address database will have Los Angeles as the city, you can assign "Los Angeles" as the default value for that field. The quotation marks are required, because the CITY field is the character data type. To use a specific date as the default value for a date field, enclose the date in curly braces: {01/01/89}. (The dBASE function DATE() will display the current date.) You can also specify .T. rather than .F. as the default value for a Logical field.

Smallest and Largest Allowed Value

You can use the Smallest Allowed Value and Largest Allowed Value options independently or together to define a range of acceptable values for a specific field in a database.

Suppose the current year is 1989 and you want the custom form for a personnel database to accept only STARTDATE values in the range January 1, 1989, to December 31, 1989. To restrict the data entered in this way, you specify {01/01/89} as the lowest acceptable value for the field and {12/31/89} as the highest acceptable value.

Later, when you use the custom form to enter data in the database, entering an invalid value will cause dBASE to beep and display the message

Range is 01/01/89 to 12/31/89 (press SPACE)

at the bottom of the screen. You must then press the Space bar and enter a new, valid value before proceeding.

Remember to use the proper delimiters for the data type of the field (for example, quotation marks for character fields and curly braces for dates).

Accept Value When

The Accept Value When edit option is similar to the Smallest and Largest Allowed Value options, but provides a little more flexibility. With Accept Value When, you can use any valid expression (such as the expressions in Table 7.6) to test the data as soon as it is entered in the field when the form is in use. Later, when you use the completed form to enter and edit data, the field will accept only entries that cause the expression to evaluate to true. Any other entry will be rejected.

For example, suppose you created a database for storing accounts receivable that included a field named DATEPAID, of the date data type. To ensure that no back-dated payments are entered into the database, you would want the DATEPAID field to accept only dates greater than or equal to the current date. To achieve this, enter DATEPAID >= DATE() as the Accept Value When expression for the DATEPAID field. Later, when you use the form to enter or edit data, any date that you enter in the DATEPAID field will have to be greater than (later than) or equal to the current date. Any earlier date will be rejected.

Unaccepted Message

The Unaccepted Message edit option lets you define a message that is displayed whenever an invalid value is entered into a field that uses the Accept Value When edit option. Suppose you created the DATEPAID field using the Accept Value When edit option, as discussed in the previous section. You could also add an Unaccepted Message such as Date must be today's date or later. (Note that you can use any character except the double quotation mark (") in your message.)

Later, when you used the custom form to enter or edit data, an unacceptable entry into the DATEPAID field would cause dBASE to beep and display the message *Date must be today's date, or later (press SPACE)* at the bottom of the screen. You would need to press the Space bar and enter a new date.

For more information, see About Expressions (Chapter 8).

Multiple-Page Custom Forms

A single dBASE IV database file can contain up to 255 fields per record. Needless to say, if you were to create a database with that many fields in it, you'd be hard pressed to squeeze all those fields onto a single screen. To solve this problem, dBASE lets you divide any custom form into several pages (or screens full) of fields.

SEQUENCE OF STEPS

Forms design screen | form: **PgDn** | **PgUp** [to scroll through pages during design and use]

USAGE

To create multiple-page custom forms, you use the standard forms design screen. Initially, the forms design screen displays only enough space to create a single page (on which you would use rows 1 through 21). However, you can use **PgDn** and **PgUp** to scroll through additional pages on the forms design screen. A single custom form can contain over 1,600 screen pages.

To prevent additional pages in a custom form from being overwritten by messages at the top of the screen or the status bar, use the following row positions (as indicated by the

Row: Col: indicator near the bottom of the forms design screen) to start and end each page of the form:

PAGE	FROM ROW	TO ROW
1	1	21
2	23	43
3	45	65
4	67	87
5	89	109
6	111	131
7	133	153

. . . and so forth.

When using a completed form that contains multiple pages, use **PgDn** and **PgUp** to scroll forward and backward through individual pages. When you are at the last page of the form, pressing **PgDn** scrolls to the next record in the database. When you are at the first page, pressing **PgUp** scrolls back to the previous database record.

Saving a Form

When saving a form, you specify a description, then a file name.

SEQUENCE OF STEPS

Forms design screen menu bar: **Layout**

Layout menu: **Edit Description of Form** ↵

Prompt box: *<description>* ↵

Forms design screen menu bar: **Save This Form** on **Layout** menu | **Save Changes and Exit** on **Exit** menu

Save as prompt: *<file name>* ↵

USAGE

Select **Edit Description of Form** from the **Layout** pull-down menu. Type a description, such as "Form for entering/editing customer information," and press ↵. Select **Save This Form** from the **Layout** menu or **Save Changes and Exit** from the **Exit** menu. When prompted, type a valid DOS file name and press ↵. After dBASE creates the appropriate form (in its own language), you'll be returned to the Control Center. You'll see the name of the new form in the Forms panel of the Control Center.

Modifying a Form

To change an existing form design, first make sure the appropriate database file is open.

SEQUENCE OF STEPS

Control Center Data panel: [highlight database name] ↵

Prompt box: **Use File** ↵

Control Center Forms panel: [highlight form name] ↵

Prompt box: **Modify Layout** ↵

USAGE

Highlight the name of the form you want to edit in the **Forms** panel of the Control Center and press ↵. Select **Modify Layout** from the menu that appears.

You can use the same techniques to make changes in the form as you did to create it. When you are done, select **Save Changes and Exit** from the **Exit** pull-down menu. (If you prefer *not* to save your changes, select **Abandon Changes and Exit** instead.) You'll be returned to the Control Center.

Using a Form

To use any custom form, you simply highlight its name on the Forms panel of the Control Center and press **F2** (Data).

SEQUENCE OF STEPS

Control Center Forms panel: [highlight form name] **F2**

USAGE

The form will appear, and you can use the usual keys, including **PgDn** and **PgUp**, to scroll through records and to enter and change information. Note that you can still use the Data key (F2) to switch back and forth between the custom form and the browse screen.

CHAPTER 8

Performing Calculations

dBASE IV lets you perform calculations in reports and queries. Adding *calculated fields* and *summary fields* to a report format lets you print neatly formatted calculated data with totals, subtotals, and other types of calculations. Performing calculations through a query enables you to experiment with data and calculations quickly without creating a report format.

Although you can add calculated fields to a custom form, using the same method as for a report, these fields are of limited value because the calculations are not updated automatically as you add new data.

Performing Calculations in Reports

The Quick Report option and the column layout format always show totals for numeric fields in the report summary band. You can also add calculated fields and summary fields to your own custom report formats.

Calculated Fields

You can place calculated fields anywhere on a report or custom form format using the usual technique of positioning the cursor and pressing F5.

SEQUENCE OF STEPS

Reports design screen: [move cursor to position for new field] **F5** | **Add Field** on **Fields** menu

Field options menu: [move to Calculated column] **<create>** ⏎

Calculated field options menu: **Name** ⏎ *<name>* ⏎

Calculated field options menu: **Description** ⏎ *<description>* ⏎

Calculated field options menu: **Expression** ⏎ *<expression>* ⏎

Keyboard: **Ctrl-End** [to record changes]

USAGE

First open the database that contains the data you wish to perform calculations on; then access the reports (or labels, or forms) design screen. Position the cursor where you want the calculation to appear and then press **F5** (Field) or select **Add Field** from the **Fields** menu. You'll see a menu of options. Select **<create>** from the Calculated column, because you want to create a calculated field.

At this point, you are given the options to define a name, description, expression, and display attributes for the calculated field. Select **Name** and enter a field name, using the rules that apply to database field names (10 characters maximum length, must begin with a letter, may not contain spaces or punctuation except for the underline (_) character).

Then select **Description** and enter a plain-English description. (The description is optional, but is useful for future reference.) Select **Expression** and enter a dBASE expression, or press **Shift-F1** to access the Expression Builder and build the expression by selecting options.

If you wish to change the display attributes of the calculated field, select the template and picture functions options (discussed in Chapter 7). When you finish defining the calculated field, press **Ctrl-End** to leave the submenu.

Figure 8.1 shows a sample report design for a database that contains a numeric field named Qty and a numeric field named UnitPrice. The last field in the Detail band is a calculated field named ExtPrice, which uses the expression **Qty * UnitPrice** to calculate and display the total sale. Figure 8.2 shows the report printed by the sample design.

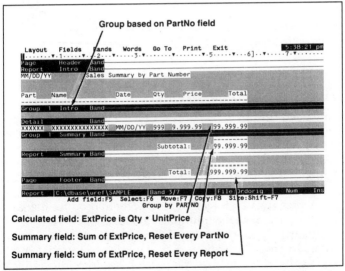

Figure 8.1: A report format with calculated and summary fields

```
06/15/89              Sales Summary by Part Number

Part      Name               Date      Qty     Price      Total
---------------------------------------------------------------
A-111     Astro Buddies      06/01/89   2      50.00      100.00
A-111     Astro Buddies      06/02/89   3      55.00      165.00
A-111     Astro Buddies      06/05/89   4      55.00      220.00
                                                         ---------
                                        Subtotal:         485.00

B-222     Mondo Man          06/01/89   2     100.00      200.00
B-222     Mondo Man          06/01/89   1     100.00      100.00
B-222     Mondo Man          06/15/88   1     100.00      100.00
                                                         ---------
                                        Subtotal:         400.00

C-333     Cosmic Critters    06/01/89   1     500.00      500.00
C-333     Cosmic Critters    06/01/89   5     500.00    2,500.00
                                                         ---------
                                        Subtotal:       3,000.00

                                                       ==========
                                        Total:         3,885.00
```

Figure 8.2: Report printed by the example design

About Expressions

Any valid dBASE expression is allowed in a calculated field. Table 8.1 displays the operators that are used in expressions. dBASE IV follows the standard mathematical order of precedence when performing calculations. That is, exponentiation takes place first, followed by multiplication and division, followed by addition and subtraction. Therefore, the expressions 2 * 5 + 1 and 1 + 2 * 5 both produce the same result, 11, because the multiplication takes place first.

When in doubt about order of precedence, use parentheses to group operations. For example, the formula (1 + 2) * 5 results in 15, because the parentheses force the addition to take place before the multiplication. When using parentheses in a mathematical formula, you must make sure that the formula contains an equal number of opening and closing parentheses. Otherwise, dBASE responds with an error message, such as *Syntax error* or *Unbalanced parentheses*.

OPERATOR	ACTION	EXAMPLE
+	Addition	2+2=4
−	Subtraction	5−3=2
*	Multiplication	3*5=15
/	Division	10/2=5
^ or **	Exponentiation	3^2=9 3**2=9
()	Grouping	(1+2)*5=15 1+(2*5)=11

Table 8.1: Arithmetic Operators

You can use calculated fields to combine character data. For example, given that City, State, and Zip are three character fields in the current database, the expression

```
TRIM(City)+", "+State+" "+Zip
```

displays the fields in the format *San Diego, CA 92067*.

You can use the + and − operators with date fields to calculate new dates or the number of days between two dates. For example, if a database contains a field named StartDate and a field named EndDate, the expression **StartDate+90** displays the date 90 days after the date in StartDate. The expression **EndDate–StartDate** displays the number of days between the two dates. The expression **EndDate–{01/01/89}** displays the number of days between the date in the End-Date field and January 1, 1989. The expression **EndDate–DATE()** displays the number of days between today's date and the date in the EndDate field.

You can use any dBASE *function* in an expression. For example, suppose a database contains two numeric fields named

Qty and UnitPrice, and also contains a logical field named Taxable. The expression

IIF(Taxable,1.07∗(Qty∗UnitPrice),Qty∗UnitPrice)

displays the quantity times the unit price with 7 percent tax added if the Taxable field contains .T. However, if the Taxable field contains .F., the field displays the quantity times the unit price without tax added.

SEE ALSO

Editing Label and Report Formats (Chapter 6), Printing Reports from Related Databases (Chapter 9), Controlling Input/Picture Functions (Chapter 7), Printing a Quick Report (Chapter 6)

Summary Fields

A summary field summarizes the information in a group of records. The summary might be a total or subtotal, an average, a count, or some other calculation. Table 8.2 lists the summary options.

SEQUENCE OF STEPS

Reports design screen: [move cursor to summary field template in Report Summary band]

Report Summary band: [move cursor to position for new field] **F5** | **Add Field** on **Fields** menu

Field options menu: [move to Summary column] **Sum** ↵

Summary field options menu: **Name** ↵ <name> ↵

Summary field options menu: **Description** ↵ <description> ↵

Summary field options menu: **Field to Summarize On** ↵ [highlight field name] ↵

Keyboard: **Ctrl-End** [to record changes]

USAGE

If a total is to appear once at the end of the report, you need to place it in the Report Summary band. Move the cursor to the appropriate column position within the Report Summary band, then press **F5** (Field) or select **Add Field** from the **Fields** menu. Then select an option from the **Summary** column (such as Average or Sum).

Next, select **Name** and enter a unique name for the field, following the same rules as for creating regular field names: 10 characters maximum, must begin with a letter, cannot contain spaces or punctuation marks other than the underline character (_). (The name is actually optional in summary fields.)

Next, select **Description** and enter a plain-English description up to 80 characters long (this too is optional in summary fields). Select **Field to Summarize On** and then select a database or calculated field name from the submenu that appears. Optionally, select **Template** and **Picture Functions** to change the appearance of the field on the report.

OPTION	OPERATION
Average	Displays the average for a group of numbers
Count	Counts the number of records in a group
Max	Displays the largest value in a group
Min	Displays the smallest value in a group
Sum	Displays the total of values in a group
Std	Displays the standard deviation (a statistical measure) for a group
Var	Displays the variance (a statistical measure) for a group

Table 8.2: Summary-Field Options

When you've finished defining the field, press **Ctrl-End**. The template for the summary field will appear on the screen. When the cursor is within the template for the summary field, the field name, the operation it performs, and the name of the field it summarizes are displayed at the bottom of the screen.

In Figure 8.1, the field template in the Report Summary Band near the bottom of the screen calculates the total sales for all customers. It uses the Sum operator, the calculated field ExtPrice as the field to summarize on, and is set to Reset Every REPORT (because it keeps accumulating totals until the report is finished).

Subtotals

To display subtotals in a report, you need to add a group band to the report format, then place a summary field to display subtotals in the Group Summary band.

SEQUENCE OF STEPS =========================

Group Summary band: [move cursor to position for new field] **F5** | **Add Field** on **Fields** menu

Field options menu: [move to Summary column] **Sum** ↵

Summary field options menu: **Name** ↵ *<name>* ↵

Summary field options menu: **Description** ↵ *<description>* ↵

Summary field options menu: **Field to Summarize On** ↵ [highlight field name] ↵

Summary field menu: **Reset Every** ↵ [*grouping field* | **Page** | **Report**] ↵

Keyboard: **Ctrl-End** [to record changes]

The basic steps for placing subtotaling fields in a report format are identical to those for placing totaling fields on the format, with two exceptions: the field must be placed in the Group Summary band rather than the Report Summary band, and the Reset Every option should be based on the field controlling the subtotals rather than on REPORT.

After designing a report format that uses subtotals, but before actually printing the report, you need to ensure that records are indexed (or sorted) into proper order (based on the subtotaling field). Otherwise, the subtotal groups may be printed in haphazard order.

For example, suppose a database contains records of sales transactions and includes the fields PartNo, Qty, and UnitPrice (among others). To design a report with sales subtotaled by part number, you first need to create a group band (in the reports design screen) based on the PartNo field.

Within the Detail band of the report, you could create a calculated field that uses the expression **Qty * UnitPrice** to calculate the total for each individual sale. (For the sake of example, assume you've named this calculated field ExtPrice.)

To display subtotals for each part number, you must then place in the Group Summary band a summary field that uses Sum as the operator and ExtPrice as the field to summarize. The Reset Every option for this field would be PartNo, because you want to reset the total to zero before subtotaling sales for each part. (See Figure 8.1 for an example.)

After saving the completed report format, but before you print the report, you need to make sure the database is in PartNo order, using either of two techniques. If the database is indexed on the PartNo field, you can transfer to the database design screen and select Order Records By Index from the Organize pull-down menu to activate the PartNo index. You can also create a query that displays records in PartNo sorted order, and activate the query, rather than the actual database, before printing the report.

| SEE ALSO |

Designing Reports/Designing a Report Format/Report Bands (Chapter 6), Activating an Index (Chapter 4)

Using Queries to Perform Calculations

You can use the queries design screen to perform calculations without going through all the steps involved in creating a form or report format. This is useful when you just want to experiment with data and calculations and do not need a neatly formatted report.

| SEQUENCE OF STEPS |

Control Center Data panel: [open database]

Control Center Queries panel: **<create>** ↵

Query design screen: **Fields**

Fields menu: **Create Calculated Field** ↵

Calculated fields skeleton: *<expression>* ↵

Keyboard: **F5** [to move calculated field to view skeleton]

View skeleton: *<calculated field name>* ↵

Keyboard: **F2** [to execute the query]

| USAGE |

First create a query for the appropriate database. Select **Create Calculated Field** from the **Fields** pull-down menu. Enter the expression (formula) required to perform the calculation, using database field names and arithmetic operators. Press **F5** (Field) to include the calculated field in the view skeleton so its results will be displayed. When prompted, enter a field name for the calculated field. A completed query is shown in Figure 8.3.

Press **F2** (Data), as usual, to see the results of the query (see Figure 8.4). The calculated field will appear in both the browse and edit screens. Remember that you can print the results of any query simply by pressing **Shift-F9** Quick Report while the results are on the screen.

You can add up to 20 calculated fields to a query. Each new calculated field will be added to the right of existing calculated fields. To remove all the calculated fields from a query, put the cursor into any calculated field and select **Remove File from Query** from the **Layout** menu.

SEE ALSO

Chapter 5: Searching a Database

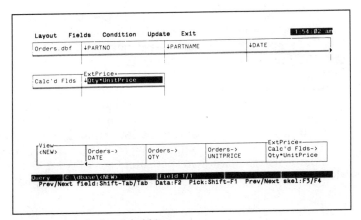

Figure 8.3: Calculated field in a query

```
   Records    Fields    Go To    Exit                          12:31:23 am
  ┌────────┬──────────────┬────────┬─────┬──────────┬──────────────────────┐
  │PARTNO  │PARTNAME      │DATE    │QTY  │UNITPRICE │EXTPRICE              │
  ├────────┼──────────────┼────────┼─────┼──────────┼──────────────────────┤
  │B-222   │Banana Man    │06/01/89│  2  │ 100.00   │        200.00        │
  │B-222   │Banana Man    │06/01/89│  1  │ 100.00   │        100.00        │
  │A-111   │Astro Buddies │06/01/89│  2  │  50.00   │        100.00        │
  │C-333   │Cosmic Critters│06/01/89│ 1  │ 500.00   │        500.00        │
  │A-111   │Astro Buddies │06/02/89│  3  │  50.00   │        150.00        │
  │A-111   │Astro Buddies │06/05/89│  4  │  50.00   │        200.00        │
  │B-222   │Banana Man    │06/15/88│  1  │ 100.00   │        100.00        │
  │C-333   │Cosmic Critters│06/15/88│ 2  │ 500.00   │       1000.00        │
  │C-333   │Cosmic Critters│06/15/88│ 1  │ 500.00   │        500.00        │
  │C-333   │Cosmic Critters│07/01/89│ 2  │ 500.00   │       1000.00        │
  │        │              │        │     │          │                      │
  └────────┴──────────────┴────────┴─────┴──────────┴──────────────────────┘
  Browse   C:\dbase\<NEW>              Rec 1/10              View
                             View and edit fields
```

Figure 8.4: Results of the query in Figure 8.3

Summary Operators

Like reports, queries offer summary operators. To use a summary operator in a query, place its name beneath the box in the appropriate field of the file skeleton (you cannot use summary operators with calculated fields). The summary operator must be spelled as listed in Table 8.3. The table also lists the data types with which each summary operator can be used.

You can combine filter conditions and summary operators in separate fields or in the same field. When combining the two in a single field, separate them with a comma, as shown in Figure 8.5. (The query in this figure counts the number of records in the database with part number A-111.) You can also combine different summary operators in a single query.

SUMMARY OPERATOR	CALCULATES	DATA TYPES
AVG or AVERAGE	Average	Numeric, float
CNT or COUNT	Count	Numeric, float, character, date, logical
MAX	Highest value	Numeric, float, character, date
MIN	Lowest value	Numeric, float, character, date
SUM	Total	Numeric, float

Table 8.3: Summary Operators Used in Queries

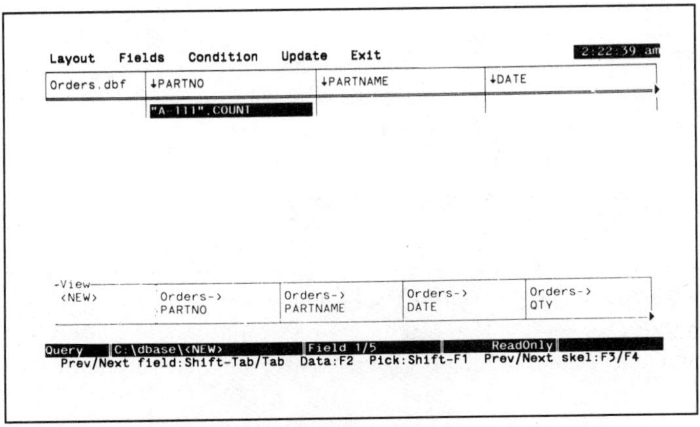

Figure 8.5: A query combining a filter condition and a summary operator in a single field

Groups and Subtotals

Queries can generate quick calculations that involve groups or subtotals, without the use of report formats or indexes. To group the results of a query, place the Group By operator in the field by which you want records grouped and include at least one summary operator to perform a calculation. For example, Figure 8.6 shows a query to total the Qty field for each PARTNAME in a sample database. The results of the query show *only* the resulting summaries, and not the individual details within each group, as Figure 8.7 shows.

For more information, see Designing Reports/Designing a Report Format/Report Bands (Chapter 6).

Figure 8.6: Query to subtotal QTY by part name

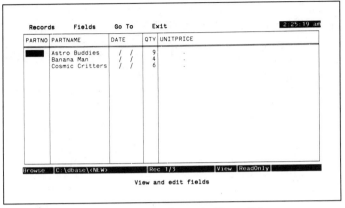

Figure 8.7: Results of the query shown in Figure 8.6

Calculating Frequency Distributions

You can combine the Group By and Count operators in a query to calculate a *frequency distribution* (a count of all records that have specific values, with the values listed by frequency of occurrence). For example, in a customer database you could find out how many customers live in each state or city.

SEQUENCE OF STEPS

Query design screen file skeleton: [place **Group By** operator in field by which records are to be grouped]

Query design screen file skeleton: [place **Count** operator in any other field]

USAGE

When performing frequency distributions, remember that the Group By operator, not the Count operator, is placed in the field of interest (see Figure 8.8). For example, to count

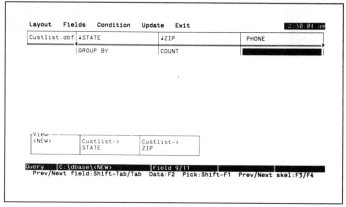

Figure 8.8: A frequency distribution query

how many customers are in each state, you would place the Group By operator in the State field. You can place the Count operator in any other field.

To ensure that the results of the query are easy to read, include only the fields that contain the Group By and Count operators in the view skeleton.

Calculating Dates

You can use basic date arithmetic in queries to isolate records that are older or newer than a specified date or to find records from between two dates. To display records that are older or newer than a specified date, use the +, −, and <= operators in the filter condition for the Date field. For example, placing the filter condition **<= {9/12/89} – 90** in a date field displays records that are 90 or more days before 9/12/89.

You can use the dBASE DATE() (today's date) function in place of a specific date in a query. If you replace the formula <= {9/12/88} –90} with the formula <= **DATE() – 90**, the query will display records with dates that are 90 or more days before today. If you then save that query, you can simply select it from the Control Center at any time in the future to see records with dates from 90 or more days ago. This feature is very handy for accounts receivable.

You can also subtract one date from another to determine the number of days between them. For instance, the formula {12/15/88} – {12/01/88} results in the number 14, because 12/15/88 is 14 days "larger than" (that is, after) 12/01/88. This kind of date arithmetic can be very useful in databases that store starting and ending dates for projects.

For more information, see Saving a Query for Future use (Chapter 5).

Comparing Fields

Once in a while, you might want to perform a query that compares values in one field to values in another field. Suppose you want to isolate records that have a difference of three or more dollars in the opening and closing prices (stored in the Open and Close fields) from a database of stock prices. To perform such a query, you need to use an *example,* or *placeholder.* The placeholder can be any letter or word. Put the placeholder in one of the comparison fields and then use the placeholder in the filter condition of the other one (see Figure 8.9). Notice that the query uses the word *Open* as the placeholder for the Open field (although the placeholder could just as easily be X or YooHoo). The Close field uses the filter condition >= **Open + 3** to isolate records that have a value in the Close field that is greater than or equal to the value in the Open field plus 3.

For more information, see Comparing Records (Chapter 5)

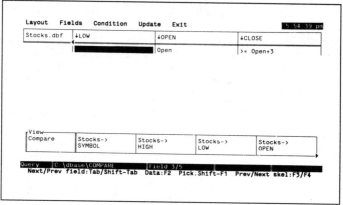

Figure 8.9: A query comparing two fields

CHAPTER 9

Managing Related Database Files

In most business applications, it is not practical to store all information in a single database file. This chapter is a reference for using multiple *related* databases.

One-To-Many Database Designs

Suppose you want to store accounts-receivable information for customer charge-account transactions, and customers can charge any number of items in a month. You can attempt to store the accounts-receivable information in a single database file using either one record per transaction or one record per customer. Neither of these approaches is satisfactory, however.

If you base each record on a single charge transaction, as in Figure 9.1, the database will store the correct information, but the database will not be efficient or convenient to use because

- Repeating names and addresses wastes both disk space and data-entry time.

- If a customer changes address, this change must be made in many different records.

If you base each record on a customer, rather than a transaction, and use multiple fields for charge transactions, you eliminate the problem of repeated names and addresses. Figure 9.2 shows an example in which charge amounts are stored in fields named Amount1, Amount2, Amount3, and AmountN, and dates are stored in similarly named fields. This second design, however, has a different set of problems:

- There is a limit to the number of fields that a database record can have, so there is a limit to the number of charges a customer can make.

- If you want to query for all charge transactions that occurred, for example, on 01/01/89, you would need to include each date field in the query (Date1=01/01/89 or Date2=01/01/89 or Date3 = 01/01/89... and so on).

- You could not easily distinguish charges that have been invoiced or paid from those that have not.

LastName	FirstName	Address	City	State	Zip	Amount	Date
Smith	John	123 A St.	San Diego	CA	92067	$276.69	01/01/89
Smith	John	123 A St.	San Diego	CA	92067	$600.26	01/01/89
Smith	John	123 A St.	San Diego	CA	92067	$962.91	01/01/89
Smith	John	123 A St.	San Diego	CA	92067	$291.88	02/02/89
Smith	John	123 A St.	San Diego	CA	92067	$972.70	02/02/89
Beach	Sandy	11 Elm St.	Portland	OR	76543	$331.77	01/01/89
Beach	Sandy	11 Elm St.	Portland	OR	76543	$100.63	01/01/89
Beach	Sandy	11 Elm St.	Portland	OR	76543	$698.52	01/01/89
Beach	Sandy	11 Elm St.	Portland	OR	76543	$183.15	02/02/89
Beach	Sandy	11 Elm St.	Portland	OR	76543	$217.41	02/02/89

Figure 9.1: A poorly designed accounts-receivable database

LastName	FirstName	Address	City	State	Zip	Amount1	Date1	Amount2	Date2	Amount3	Date3
Smith	John	123 A St.	San Diego	CA	92067	$468.39	01/01/89	$926.61	01/01/89	$54.66	01/01/89
Adams	Annie	345 Ocean St.	Santa Monica	CA	92001	$702.02	01/01/89	$253.07	01/01/89	$684.76	01/01/89
Mahoney	Mary	211 Seahawk	Seattle	WA	88977	$632.50	01/01/89	$351.02	01/01/89	$702.53	01/01/89
Newell	John	734 Rainbow	Butte	MT	54321	$665.33	01/02/89	$892.19	01/02/89	$294.24	01/02/89
Beach	Sandy	11 Elm St.	Portland	OR	76543	$75.96	01/02/89	$970.92	01/02/89	$99.69	01/02/89
Kenney	Ralph	1101 Rainbow	Los Angeles	CA	96607	$582.68	01/02/89	$307.47	01/02/89	$523.95	01/02/89
Schumack	Susita	47 Broad St.	Philadelphia	PA	45543	$990.16	01/03/89	$598.00	01/03/89	$943.32	01/03/89

Figure 9.2: An improved, but still inadequate design for the accounts-receivable database

At the heart of this accounts-receivable problem is the fact that there is a natural *one-to-many* relationship between customers and their charges. Any *one* customer may have many charges, and in fact may have an *unpredictable* number of charges.

The best way to store information when there is a one-to-many relationship is to place the information in two separate databases to minimize repetition of information. Hence, the best way to store information about customers and their charges is to use two separate database files: one for names and addresses and another for charge transactions. That way, you will not need to repeat information unnecessarily, and the number of charge transactions that you can record for a customer will not be limited.

However, separating customers and their transactions into two separate database files does create one new problem. How do you ensure that each charge in the charge-transaction database is billed to the correct customer? To *relate* each charge to the appropriate customer, you create a *common field*—one that exists in both databases, with the same name, data type, width, and number of decimal places. (It's also a good idea to index this field in both databases, as this will speed up later operations.)

The common field must contain information that is unique to each customer, or problems will arise. For example, if you use the customer's last name to link charges to customers, dBASE can look at any single charge and link it to a specific customer, such as Smith. But if there are two or more Smiths, how does dBASE decide which Smith gets the bill? Linking on an additional field, such as the customer's first name, still does not ensure a unique identification, and you're starting to repeat too much information from the Customer database in the Charges database.

The best way to relate the two databases is to assign each customer a unique customer number, or code, and to store this code with each record in the Charges database. As long as no two customers have the same customer number, there can be no confusion about who is responsible for each charge transaction. Figure 9.3 shows a simple example in which a field named Custno exists in both the Charges database and the Customer database (in a real Charges database, you would probably want to add fields to store more information about each charge).

There is always the temptation to put hidden meanings into common fields that relate two files. For example, you might assign each customer a code such as SD41289, where SD stands for San Diego, 4 stands for an excellent credit rating, and 1289 stands for a starting date. If you try to use a scheme like this and have two or more San Diego residents with credit ratings of 4 and start dates of 12/89, you may wind up assigning the same number to multiple customers. Using an arbitrary and meaningless number is the best (albeit most impersonal) way to relate two files.

Even after you add a Custno field to both databases, dBASE does not automatically "know" that the Custno field in the Customer database is in any way related to the Custno field in the Orders database. You must use the common Custno field to create a view that links the two databases.

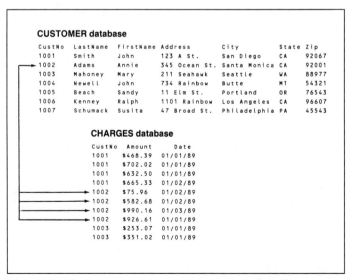

CUSTOMER database

CustNo	LastName	FirstName	Address	City	State	Zip
1001	Smith	John	123 A St.	San Diego	CA	92067
1002	Adams	Annie	345 Ocean St.	Santa Monica	CA	92001
1003	Mahoney	Mary	211 Seahawk	Seattle	WA	88977
1004	Newell	John	734 Rainbow	Butte	MT	54321
1005	Beach	Sandy	11 Elm St.	Portland	OR	76543
1006	Kenney	Ralph	1101 Rainbow	Los Angeles	CA	96607
1007	Schumack	Susita	47 Broad St.	Philadelphia	PA	45543

CHARGES database

CustNo	Amount	Date
1001	$468.39	01/01/89
1001	$702.02	01/01/89
1001	$632.50	01/01/89
1001	$665.33	01/02/89
1002	$75.96	01/02/89
1002	$582.68	01/02/89
1002	$990.16	01/03/89
1002	$926.61	01/01/89
1003	$253.07	01/01/89
1003	$351.02	01/01/89

Figure 9.3: The best way to store accounts receivable data

You can then use this view to search for information or print reports.

A one-to-many database design can include more than two databases linked with a common field. For example, you might want to create a Payments database and use the Custno field to identify the customer to whom each payment belongs. Linking three or more files with a view is no more difficult than linking two.

Many-to-Many Database Designs

Another common database design is based on a *many-to-many* relationship. This type of relationship occurs quite often in applications that involve scheduling. For example, a school offers many different courses, and each course is attended by many different students. To set up a database design for such an application, you need three database files: one to list students, one to list courses, and one to list students' numbers and the courses in which they are enrolled. The design assumes that each student and each course has a unique number.

Figure 9.4 shows the three databases and the links among them. The common field between the Students and Linker databases is StudentID, a Character field that is 11 spaces wide in both databases. The common field linking Courses to Linker is CourseID, a Character field that is 5 spaces wide in both databases. (Although the course IDs shown are not completely arbitrary, as long as each department in the school has a unique abbreviation and each course in each department has a unique number, each course will be ensured a unique code.)

Just like databases with a one-to-many relationship, these databases can be linked with a *view*, which is then used to find information or print reports.

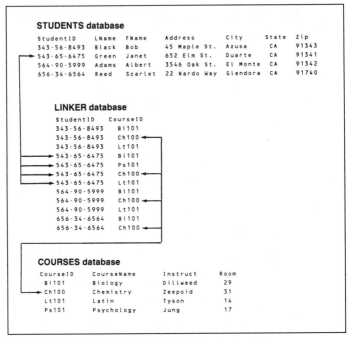

Figure 9.4: Three related databases used for scheduling

Creating Views with Multiple Databases

A view is essentially a query that includes two or more file skeletons and an *example* (or *placeholder*) to relate the common fields. The example used in the query design screen must show dBASE that records with identical values in the common field on both databases are related.

Control Center Data panel: [open one database]

Control Center Queries panel: **<create>** ↵

Query design screen menu bar: **Fields**

Fields menu: **Include Indexes** [change setting to **Yes**] ↵

Menu bar: **Layout**

Layout menu: **Add File to Query** ↵

File options menu: [highlight second database name] ↵

Menu bar: **Fields**

Fields menu: **Include Indexes** [change setting to **Yes**] ↵

File skeleton for second database: [move to common field]

Menu bar: **Layout**

Layout menu: **Create Link by Pointing** ↵

File skeleton for first database: [move to common field] ↵

View skeleton: [press F5 to add appropriate fields from second database]

Keyboard: **F2** [to execute the query]

| USAGE |

Open one database to be viewed from the Control Center **Data** panel. To start building the view, highlight **<create>** in the **Queries** panel and press ↵, which brings you to the query design screen. Select **Include Indexes** from the **Fields** pull-down menu and change its setting to **Yes** (a # symbol appears next to the indexed field).

Now, to bring a file skeleton of the second database into the design screen, select **Add File to Query** from the **Layout** pull-down menu. From the submenu that appears, select the database name. Activate the appropriate index by selecting **Include Indexes** again.

To tell dBASE that the two databases are related through the common field, press **Tab** to move the highlight to that field in the second file skeleton and select **Create Link By Pointing** from the **Layout** pull-down menu. Press **F3** (Previous) and **Tab** to move the highlight to the common field in the first file skeleton. Press ↵ to complete the link.

dBASE adds the placeholder LINK1 to the common field of each file skeleton (see Figure 9.5). The query presents an example in which the common field from each database contains the same placeholder. When you execute the query, dBASE will follow this example and display records that have the same value in the common field. The Create Link by Pointing option uses LINK1 as the placeholder, but you can, instead, type any letter or word into the common fields, as long as you use the same letter or word in both file skeletons.

You can use this method to link two or more files in a one-to-many or many-to-many design, as long as they include the proper common fields. Just include file skeletons for all the files (using the **Add File to Query** option), and select **Create Link by Pointing** (or insert placeholders) for each file. Figure 9.6 shows a query to display data from three

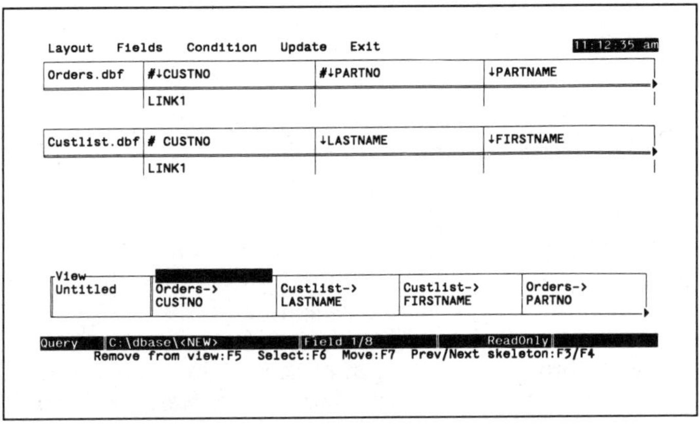

Figure 9.5: A query linking two databases

many-to-many related files. Notice that there are two placeholders: LINK1 and LINK2. (In this sample view, the Asc1 operator is also used, so that the resulting display will sort records into StudentId order.)

When you create a query that links two or more files, you can still use filter conditions to isolate records that meet a particular search criterion. If the filter condition is based on one of the linking fields, enter the LINK example first, followed by a comma and the filter condition. You can place filter conditions in any of the other field boxes in the usual manner and use the rows from each file skeleton to create AND and OR relationships. Placing different filter conditions in the top rows of two file skeletons creates an AND query; placing the filters on different rows creates an OR query.

Before you execute the query, you need to adjust the view skeleton (using **F5**) to include the appropriate fields from each database. Copy the fields into the view skeleton and rearrange them the way you want to see the data. Press **F2** (Data) to execute the query. A browse (or edit) screen will appear showing all the fields you specified in the view skeleton, *as though* a single database contained repetitive information from the two database files.

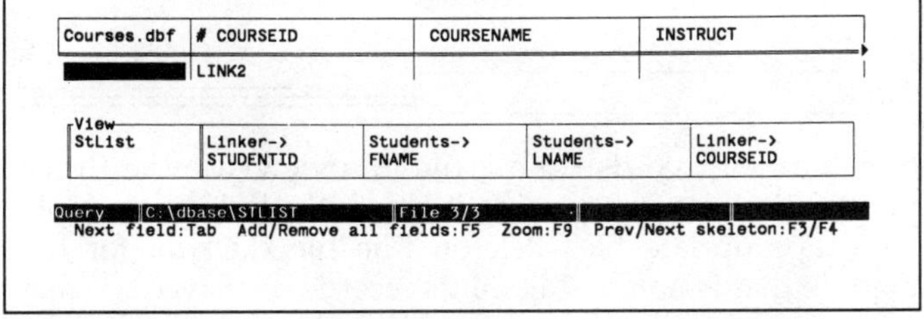

Figure 9.6: A query linking three many-to-many related files

When a browse or edit screen is displaying a view, you cannot make changes. That's why the message *ReadOnly* appears in the status bar near the bottom of the screen. If you attempt to make changes through a view, dBASE will beep and ignore your keystrokes. If you wish, you can save the query and use it as a basis for developing report formats.

SEE ALSO

Chapter 5: Searching a Database

Viewing Every Record

Normally a view presents only records that have a common field in both databases. For example, if you have a Customer database and an Orders database linked on a Custno field, and customers 1007 to 1009 have no records in the Orders database, they will not be included in a view. However, in some situations you might want to include all records from a database file, even if the related file contains no information for some records.

SEQUENCE OF STEPS

Query design screen: [highlight common field in desired file skeleton]
Common field box: **Every LINK1** ↵

USAGE

To include all records from a file in a view, use the **Every** operator in the query, placing it before the linking example in the appropriate file skeleton (the file skeleton for the database that is not having all its records displayed). When you execute the query, fields from the other database will be empty because there is no related information.

| SEE ALSO |

Searching with Relational Operators (Chapter 5)

Limited Links

Usually, a query will find every record that matches the linking value. For example, if there are a dozen records for customer number 1111, dBASE will display all of them. Sometimes, however, you want to see just the first record.

| SEQUENCE OF STEPS |

Query design screen: [highlight common field in
desired file skeleton]

Common field box: **First LINK1** ⏎

| USAGE |

To view only the first record that matches a linking value, place the **First** operator before the linking example in the appropriate file skeleton. If you have a Customer and an Orders database linked on the Custno field, a view using **First** would show only the first record for customer 1111, the first record for customer 1112, and so on.

| SEE ALSO |

Searching with Relational Operators (Chapter 5)

Printing Reports from Related Databases

You can use a view to print reports from multiple databases that are related in a one-to-many or many-to-many design.

SEQUENCE OF STEPS

Query design screen: [create query that links the databases]

Keyboard: **F2** [to test the query]

Keyboard: **Shift-F2** [to return to the query design screen]

Query design screen menu bar: [save query]

Reports design screen: [create report as if you were using a single database]

Reports design screen menu bar: [save report]

USAGE

To print a report from two or more databases, you first need to create a query that links the databases. Also, make sure that all the fields you need in the printed report are included in the view skeleton. If the report involves any groups (subtotals), be sure to use the **Sort on This Field** option from the query **Fields** menu to arrange the records into proper order for the grouping.

After creating the query, test it by pressing **F2** (Data). If you are satisfied with the results, press **Shift-F2** (Design) to return to the query design screen and save the query in the usual fashion. (If you are not satisfied with the query, you can easily make changes, and press F2 to try out the modified query.)

Next you need to use the view as the basis for building a report format. Make sure the view name is above the line in the Queries panel of the Control Center. Then select **<create>** from the Reports panel. As far as the reports design screen is concerned, a view is no different from a database file, so you are now free to use the same techniques you use with a single database file to design a report format to your liking.

After you save the report format, you need to follow two steps to print the actual report:

- First activate the view by highlighting its name in the Queries panel, pressing ↵, and selecting Use View.
- Next, highlight the report name in the Reports panel, press ↵, and select Print Report.

You can also use a view to lay out a custom form. But remember, when the view is active, you cannot change any data in the database. Hence, your custom form would be useful only for viewing data on the screen.

SEE ALSO

Chapter 5: Searching a Database, Chapter 6: Labels and Reports

---

Automatic Updating

In many business applications, you'll want dBASE to update information automatically in one database file based on information in another database file.

SEQUENCE OF STEPS

Query design screen: [create query to link databases]
Box containing target database name: **Replace** ↵
Box for field to be updated: **With** *<field name>* ↵
Query design screen menu bar: **Update**

Update menu: **Perform the Update** ↵

Update options menu: **Replace Values In** ↵ *<file name>* ↵

Keyboard: **F2** [to see results]

USAGE

To understand how automatic updating works, suppose you work for a business that purchases items to sell. You have three database files, named Master, Sales, and Purchase. The Master database stores information about each item in the inventory, including the part number, part name, in-stock quantity, unit price, and reorder point, as well as other useful information. The Partno field is indexed and is the common field used to link transactions to the Sales and Purchase databases. The Sales database stores orders, including the part number, quantity sold, and date of sale, and is also indexed on the Partno field. All completed purchase transactions are stored in the Purchase database, which has the same fields as Sales and is also indexed on the common field, Partno.

To calculate the true in-stock quantity for each product in the inventory, you need to subtract the quantities of items sold in the Sales database from in-stock quantities in the Master database. This is done with an *update query* that links the two databases (see Figure 9.7).

Notice that the Master file (the one containing the **Replace** operator) is the target of the replacements. The Qty-Sold field contains the placeholder **Sold.** The In-Stock field uses the expression **With In-Stock – Sold** to subtract the quantity sold from the quantity in stock. When you select **Perform the Update** from the **Update** menu to execute this query, dBASE will step through each record in the non-target database (Sales), look for a record in the target database (Master) that has the same part number (because LINK1 sets up the link), and then perform the With calculation in the In-Stock field.

To update the Master database using the quantities in the Purchase database, you need to add the quantities received to the in-stock quantities and subtract them from the on-order quantities. (Presumably the items received were previously on order, but now the on-order quantity needs to be decreased accordingly.)

The query to perform the update appears in Figure 9.8. The **Replace** update operator specifies a replacement update. The word **Recvd** is a placeholder for the value in the Qty-Recvd field. The expression **With In-Stock + Recvd** replaces the in-stock value with its current value plus the quantity received. The expression **With On-Order – Recvd** replaces the on-order value with its current value minus the quantity received. Again, because the Partno fields in the two file skeletons contain the same LINK1 placeholder, the replacement takes place only in the Master file record that has the same part number as the record in the Sales database.

SEE ALSO

Chapter 5: Searching a Database

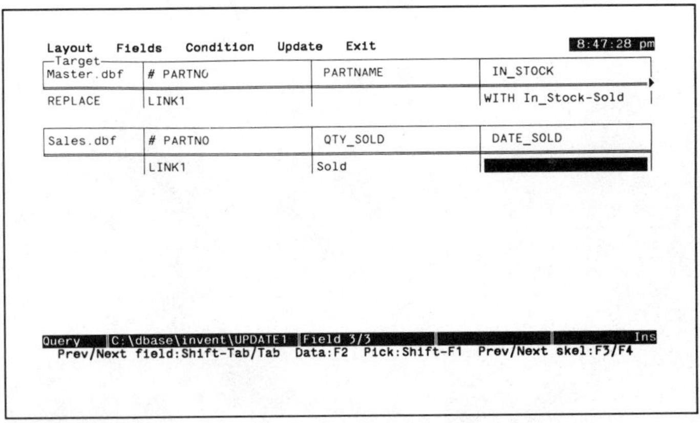

Figure 9.7: *Query to subtract sold quantities from in-stock quantities*

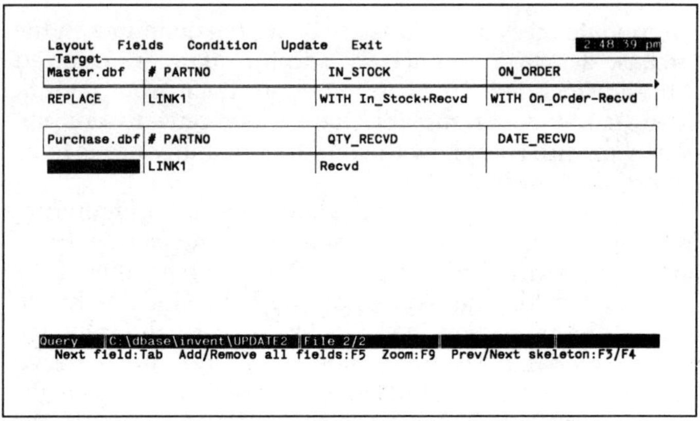

Figure 9.8: Query to update in-stock and on-order quantities

CHAPTER 10

Catalogs and Files

This chapter presents general techniques for managing catalogs and files, as well as techniques for interfacing with the file-management capabilities of DOS. It also describes how to import and export dBASE data.

Managing Catalogs

A *catalog* is a tool for helping you keep the names of files that belong together visible in the Control Center. Any time you create a file (be it a database file, report format, custom screen, or whatever), dBASE automatically adds the new file name to the current catalog, and that name appears in the Control Center.

Because a catalog consists only of the names of files, you can include the same file name in more than one catalog. As you create and work with multiple catalogs, you may eventually want to add, change, or delete file names in them. The Catalog pull-down menu in the Control Center offers all the options you'll need.

Creating a New Catalog

The general steps for creating a catalog are simple.

SEQUENCE OF STEPS

Control Center menu bar: **Catalog**

Catalog menu: **Use a Different Catalog** ↵

Catalog options menu: **<create>** ↵

Prompt box: *<file name>* ↵

USAGE

Pull down the **Catalog** menu from the Control Center menu bar. Highlight the **Use a Different Catalog** option and press ↵. The screen displays a submenu of existing catalog names as well as the option to create a new catalog, as shown in Figure 10.1. Highlight the **<create>** option and press ↵.

The screen displays the prompt *Enter name for new catalog:*. The name you enter must follow these rules:

• It may be no more than eight characters long.

• It may contain numbers (0 to 9) but may not contain any blank spaces or punctuation marks, such as ?, *, ., $, :,

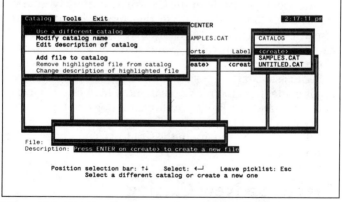

Figure 10.1: The Catalog menu and a submenu of catalog names

or ;. The underline character (_) is the only special character allowed.

- You may use upper- or lowercase letters, but lowercase
letters are automatically converted to uppercase.

Type the new catalog name and press ↵. dBASE automatically adds the extension .CAT to the name you provide.

The new catalog will become the current catalog, and the
panels in the Control Center will be empty. Any new files
you create while using the new catalog will be listed in the
catalog automatically.

Adding a Catalog Description

It's helpful to have a short description of a catalog's contents.

SEQUENCE OF STEPS

Control Center menu bar: **Catalog**

Catalog menu: **Edit Description of Catalog** ↵

Prompt box: *<description>* ↵

USAGE

To add or change a catalog description, select **Edit Description of Catalog** from the **Catalog** pull-down menu. Use the
usual editing keys to type a new description (or change
the old one) and press ↵. The description of the catalog appears when you scroll through catalog names after selecting
Use a Different Catalog.

Changing the Name of the Current Catalog

If you start dBASE IV from a directory that contains no
catalogs, it will automatically create a catalog named UN-
TITLED.CAT, which includes all of the dBASE IV database

files on the current directory. You will probably want to change this to a more meaningful name.

SEQUENCE OF STEPS

Control Center menu bar: **Catalog**

Catalog menu: **Modify Catalog Name** ↵

Prompt box: *<file name>* ↵

USAGE

To change the name of the current catalog, select **Modify Catalog Name** from the **Catalog** pull-down menu. Press **Backspace** to erase the current name and then enter the new name. Do not enter any extension; dBASE will add the .CAT extension automatically.

Selecting a Catalog

When working with multiple catalogs, you can switch from one to another.

SEQUENCE OF STEPS

Control Center menu bar: **Catalog**

Catalog menu: **Use a Different Catalog** ↵

Catalog options menu: [highlight catalog name] ↵

USAGE

Pull down the **Catalog** menu from the Control Center menu bar. Highlight **Use a Different Catalog** and press ↵. Select the name of the catalog you want to use from the submenu that appears.

Adding a File Name to a Catalog

If you create a file while using one catalog, you can add that file name to a different catalog.

SEQUENCE OF STEPS

Control Center menu bar: **Catalog**

Catalog menu: **Use a Different Catalog** ↵

Catalog options menu: [highlight catalog name] ↵

Control Center: [move highlight to panel for type of file]

Control Center menu bar: **Catalog**

Catalog menu: **Add File to Catalog** ↵

File options menu: [highlight file name] ↵ ↵

USAGE

To add a file name to a catalog, select that catalog and then move the highlight to the panel that describes the type of file you want to add. For example, if you are adding a database file name to the current catalog, move the highlight to the **Data** panel.

Next, select **Add File to Catalog** from the **Catalog** pull-down menu. A submenu will list all files in the current directory that match the type of file you are adding (for example, all .DBF files if the highlight is in the Data panel) along with options to change to a different disk drive, to the parent directory, or to another subdirectory. If necessary, switch to the appropriate directory to locate the file name. Then select the file name from the submenu.

You can either edit the description of the file or just press ↵ to use the current description. The name of the file will appear in the appropriate panel of the Control Center.

If you are adding a query, form, report, or label file name to the current catalog, the submenu will display every file name with every extension (such as CUSTFORM.FRM and CUSTFORM.SCR). You need select only one of these multiple names, using the appropriate extension, as listed in Table 10.1.

Note that if you add the name of a file that is stored on a floppy disk to a particular catalog, that floppy disk must be in its disk drive whenever you use that catalog; adding a file name to a catalog does not copy the file to the current drive or directory. However, you can copy the file from the floppy disk onto your hard disk, then add the file name to the hard-disk catalog.

FILE TYPE	EXTENSION TO SELECT
Query	.QBE
Update query	.UPD
View query	.VUE
Form	.SCR
Report	.FRM
Labels	.LBL
Application	.APP

Table 10.1: File Name Extensions to Select for Catalogs

Changing a File Description

To change the description you've assigned to a file, first highlight the file name in the Control Center.

SEQUENCE OF STEPS

Control Center menu bar: **Catalog**

Catalog menu: **Change Description of Highlighted File** ↵

Prompt box: *<description>* ↵

USAGE

Select **Change Description of Highlighted File** from the **Catalog** pull-down menu. Use the arrow and Backspace keys to position the cursor and erase, as needed, and then save the new description by pressing ↵. The new description will appear below the Control Center panels whenever the file name is highlighted.

Removing a File Name from a Catalog

To remove a file name from the current catalog, first highlight it in the Control Center.

SEQUENCE OF STEPS

Control Center menu bar: **Catalog**

Catalog menu: **Remove Highlighted File from Catalog** ↵

Prompt box: **Yes** ↵

Prompt box: **Yes | No** ↵

USAGE

Select **Remove Highlighted File from Catalog** from the **Catalog** pull-down menu. dBASE will double-check your request by asking *Are you sure you want to remove this file from the catalog? No Yes*. Select **Yes** if you do want to remove the file. Next, dBASE will ask *Do you also want to delete this file from the disk? No Yes*. If you select **No,** the file name is removed from the catalog, but the file remains intact on the disk (and its name can be added to some other catalog). If you select **Yes,** the file is permanently removed from the disk and cannot be recovered. (So use this option with caution!)

Managing Files

The computer's disk operating system (DOS) handles all basic file-management tasks, including saving, retrieving, copying, moving, and deleting files as well as managing directories. dBASE IV lets you interact with DOS to manage files on your own via the *DOS utilities screen.*

The DOS Utilities Screen

Whereas the Catalog pull-down menu lets you manage the file *names* that appear in a catalog, the DOS utilities screen offers options for performing DOS operations on files.

SEQUENCE OF STEPS

Control Center menu bar: **Tools**

Tools menu: **DOS Utilities** ↵

USAGE

To get to the DOS utilities screen, select **DOS Utilities** from the **Tools** pull-down menu at the Control Center. Like other dBASE screens, the DOS utilities screen has a status bar, a clock, and a menu bar. The options on the menu bar are DOS, Files, Sort, Mark, Operations, and Exit.

The main part of the screen contains a *file list* that includes all subdirectory names (directories beneath the current directory) and files, as shown in Figure 10.2. You use PgDn, PgUp, **End**, and **Home** to scroll through the file names.

The current drive and directory, C:\DBASE in this example, are displayed at the top of the box. Within the file list, the Name/Extension column lists subdirectory names and file names. The Size column displays the number of characters in the file (or <DIR> for directory names). The Date & Time column shows the date and time that the file was created or last changed.

The Attrs (Attributes) column lists the DOS attributes assigned to each file, in the order Archive, Hidden, Read-Only, and System. The Space Used column shows how much real disk space the file occupies. This information differs from that in the Size option because DOS stores files in clusters, which have some minimal size. For example, if your computer uses a cluster size of 2,048 bytes, then even the smallest file occupies at least 2,048 bytes.

The Total Marked information at the bottom of the box lists the total size and number of files that are currently marked (zero in the figure). The Total Displayed information lists the size and number of files displayed.

The indicator *Files:*.* means that all files are currently displayed. (*.* means "files with any name with or without an extension.") The *Sorted by: Name* indicator means that file names are currently sorted by name (though subdirectory names are listed above file names).

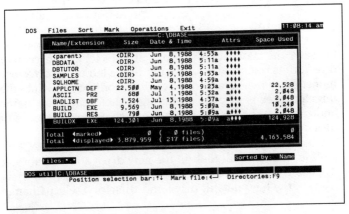

Figure 10.2: The DOS utilities screen

When you are done working with the DOS utilities screen, you can return to the Control Center by choosing **Exit to Control Center** from the **Exit** pull-down menu.

Changing the Default Drive and Directory

You can change the default drive and directory for all operations in the current dBASE session.

SEQUENCE OF STEPS

DOS utilities screen menu bar: **DOS**

DOS menu: **Set Default Drive:Directory** ⏎

Prompt box: *<drive\directory>* ⏎|**Shift-F1** [highlight directory] ⏎

USAGE

Select **Set Default Drive:Directory** from the **DOS** pull-down menu on the DOS utilities screen. You can then either type the name of the new drive and directory to log on to, or press **Shift-F1** (Pick) to select an option from a directory tree (see Figure 10.3).

In the directory tree, the subdirectory names are indented beneath the name of their parent directory. The current directory is indicated by a pointer to the left of the directory name. To switch to any directory or subdirectory while the directory tree is displayed, highlight the appropriate name and press ⏎. The file list will appear, showing the names of files on the new current directory.

Changing the default drive and directory tells dBASE to look for and save all files on the new drive and directory; it does not immediately affect the current files list. To view files on the new default drive and directory, select **Change**

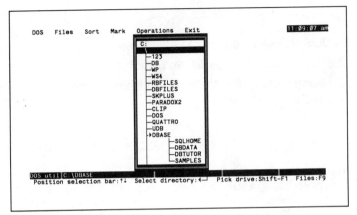

Figure 10.3: A directory tree

Drive:Directory from the **Files** pull-down menu and type or select the name of the new default drive and directory.

After you leave the DOS utilities screen and return to the Control Center, you'll see, by the catalog name, that dBASE is logged on to the new drive and directory. dBASE will search only this new default directory for any files you request and will also save any new files you create on the new drive and directory.

Changing Directories Temporarily

You can temporarily switch to a different directory or subdirectory to use in the DOS utilities screen. This does *not* change the default drive and directory for all operations in this dBASE session.

SEQUENCE OF STEPS

DOS utilities screen file list: [highlight subdirectory name | **<parent>**] ↵ | **F9** [highlight directory | subdirectory name] ↵ [highlight option] ↵

or

    DOS utilities screen menu bar: **Files**

    Files menu: **Change Drive: Directory** ⏎

    Prompt box: *<directory name>* | **Shift-F1** [highlight directory | subdirectory name] ⏎

USAGE

You can use ↑ and ↓ to move the highlight through the file list. To switch to a subdirectory, select the subdirectory name using the usual technique of highlighting and pressing ⏎. To switch to the parent directory, select **<parent>**.

To get a better view of the overall directory structure, press **F9** (Zoom). This brings up the same directory tree shown when you press **Shift-F1** (Pick).

You can also switch to a new drive and directory by selecting **Change Drive:Directory** from the **Files** pull-down menu. When you select this option, you'll be given the opportunity to enter a new drive and directory or press **Shift-F1** (Pick) to view the directory tree.

Note that the techniques discussed in this section affect only the DOS utilities screen display. When you return to the Control Center, the directory that was in effect before you went to the DOS utilities will still be in effect.

Selecting Files to Display

You can limit the file names displayed on the DOS utilities screen to only those that match some wildcard pattern. As with searches, you can use ? to stand for any single character and * to stand for any group of characters.

SEQUENCE OF STEPS

    DOS utilities screen menu bar: **Files**

    Files menu: **Display Only** ⏎

Prompt box: *<wildcard pattern>* ↵

USAGE

To change the wildcard pattern, select **Display Only** from the **Files** pull-down menu and type the new pattern. For example, to view only database file names (those with the extension .DBF), change the wildcard pattern to *.DBF. Note that subdirectory names and the <parent> option are still displayed, regardless of the wildcard pattern you use.

Sorting File Names

The Sort pull-down menu lets you select a sort order for viewing file names.

SEQUENCE OF STEPS

DOS utilities screen menu bar: **Sort**

Sort menu: **Name | Extension | Date & Time | Size** ↵

USAGE

When you highlight **Sort** on the menu bar, you'll be given a menu containing the options Name, Extension, Date & Time, and Size (see Table 10.2). Highlight an option and press ↵. The files in the file list will be sorted in the selected order, and the sort indicator at the bottom of the screen will change.

Marking Files

Sometimes you may want to perform operations on groups of files. dBASE provides several techniques for marking files.

OPTION	EFFECT
Name	Lists files alphabetically by file name (the default setting)
Extension	Lists file names alphabetically by extension
Date & Time	Lists file names in ascending order by date and time
Size	Lists files by size, from smallest to largest

Table 10.2: File-Sorting Options

SEQUENCE OF STEPS
═══════════════

DOS utilities screen file list: [highlight file name] ↵

or

DOS utilities screen menu bar: **Mark**
Mark menu: **Mark All | Unmark All | Reverse Marks** ↵

USAGE
═══════════════

The simplest approach is to scroll the highlight to the file you want to mark and then press ↵. A triangular marker appears at the left edge of the file listing. You can mark as many files as you wish in this manner. Note that ↵ works as a toggle: Each time you press it, it either marks or unmarks the current file name.

You can also use options from the **Mark** pull-down menu to mark and unmark records. The **Mark All** option marks all currently displayed file names. Hence, if the wildcard pattern CUST*.* is in effect and you select Mark All, all files beginning with the letters CUST will be marked. Changing the wildcard pattern does not affect the marks, so you can mark several groups of files by changing the wildcard pattern and selecting Mark All. The **Unmark All** option on the

Mark pull-down menu unmarks all currently displayed file names.

The **Reverse Marks** option swaps the file marks, so that unmarked files are marked and marked files become unmarked. This option is handy when, for example, you want to copy two groups of files to two floppy disks. You could mark one set of files and copy those files to one floppy disk. Then you could reverse the marks and copy the now-marked files to another floppy disk.

Copying, Moving, Renaming, and Deleting Files

To copy, move, rename, or delete files, you first select the files to include in the operation. Next, select the appropriate option from the Operations pull-down menu. Finally, you provide the information dBASE needs to perform the operation.

Selecting an Operation and the Files to Include

The options for including files in an operation are the same for copying, moving, renaming, and deleting.

SEQUENCE OF STEPS

DOS utilities screen menu bar: **Operations**

Operations menu: **Copy** | **Move** | **Rename** | **Delete** ↵

Operations submenu: **Single File** | **Marked Files** | **Displayed Files** ↵

USAGE

After you select **Copy, Move, Rename,** or **Delete** from the **Operations** menu, you'll see a submenu with three options for including files: Single File, Marked Files, and Displayed Files (see Table 10.3).

Note that the phrase "currently displayed," as used in Table 10.3, refers to all files that match the current wildcard pattern. Hence, any file names that are not visible at the moment, simply because they are scrolled off the bottom of the screen, are still included in the operation. The **Marked Files** option includes only marked files that are currently displayed (that is, marked files that match the current wildcard pattern).

If the highlight is on a directory name when you choose a group of files for an operation, and you select **Single File,** the operation will be performed on all files in that directory.

Copying Files

If you select Copy as the file operation, you will be prompted to specify a destination and file names.

SEQUENCE OF STEPS ═══════════════

Prompt box: *<drive\directory>* ↵ | **Shift-F1** [highlight directory] ↵ *<file name>* ↵

Keyboard: **Ctrl-End** [to begin the copy operation]

OPTION	EFFECT
Single File	Includes only the currently highlighted file in the operation
Marked Files	Includes all currently marked files in the operation
Displayed Files	Includes only the currently displayed files in the operation

Table 10.3: Options for Files to Include in Operations

USAGE

Enter the appropriate disk drive and directory for the copy operation in the Drive:Directory area of the prompt box or press **Shift-F1** (Pick) to use the directory tree. Press ↵. After you choose a drive and directory, the highlight will move to the Filename area.

If you are copying a single file, its name will be displayed as the name for the copied file. You can change that name (so that the copied file has a different name than the original) or press ↵ to use the same name. If you are copying a group of files, you can either enter *.* as the destination file name to ensure that copied files have the same names as the original files, or you can assign new names to the copied files. In the destination file name, use a combination of the new name (for that part of the file name that you want to change) and a wildcard (for the part that you want to remain the same). For example, suppose you mark the files CUSTLIST.DBF and CUSTLIST.MDX as the file group to copy. If you enter CUSTBAK.* as the destination file name, the copied files will have the names CUSTBAK.DBF and CUSTBAK.MDX.

If you want to place copied files in the same directory as the original files, you must specify a new name for the copied files (a directory cannot have two files with the same name).

When you have finished filling in the destination and file name for the copy, press **Ctrl-End** to begin the copy operation. Note that you can also copy a single file by highlighting its name in the file list and pressing **F8** (Copy).

Moving Files

The Move option lets you move a file from one disk drive or directory to another. This option works in the same manner as Copy, except that the original file is deleted from its original drive and directory after being copied to its new destination.

SEQUENCE OF STEPS

Prompt box: *<drive\directory>* ↵ | **Shift-F1** [highlight directory] ↵ *<file name>* ↵

Keyboard: **Ctrl-End** [to begin the move operation]

USAGE

After you select **Move,** you specify a disk drive or directory to move the file to or press **Shift-F1** (Pick) to select a new directory from the directory tree. You'll then be prompted to enter a new name for the moved file. If you are moving a single file, its name will be displayed, and you can just press ↵ to retain the name. If you are moving a group of files, enter the wildcard pattern ***.*** to move all files and retain their current names.

Press **Ctrl-End** after responding to both prompts (or press **Esc** to abort the operation). You can also move a single file by highlighting its name in the file list and pressing **F7** (Move).

Renaming Files

The Rename option lets you change the name of a file, group of files, or a subdirectory.

SEQUENCE OF STEPS

Prompt box: *<file name>* ↵

Keyboard: **Ctrl-End**

USAGE

When you select **Rename,** you'll be prompted to enter the new name. If you are renaming a group of files, be sure to use a wildcard character in the new file name. For example, if you want to rename all files named CUSTBAK to OLDCUST, enter **OLDCUST.*** as the new file name. Each file previously named CUSTBAK will be renamed OLDCUST, but will still have the original extension.

If the new name you assign to a file is the same as an existing file name, an information box will warn you that the existing file will be erased. The screen will display options to overwrite the existing file or to skip the renaming operation. Unless you are absolutely sure that you wish to replace the currently named file with the new one, select **Skip.**

Deleting Files

Before deleting all marked or displayed files, use PgDn and PgUp to scroll through the file list to make certain that you know exactly which files will be deleted. If you select Delete as the operation, dBASE displays the options Proceed and Cancel. If you are sure you want to delete all the files described, select Proceed. But use this option with caution, because once you delete a file, you cannot retrieve it. If you are unsure about deleting the files, select Cancel.

You can also delete any single file by moving the highlight to the appropriate file name in the file list and pressing Del. You'll still be given the option to proceed or cancel.

Viewing and Editing Files

The View option on the Operations menu enables you to display the highlighted file's contents in the display area for quick review. Any nontextual characters are filtered out. Press the Space bar to view the next screen of text or ↵ to keep scrolling the file until you press the Space bar or ↵ again. Press **Esc** when you want to stop the display. The Edit option on the same menu allows you to use the program editor on the highlighted file.

Accessing DOS

dBASE IV offers two techniques for accessing DOS commands without quitting dBASE. Both are available from the DOS utilities screen.

SEQUENCE OF STEPS

DOS utilities screen menu bar: **DOS**

DOS menu: **Perform DOS Command** ↵

Prompt box: *<command>* ↵

Keyboard: *<key>* [to return to dBASE]

or

DOS utilities screen menu bar: **DOS**

DOS menu: **Go to DOS** ↵

DOS prompt: *<commands>*

DOS prompt: **EXIT** ↵

USAGE

The **Perform DOS Command** option lets you enter a single DOS command. When the DOS command completes its job, you'll be prompted to press any key to return to dBASE IV.

The **Go to DOS** option temporarily leaves dBASE IV and displays the DOS prompt. If any marked files are currently in the file list, dBASE will warn you that all marked files will be unmarked and ask whether to proceed or to cancel the operation. Whenever you select **Go to DOS,** be sure to return to dBASE IV and exit dBASE in the usual manner before turning off your computer.

SEE ALSO

Exiting dBASE (Chapter 1)

Importing and Exporting Data

dBASE IV offers several options for importing and exporting data directly in a variety of formats. In some cases, you may want to transfer data to software products that dBASE IV does not support. In those situations, you will need to use one of the following alternative methods to complete the transfer.

If the foreign software product has the ability to transfer dBASE IV, dBASE III, or dBASE III PLUS database files, use its transfer capabilities (dBASE IV can read dBASE III and dBASE III PLUS database files directly). If the foreign software product does not support dBASE file transfers but does allow exporting of ASCII text files, use the ASCII text files as intermediary files to complete the transfer.

Built-In Import Options

dBASE IV provides options for importing files from Rapid-File, dBASE II, Framework II, Lotus 1-2-3, and PFS:File.

SEQUENCE OF STEPS

Control Center menu bar: **Tools**

Tools menu: **Import** ↵

Format options menu: [highlight format] ↵

File options menu: [highlight file name] ↵

USAGE

Pull down the **Tools** menu from the Control Center menu bar. Select the **Import** option and a file format from the submenu. Then select the file to import from the list of names that appears.

When the file is imported, dBASE gives it the extension .DBF. If a database file with the same name already exists, dBASE will ask for permission to overwrite it. Select **Overwrite** to proceed (and lose any data in the original database). You'll be returned to the Control Center, with the name of the new database above the line in the Data panel. You can then press **F2** to see the database's contents.

You may have to alter the new file in various ways both
before and after importation. For example, database files
store data in even rows and columns, whereas spreadsheets
allow data to be stored in any format. If you want to import
data from a spreadsheet to a dBASE IV database, you should
import only that portion of the spreadsheet that stores data
in even rows and columns. Use the spreadsheet program's
editing and export commands to extract the correct data.

Once you have imported the file into dBASE, you may
want to change data types, mark fields for indexing, and
(*after* saving these changes) rename, add, or delete fields. At
this point, the importation is complete, and you can use the
imported data just as you would any dBASE IV database
file. If you wish to change the name of the imported
database, use the Rename option on the Operations menu in
the DOS utilities screen.

Importing ASCII Text Files

If neither dBASE IV nor a foreign software product provides
built-in options for interfacing, you'll usually need to use an
ASCII text file as an intermediary file for the transfer operation. Most software products, even those with very limited
interfacing capability, have some means of storing data in an
ASCII text file. Chances are that you can import that text file
into a dBASE IV database.

SEQUENCE OF STEPS

Foreign program: [create ASCII text file]

DOS prompt: **TYPE** [to view file contents]

Pencil and paper: [plan database structure]

DOS prompt: **COPY** <file name> C:\DBASE\<file
name>.TXT

DOS prompt: **CD\DBASE**

DOS prompt: **DBASE**

Control Center Data panel: **<create>** ↵

Database design screen: [design database]

Database design screen menu bar: **Layout**

Layout menu: **Save This Database File Structure** ↵

Prompt box: *<file name>* ↵

Database design screen menu bar: **Append**

Append menu: **Copy Records from Non-DBASE File** ↵

Format options menu: [highlight format] ↵

File options menu: [highlight file name] ↵

Database design screen menu bar: **Exit**

Exit menu: **Save Changes and Exit** ↵

USAGE

Suppose you are using a product, which we'll name Flash-Base, to store data, and you want to transfer copies of that data to a dBASE IV database. Use whatever technique Flash-Base provides for creating ASCII text files, either through a file exporting option or by storing printed reports or data on disk files. Create the file and note the disk drive, directory, and complete file name of the exported ASCII text file.

Next, ascertain the structure of the ASCII text file. To do so, starting from the DOS prompt, log on to the directory where the file is stored and use the DOS **TYPE** command to look at the contents of the file. (You can also use the View option on the Operations pull-down menu in the dBASE IV DOS Utilities screen to view the contents of the file.)

Most likely, the file will be in one of three formats: *delimited, blank delimited,* or *fixed field length* (also called *structured data format,* or *SDF*). Delimited ASCII files generally place a comma between each field and surround character strings with quotation marks or some other character. Blank-delimited files separate each field with a single blank space, and individual fields contain no blank spaces. Fixed field-length storage places each field in evenly spaced columns. Figure 10.4 shows examples of these three formats.

In Figure 10.4, the delimited file uses double quotation marks as delimiters. If, while viewing the file, you notice that some other character is used to delimit character strings, make a note of this character to remind yourself later.

If you find that the file uses none of the formats discussed in this section, you may need to write a program to perform the conversion. For example, WordPerfect secondary (mail-merge) files use a format that cannot be easily imported into or exported from dBASE IV database files.

While viewing the contents of the ASCII text file on your screen, plan a structure for the dBASE IV database. Assign a name, data type, width, and number of decimal places (for numbers) to each field. Be sure to list file names in the same order that they are listed, from left to right, in the text file.

If the fields in the file are separated by commas or single blank spaces, you can assign any width you wish to each field. If, however, the file has the SDF structure, the width you assign to each field in your dBASE IV database must exactly match the width of the corresponding field in the ASCII text file.

Delimited (with ") format:

```
1001,"Smith","John","ABC Co.","123 A St.","San Diego","CA"
1002,"Adams","Annie","","3456 Ocean St.","Santa Monica","CA"
```

Blank-delimited format:

```
1001 Smith John CA 92067 (619)555-1234 19881115 Y
1002 Adams Annie CA 92001 (714)555-0123 19890101 F
```

Fixed field-length (SDF) format:

```
1001 Smith        John           ABC Co.
1004 Newell       John           LoTech Co.
```

Figure 10.4: Examples of ASCII file formats

Next, copy the file to the C:\DBASE directory and change the extension to .TXT. (If you have a DOS redirect or move utility, you can move the file instead.) Now you can log on to the DBASE directory and run dBASE by entering the usual commands.

When the Control Center appears, select **<create>** from the **Data** panel. In the database design screen, lay out a database with the field names and data types that you noted earlier. Save the database structure using the **Save This Database File Structure** option on the **Layout** pull-down menu. Then select **Copy Records from Non-dBASE File** from the **Append** pull-down menu, and then the appropriate format option from the submenu that appears (see Figure 10.5). Select the name of the text file from the submenu that appears. Finally, select **Save Changes and Exit** from the **Exit** pull-down menu.

The importation is now complete. You can press **F2** to switch to the browse screen and use the **PgDn, PgUp,** and arrow keys to scroll through the database and verify that all appropriate records were imported.

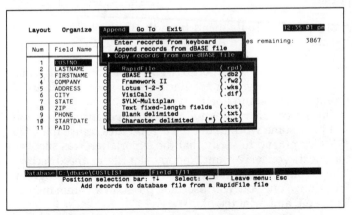

Figure 10.5: Menu for importing data into a database file

| SEE ALSO |

The Database Design Screen (Chapter 2)

Built-In Export Options

To export data from a dBASE IV database to a format used by another program, select the Export option from the Tools pull-down menu. You will see a submenu of exporting formats, each of which is summarized in Table 10.4.

| SEQUENCE OF STEPS |

Control Center menu bar: **Tools**

Tools menu: **Export** ↵

Export options menu: [highlight export option] ↵

File options menu: [highlight file to export] ↵

| USAGE |

Pull down the **Tools** menu from the Control Center menu bar and select **Export**. A submenu listing dBASE's export options will appear. Highlight the desired option and press ↵. Then select the file to export from the submenu that appears. If a file with the same name already exists, you'll be prompted for permission to overwrite it.

This procedure creates a file in the proper format, but you still have some work to do. It's a good idea to use the DOS **TYPE** command to verify that the exportation was successful. Next, you may want to copy the file to the directory where you store the files you use with the foreign program. From now on, you will use that program's commands to load, edit, and print the file.

OPTION	EFFECT
RapidFile	Copies data to the format used by RapidFile and assigns the extension .RPD to that file.
dBASE II	Copies data to dBASE II format and assigns the extension .DB2 to the file. Do not change the name of the .DB2 file to the .DBF extension until you've moved it to another directory, disk drive, or computer. Otherwise, you may overwrite your original dBASE IV database.
Framework II	Copies data in a dBASE IV database to a file with the extension .FW2, which can be used in Framework II.
Lotus 1-2-3	Copies a dBASE IV database to a file with the extension .WKS, which can be used by Lotus 1-2-3 (as well as Symphony and Quattro). Different versions of 1-2-3 and Symphony require different extensions (for example, version 2 of 1-2-3 uses the .WK1 extension).
VisiCalc	Copies a dBASE IV database to a VisiCalc .DIF file.
PFS:FILE	This option copies a dBASE IV database to a format that can be read by PFS:FILE. The name of the copied file will have no extension.

Table 10.4: File Export Options

OPTION	EFFECT
SYLK-Multiplan	Copies a dBASE IV database to a Multiplan SYLK file. The file name for the copied file will not include an extension.
Text Fixed-Length Fields	Copies a dBASE IV database to an ASCII text file that lists fields in equal-width columns (called SDF format in earlier versions of dBASE). The copied file with have the extension .TXT.
Blank Delimited	Copies a dBASE IV database to an ASCII text file that includes a single blank space between each field. The copied file will have the exten sion .TXT.
Character delimited (")	Copies a dBASE IV database to an ASCII delimited text file with a general format that most software packages can import. When you select this option, you can specify a delimiter other than the default quotation marks.

Table 10.4: File Export Options (continued)

Exporting Printed Reports

In some situations, you may want to export printed, for-matted data rather than raw data from a database file. For example, suppose you create a report format to display to-tals and subtotals and wish to embed a copy of the report in a document you created with WordStar, WordPerfect, or some other word processing program. To do so, you need only send the printed report to a disk file and then read that file into the appropriate word-processing document (or into a new one).

| SEQUENCE OF STEPS |

Control Center Data panel: [highlight database name] ↵

Prompt box: **Use File** ↵

Control Center Queries panel: **<create>** ↵

Query design screen: [create query that displays appropriate records]

Keyboard: **F2** [to check query results]

Control Center Reports panel: [highlight report format name] ↵

Prompt box: **Print Report** ↵

Print menu: **Destination** ↵

Destination menu: **Write To** [use **Space** bar or ↵ to change setting to **DOS File**]

Destination menu: **Name of DOS File** ↵

Prompt box: *<file name>* ↵

Destination menu: **Echo to Screen** ↵ [use **Space** bar or ↵ to change setting to **Yes**]

Keyboard: **Ctrl-End** [to save changes]

Print menu: **Begin Printing** ↵

Control Center menu bar: **Exit**

Exit menu: **Quit to DOS** ↵

DOS prompt: **TYPE** ↵ [to verify that the DOS file exists]

DOS prompt: [start foreign program]

Foreign program: [select word processing file and import report]

These are the general steps for creating a text file from a report or label format. Open the database by highlighting its name in the **Data** panel of the Control Center, pressing ↵, and selecting **Use File.** To export only certain records or to sort the database, create a query or use an existing query to display the appropriate records. Press **F2** to verify the query and then return to the Control Center. Highlight the name of the report format in the **Reports** panel, press ↵, and select **Print Report.** This brings up the **Print** menu. Select **Destination**, which brings up the **Destination** menu.

Highlight **Write To** and press the **Space** bar or ↵ to change the setting to **DOS File.** Then select **Name of DOS File** and note the suggested file name or change the drive, directory, or suggested file name. To view the report on the screen as it is stored on disk, select **Echo to Screen** and press the **Space** bar or ↵ to change the setting to **Yes.** Press **Ctrl-End** to save your settings. Then select **Begin Printing** from the **Print** menu.

When you get back to the Control Center, select **Quit to DOS** from the **Exit** pull-down menu to leave dBASE IV. You can use the DOS **TYPE** command to verify that the file exists. You should see the entire formatted report. Now you must bring up your word processor and issue the appropriate commands to read the printed report into a new or existing file. The formatted report will appear in your document.

SEE ALSO

Printing Labels and Reports (Chapter 6)

CHAPTER 11

Managing Your Workspace

This chapter discusses techniques for managing your workspace, such as customizing dBASE by fine-tuning environmental settings and display options, as well as using keystroke macros to speed up your work.

Customizing Your Environment

dBASE provides a Settings screen, which you can use to display colors on a color monitor.

Environmental Settings

A variety of commonly used settings, for example the setting that turns the Instruct mode on and off, are available on the Options menu. These settings affect only the current dBASE IV session. When you exit and then return to dBASE later, the settings originally created with the DBSETUP program during installation will be in effect.

SEQUENCE OF STEPS

Control Center menu bar: **Tools**

Tools menu: **Settings** ⏎

Settings menu bar: **Options** ⏎

Options menu: [highlight option and scroll through settings with space bar | ⏎ | enter value in prompt box ⏎]

Settings menu bar: **Exit**

Exit menu: **Exit to Control Center** ⏎

USAGE

Pull down the **Tools** menu from the Control Center menu bar and select **Settings**. You'll see a Settings menu bar with three pull-down menus: Options, Display, and Exit. The environmental settings are on the **Options** menu (see Figure 11.1). The effects of changing the settings are described in Table 11.1. Highlight each option you want to change and scroll through the multiple-choice settings with the Space bar or ⏎. Some options require you to enter a value in a prompt box. When the options are set to your satisfaction, use the **Exit** menu to return to the Control Center.

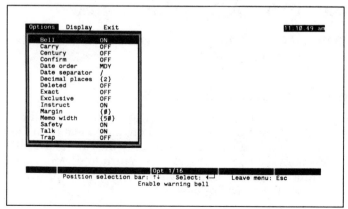

Figure 11.1: The Options menu

OPTION	**ACTION**
Bell	When on, beeps whenever a field on an edit screen or custom form is filled or an error occurs. When off, doesn't beep.
Carry	When on, copies all information from the current record to the next new record while you are entering new data. When off, starts each new record with blank fields.
Century	When off, displays dates with two-digit years (for example, 12/31/89). When on, displays dates with four-digit years (for example, 12/31/1989).
Confirm	When off, automatically moves the cursor to the next field when you fill a field during data entry or editing. When on, keeps the cursor in the current field until the ↵ key is pressed.
Date Order	Lets you determine the order of month, day, and year in date displays (press the Space bar to scroll through the options). Options are MDY (12/31/89), DMY (31/12/89), and YMD (89/12/31).
Date Separator	Determines the character used in date displays (Space bar scrolls through options). Slash (/) displays dates as 12/31/89, hyphen (-) displays dates as 12-31-89, and period (.) displays dates as 12.31.89. Can be used in conjunction with Date Order to create various international date formats (for example, 89.12.31).

Table 11.1: Setting Options

OPTION	ACTION
Decimal Places	Determines the number of decimal places displayed in the results of calculations, in the range 0 to 18. The default setting is 2.
Deleted	When off, displays records that are marked for deletion. When on, hides records marked for deletion from view and from all operations.
Exact	When off, matches strings of different lengths in a search. When on, matches only strings of the same length. Hence, when Exact is off, a search for **"AB"** locates "ABC Co." When on, a search for **"AB "** matches only "AB".
Exclusive	When off, lets other network users access the file you are currently using. When on, does not let other network users access the file you are currently using.
Instruct	When on, displays information boxes each time you use a feature for the first time. When off, does not display information boxes.
Margin	Adjusts the left margin for all printed output, as measured in characters. Thus, entering **10** adds a one-inch margin to the left side of the page (assuming that 10 characters to the inch are printed).

Table 11.1: Setting Options (continued)

OPTION	ACTION
Memo Width	Adjusts the default width of memo field displays during certain operations. Can accept a value in the range 5 to 250. (Widths defined in custom forms and reports override this setting.)
Safety	When on, displays a warning before dBASE overwrites an existing file and provides an option to cancel the operation. When off, displays no warning and immediately overwrites the existing file.
Talk	When on, displays results of various dBASE operations on the screen. When off, does not display results on the screen (used mainly in custom programming).
Trap	In custom programming, determines whether the dBASE IV debugger is activated when an error occurs in a program.

Table 11.1: Setting Options (continued)

SEE ALSO

The Instruct Mode (Chapter 1)

Display Options

If you have a color monitor, you can use the options on the Display pull-down menu to change display colors. The available color options depend on the type of monitor you have. If you have a monochrome monitor, your scope is more limited, but you can change the appearance of your screen to some extent.

Options you select from the Display menu affect only the current dBASE session. To change the colors used in all dBASE sessions, use the DBSETUP program.

SEQUENCE OF STEPS

Control Center menu bar: **Tools**

Tools menu: **Settings** ↵

Settings menu bar: **Display** ↵

Color areas menu: [highlight area option] ↵

Color menu: [highlight foreground color option] ↵

Color menu: [highlight background color option] ↵

Keyboard: **Ctrl-End** [to save changes]

Settings menu bar: **Exit**

Exit menu: **Exit to Control Center** ↵

USAGE

To get to the **Display** menu from the Control Center, pull down the **Tools** menu and select **Settings**. From the Settings menu bar, select **Display**. The Display pull-down menu provides a list of areas to color. When you select an area, you'll see a list of possible foreground and background colors for that area, as shown in Figure 11.2.

The **Standard-All** option affects the general color of text and background on normal (that is, unhighlighted) sections of the screen. The **Enhanced-All** option sets the general color for all highlighted text, such as text in the menu, status bar, and input fields of a custom form. You can color more specific areas by selecting options under Standard-All and Enhanced-All (see Figure 11.3).

After you select an area to color, the menu of foreground and background options appears. A small square indicates the current foreground color. You can use ↑ and ↓ to scroll up and down and select a different foreground color.

After selecting a foreground color, press → to move the background options. Once again, you can scroll through color options using ↑ and ↓. As you scroll through foreground and background colors, the screen adjusts to show the color combinations. You can switch back and forth between the Background and Foreground columns by pressing

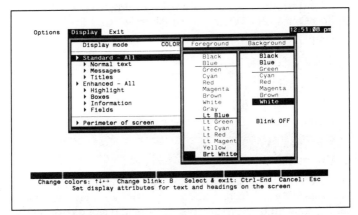

Figure 11.2: Display menu and color options

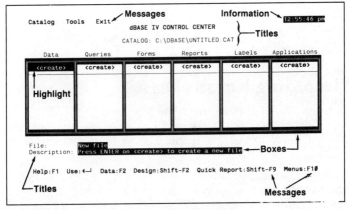

Figure 11.3: Some areas that can be colored

← and → to try different combinations until you find one you like. To save the current color combination, press **Ctrl-End**. You can color as many areas as you wish and then select **Exit to Control Center** from the **Exit** pull-down menu.

If you have a monochrome monitor, a few display options are still available. Selecting an area from the first display menu brings up a submenu with the display options Intensity, Underline, Reverse (video), and Blink. Use ⏎ to turn an option **On** or **Off**. When you finish, press **Ctrl-End.**

SEE ALSO

Making Your Form More Attractive (Chapter 7)

Keystroke Macros

Some frequently used operations require many keystrokes. As an alternative to repeating the entire key sequence each time you want to perform one of these, you can record all the necessary keystrokes in a *keystroke macro*, and then play them back at any time.

The Macros menu, which you reach from the Control Center, contains a full set of options for working with macros. You can also quickly record (or play back) a macro from anywhere in dBASE IV, then return to the Control Center to save or modify it.

Recording Keystrokes

You can record a macro from the Macros menu in the Control Center, or from a prompt box that contains an abbreviated version of this menu. Follow these steps to start recording keystrokes.

SEQUENCE OF STEPS

Control Center menu bar: **Tools**

Tools menu: **Macros** ↵
or, from anywhere in dBASE: **Shift-F10** [to bring up macros prompt box]

Macros menu or prompt box: **Begin Recording** ↵

Keyboard: [press key to assign to macro]

Keyboard: [enter keystrokes to be recorded]

Keyboard: **Shift-F10**

Prompt box: **End Recording** ↵

USAGE

If you are using the Macros menu, pull down the **Tools** menu from the Control Center menu bar, select **Macros,** then select **Begin Recording**. If you are not using the Macros menu, you can press **Shift-F10** from anywhere in dBASE to display the macros prompt box, which contains the options Begin Recording and Cancel. To start recording your keystrokes, select **Begin Recording.**

A submenu will appear, as in Figure 11.4, instructing you to choose the key that will activate the macro once it is recorded. You can enter any available letter or function key to call your macro. If you select one that is already assigned to a macro, the screen displays the message *Do you really want to overwrite <letter>? (Y/N)*. If you select **No,** the operation is canceled and you can start over. If you select **Yes,** dBASE begins recording keystrokes immediately.

The navigation line informs you that keystrokes are now being recorded, so type the keystrokes you want to save. You can save text (for example, your company name); menu options (including file and field names); the arrow keys, function keys, and other keys you regularly use in dBASE; and keystrokes that call other macros (calling a macro inside another macro is called *nesting*). The keystrokes you use to

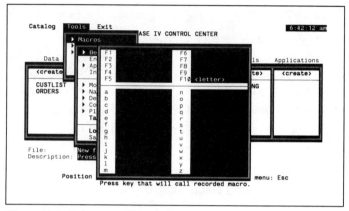

Figure 11.4: Submenu of keystroke macros

select recording options, such as Shift-F10, are not recorded as part of the macro.

If you record keystrokes that access pull-down menus, use Alt-*<first letter>*, rather than F10, to access the menus. Alt-*<first letter>* always pulls down a specific menu, whereas F10 pulls down the last-used menu. Similarly, when selecting options from pull-down menus, type the first letter of the option rather than highlighting it and pressing ↵. In this way, you ensure that the macro will not select the wrong option because the highlight is in a different position during playback.

If you want the macro to select an option from a submenu of file names or field names, type out the name rather than selecting it. Submenus of file and field names change as you add and delete objects, so the position of a name may vary.

You can record a break for user input while the macro is played back. Press **Shift-F10** while recording the macro using either method, and select **Insert User-Input Break** from the prompt box. Then continue recording. When you use the macro, press **Shift-F10** to get the macro going again after you enter the input. When you've finished recording your keystrokes, type **Shift-F10** and select **End Recording.**

If you wish to save a recorded macro for use in future dBASE sessions, you must use the Save Library option on the Macros menu (see below).

Playing Back a Macro

You can play back a recorded macro from either the Macros menu in the Control Center, or anywhere in dBASE.

SEQUENCE OF STEPS

Control Center menu bar: **Tools**

Tools menu: **Macros** ↵

Macros menu: **Play** ↵

Keyboard: [press key assigned to macro]

or

Anywhere in dBASE: **Alt-F10**

Keyboard: [press key assigned to macro]

USAGE

From the Control Center, select **Macros** from the **Tools** pull-down menu. Select **Play** from the submenu that appears. Type the letter or function key you assigned to the macro. dBASE plays back the recorded keystrokes, then returns to normal.

To play back a recorded macro without using the Tools menu, press **Alt-F10**. You will be asked to *press an alphabetic key of the macro to play back*. Type the letter name you assigned to the keystroke macro to start it playing back. If you assigned one of the function keys to a macro, you can play back that macro by holding down the **Alt** key and pressing the function key. For example, if you assigned F5 as the macro name when you began recording, you can play back the macro by simply pressing Alt-F5.

Keep in mind that when you play back a macro, it repeats the exact sequence of *keystrokes* that were recorded, not the exact sequence of recorded *operations*. Therefore, you must start playing a macro from the exact same situation that you started recording the keystrokes in. For example, If you recorded keystrokes while in the Forms Design screen, you should be in the Forms Design screen when you play back the macro.

To display the macro text as the macro is executed, set the **Talk** option on the **Macros** menu to **On**. The text appears in the navigation line or the top of the screen. You can decrease or increase the speed at which the macro is played back by pressing the < or the > key.

Saving a Macro

When you first save recorded keystrokes in a macro, they are stored only in RAM, not on disk. To save a keystroke macro for all future sessions with dBASE, store it in a *macro library* on disk.

SEQUENCE OF STEPS

Control Center menu bar: **Tools**

Tools menu: **Macros** ↵

Macros menu: **Save Library** ↵

Prompt box: *<file name>* ↵

USAGE

Select **Macros** from the **Tools** pull-down menu above the Control Center. Then select **Save Library** from the submenu that appears. Enter a valid DOS file name with no extension (such as MYMACROS) and press ↵. dBASE assigns the extension .KEY by default. A single macro library can contain up to 36 macros.

Loading a Macro Library

When you want to use a saved macro library or add more macros to an existing library, you must first load the macro library from disk into active memory.

SEQUENCE OF STEPS

Control Center menu bar: **Tools**

Tools menu: **Macros** ↵

Macros menu: **Load Library** ↵

Library options menu: [highlight library name] ↵

USAGE

From the Control Center, select the **Macros** option from the **Tools** pull-down menu. Select **Load Library**. Then select the macro library name from the submenu that appears.

Now you can either play one of the previously recorded macros by selecting Play, or add a new macro by selecting Begin Record and a name (key) for the macro. Optionally, press Esc to return to the Control Center. The macro library stays loaded for the duration of the current dBASE session or until you load a different library.

Naming a Macro

Initially, all macros have only the single-letter name you assign. If you need a reminder as to what a particular macro does, you can add an additional name.

SEQUENCE OF STEPS

Control Center menu bar: **Tools**

Tools menu: **Macros** ↵

Macros menu: **Name** ↵
Keyboard: [press key assigned to macro]
Prompt box: *<macro name>* ↵

USAGE

Select **Macros** from the **Tools** pull-down menu and **Name** from the **Macros** menu. Type the letter of the macro to which you want to add a name. You'll be prompted to enter a macro name up to 10 letters long. The additional macro name appears in the list of macros for the current library, but you still use the single-letter name to play back the macro.

Modifying a Macro

You can edit a macro using dBASE's *macro editor* or any foreign editor that works with ASCII files. You can also add some keystrokes to the end of a macro using the Append to Macro option on the Macros menu.

SEQUENCE OF STEPS

Control Center menu bar: **Tools**
Tools menu: **Macros** ↵
Macros menu: **Modify** ↵
Keyboard: [press key assigned to macro]
Macro editor screen: [make changes]
Macro editor screen menu bar: **Exit**
Exit menu: **Save Changes and Exit** ↵

or

Control Center menu bar: **Tools**
Tools menu: **Macros** ↵
Macros menu: **Append to Macro** ↵

Keyboard: [press key assigned to macro]
Keyboard: [enter new keystrokes]
Keyboard: **Shift-F10**
Prompt box: End Recording ↵

USAGE

To reach the macro editor screen, select **Modify** from the **Macros** menu. The macro editor screen has a clock, status bar, and a menu bar with the options Layout, Words, GoTo, Print, and Exit. You use this screen pretty much like the dBASE word-wrap editor.

Any letters you type in the macro editor will be entered in the macro as regular letters. Spaces are used as spaces in the macro. However, special characters, such as ↵ and the Tab key, must be entered using keywords in curly braces, in either lower- or uppercase letters (see Table 11.2). For example, the Tab key may be entered as {Tab} or {TAB}.

You can use the macro editor to nest macros, up to 16 levels deep. You cannot, however, nest a macro inside itself.

When you are finished editing a macro, select **Save Changes and Exit** from the **Exit** pull-down menu.

Choosing the **Append to Macro** command from the **Macros** menu enables you to add keystrokes to an existing macro, just as if you were creating a new macro from the Control Center. You can start appending in the Control Center, move to another dBASE screen, then use the macro editor to remove the keystrokes you used to leave the Control Center.

SEE ALSO

Editing Label and Report Formats/Formatting Fields/The Word-Wrap Editor (Chapter 6)

KEY	KEY LABEL NAME
←	{LeftArrow}
→	{RightArrow}
↑	{UpArrow}
↓	{DownArrow}
Backspace	{BackSpace}
Ctrl	{Ctrl-}
Alt	{Alt-}
Shift	{Shift-}
Del (or Delete)	{Del}
End	{End}
Escape	{Esc}
Home	{Home}
Ins (or Insert)	{Ins}
PgDn	{PgDn}
PgUp	{PgUp}
Tab	Tab
F1 to F10	{F1} to {F10}

Note: The {Ctrl-}, {Alt-}, and {Shift-} keys should be combined within the same braces for a two-key combination. For example, {Ctrl-A} types Ctrl-A, {Shift-Tab} presses Shift-Tab.

Table 11.2: Keywords for Special Characters in Macros

Copying a Macro

Sometimes you may want to edit a version of a macro while retaining the original version. The Copy command on the Macros menu enables you to copy a macro to a new key and give it a new descriptive name.

SEQUENCE OF STEPS

Control Center menu bar: **Tools**

Tools menu: **Macros** ↵

Macros menu: **Copy** ↵

Keyboard: [press key assigned to macro]

Keyboard: [press key for position of copy]

Prompt box: *<macro name>* ↵

USAGE

Select the **Copy** option from the **Macros** menu. The macro submenu for the library you are using appears. Press the key assigned to the macro, then press the key assigned to the copy position on the submenu. You will be prompted for a unique descriptive name, just as when you are using the Name command. dBASE then copies the macro to the new position on the submenu with the new name. You are now free to modify the macro as you wish.

Deleting a Macro

As with other objects in dBASE, it's a good idea to delete macros you no longer need.

SEQUENCE OF STEPS

Control Center menu bar: **Tools**

Tools menu: **Macros** ↵
Macros menu: **Delete** ↵
Keyboard: [press key assigned to macro]
Keyboard: **Y** ↵ [to confirm deletion]

USAGE

Select **Delete** from the **Macros** menu. The macro submenu appears. Press the key assigned to the macro. dBASE displays the message *Do you really want to delete <macro>? (Y/N)*. Just say Yes by typing a lower- or uppercase **Y** and pressing ↵.

CHAPTER 12

The Applications Generator

This chapter summarizes the techniques and options available for using the dBASE IV Applications Generator. Before you use the applications generator, you should create a new catalog to store various database objects that will be used in the application, such as database files, queries, reports, labels, and custom forms. Then use the various design screens to create the objects.

Starting the Applications Generator

Before you enter the Applications Generator, make sure the catalog containing the objects needed for your application is current.

SEQUENCE OF STEPS

Control Center Applications panel: **<create>** ↵

Prompt box: **Applications Generator** ↵

USAGE

Select **<create>** from the Applications panel in the Control Center. From the prompt box that appears, select **Applications Generator.** To modify an existing application, highlight its name in the Applications panel of the Control Center and press **Shift-F2** (Design) or press ↵ and select **Modify Application** from the dialog box.

Defining the Application

If you are creating a new application, you'll first see the Application Definition dialog box, as shown in Figure 12.1.

SEQUENCE OF STEPS

Dialog box Application Name prompt: *<application name>* ↵

Dialog box Description prompt: *<application description>* ↵

Dialog box Main Menu Type prompt: **Bar** | **Pop-Up** | **Batch** [scroll through options with space bar] ↵

Dialog box Main Menu Name prompt: *<menu name>* ↵

Dialog box Database/View prompt: *<database | view name>* ↵

Dialog box Set Index To prompt: *<index file name>* ↵

Dialog box Order prompt: *<index name>* ↵

Keyboard: **Ctrl-End** [to save settings]

USAGE

The prompts in the Application Definition dialog box are Application Name, Description, Main Menu Type, Main

Menu Name, Database/View, Set Index to, and Order. This section discusses the meaning of each prompt.

Specifying the Application Name

Each application must have a unique name. Enter a valid DOS file name (eight characters maximum, no spaces or punctuation). Use a name that will be easy to remember and that reflects the purpose of the application, such as INVMGR for an inventory manager or PAYROLL for a payroll system. The name you assign here is the one that appears in the Applications panel of the Control Center after you create the application.

Entering an Application Description

The description of the application is entirely optional and is provided mainly to help you remember what the application is. It appears in the description line in the Control Center when the application name is highlighted. Enter any text, but do not use double quotation marks.

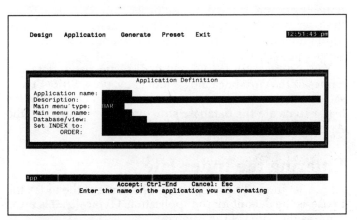

Figure 12.1: The Application Definition dialog box

Choosing the Main Menu Type

Press the Space bar to scroll through options for the application main menu (the first menu to appear when the user runs the application). Your options are

OPTION	EFFECT
Bar	Presents a horizontal bar menu as the main menu
Pop-Up	Presents a vertical pop-up menu as the main menu
Batch	Executes a batch file as soon as the user runs the application

Naming the Main Menu

Assign a valid, unique file name to the main menu for the application.

Selecting the Database or View

Enter the name of the database or view to open as soon as the user runs the application. This database is kept open throughout all other menu options, except those you later specify to override the default.

You can press **Shift-F1** (Pick) to display a list of database names in the current catalog. Optionally, press **Shift-F1** and select **<create>** to create a new database structure. (But it's better to create the database structure before you enter the Applications Generator.)

Entering the Index File

At the Set Index To prompt, enter the name of the index file to use as the default for the application. (Typically, this is the same as the name of the database.)

Specifying the Sort Order

At the Order prompt, enter the name of the index to determine the default sort order. (Typically, the index name is simply the name of any indexed field in the database.) You can override this sort order later when assigning actions to specific menu options.

After filling out the Application Definition dialog box, press **Ctrl-End** to access the application design screen.

The Application Design Screen

The application design screen is where you create the application objects that make up the application. The application objects include the menus, batch processes, and optional sign-on banner. Note that the application objects are those that you create using the Applications Generator, unlike the database objects that you create from the Control Center.

The application design screen is shown in Figure 12.2. It has a menu bar, a status bar, a navigation line, and a clock. It also has line numbers on the left side and a ruler at the bottom. Lastly, the work area in the middle contains an application object that you can convert into a sign-on banner (see below).

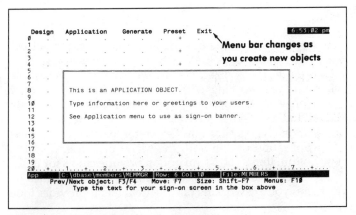

Figure 12.2: The application design screen

Table 12.1 summarizes all the navigation and function keys used in the application design screen. The *current object* always has its frame highlighted and overlays any other objects on the screen. A *full-screen editing frame* is a text frame, such as you use when creating a custom help screen. Note that the exact role played by a key depends on the type of activity in progress. The navigation line near the bottom of the screen reminds you of the effects of special keys at any given time.

Applications Generator Menus

The application design screen, like other dBASE screens, has a menu bar at the top, pull-down menus, and submenus. You select menu options using the same techniques as in other dBASE screens.

SEQUENCE OF STEPS

Application design screen menu bar: [highlight option] ⌐ | **Alt**-<*first letter of menu name*>

Pull-down menu: [highlight option] ⌐ | <*first letter of option*>

USAGE

The Applications Generator main menu is somewhat different from other dBASE IV menus, partly because it changes with the type of object you are working on. For example, when you are working with the sign-on banner, the main menu presents the options Design, Application, Generate, Preset, and Exit. When you are developing a menu for your application, the Applications Generator main menu replaces the Application option with the Menu option and adds a new option, Item. The Menu option provides tools for defining such characteristics as screen colors and file names for the menu you are working on. The Item menu provides tools

KEY	EFFECT
→	Moves the cursor one position to the right in an object, editing frame, or dialog box. Moves the cursor one option to the right in a bar menu and opens an attached pull-down menu. Wraps through options.
←	Moves the cursor one position to the left in an object, editing frame, or dialog box. Moves the cursor one option to the left in a bar menu and opens an attached pull-down menu. Wraps through options.
↓	Moves the cursor one position down in an object, editing frame, or dialog box. Moves one option down in a pop-up menu. Wraps around in menus.
↑	Moves the cursor one position up in an object, editing frame, or dialog box. Moves one option up in a pop-up menu. Wraps around in menus.
PgDn	Moves the cursor to the next item in a menu or batch process in the Item menu. Moves one page down in a list.
PgUp	Moves the cursor to the previous item in a menu or batch process in the Item menu. Moves one page up in a list.
End	Moves to the last field or option in a dialog box or list. Moves to the end of the line in a full- screen editing frame.
Home	Moves to the first field or option in a dialog box or list. Moves to the beginning of the line in a full-screen editing frame.
Del	Deletes the current character.
Backspace	Deletes the previous character in an object, full-screen editing frame, or dialog box.

Table 12.1: Keys Used to Design an Application

KEY	EFFECT
Ins	Turns the Insert mode on and off.
F1	Provides help.
F3	Moves the cursor to the previous object on the work surface, making that object current.
F4	Moves the cursor to the next object on the work surface, making that object current.
F5	Marks the beginning and end of an item when you enter it in a horizontal bar menu (you can use ↵ instead of the second F5). screen editing frame, or dialog box.
F7	Moves an object to a new location on the work surface. Moves an item and all its attributes to a new location in an object or to a different object of the same type.
F8	Copies an item to a new location in an object or to a different object of the same type.
F9	Displays or removes the Applications Generator menu bar and information lines.
F10	Moves the cursor from an object on the work surface to the Applications Generator menu bar. Selects the current option in a menu.
Shift-F1	Displays a list when the cursor is on a field that allows selection.
Shift-F2	Displays selected application when used from the Control Center.
Shift-F7	Changes the size of the frame that encloses an object.

Table 12.1: Keys Used to Design an Application (continued)

for defining actions and characteristics for a specific menu option in your application.

A second difference between standard dBASE IV menus and Applications Generator menus is that many menus offer apparently identical options. For example, the Preset, Application, Menu, and Item pull-down menus on the Applications Generator main menu each let you define display options (such as colors). At first, these options may appear to be redundant. However, each actually has a unique effect because it defines a setting for a particular *level* within the application. The four levels of an application are Preset, Application, Menu, and Item (each corresponding to the menu option with the same name). The levels are summarized in Table 12.2.

Note that the second menu option, Menu, might also be displayed as Batch or List depending on the type of object you are currently developing. But this variation does not affect the hierarchical relationship among settings. For example, settings you assign to a batch process override Preset and Application settings, but not Item settings.

LEVEL	EFFECT
Preset	Assigns characteristics to all applications.
Application	Overrides Preset settings and assigns characteristics that are specific to the application you are currently developing.
Menu	Overrides the Preset and Application settings and assigns characteristics to the specific menu you are currently developing.
Item	Overrides the Preset, Application, and Menu settings and assigns characteristics to the specific menu option you are currently developing.

Table 12.2: Levels for Display Options

Creating a Sign-On Banner

The sign-on banner is always displayed in the center of the application design screen. You can modify the text in the sign-on banner and use it to display information to the user when he or she first runs the application.

SEQUENCE OF STEPS

Application design screen: [modify sign-on banner]

Application design screen menu bar: **Application**

Application menu: **Display Sign-On Banner** ⏎

Dialog box: **Yes** | **No** ⏎

USAGE

You can type the application title, a description, an author name, a copyright notice, or any other text into the sign-on banner. (However, do not use double quotation marks.) To delete information from the sign-on banner, use the **Ctrl-Y** key.

You can also resize and move the frame that contains the sign-on banner (as well as the frames for most other objects you create). To change the size of the frame, press **Shift-F7** (Size). The border will blink. Use the arrow keys to expand or reduce the frame, then press ⏎. To move the sign-on banner, press **F7** (Move), use the arrow keys to move the frame, and press ⏎ when you are done.

By default, the sign-on banner is not displayed when the user runs the application. To display the sign-on banner in the completed application, select **Display Sign-on Banner** from the **Application** pull-down menu and **Yes** from the dialog box that appears.

The Design Menu

The Design pull-down menu on the application design screen presents the following options for creating and modifying application objects: Horizontal Bar Menu, Pop-Up Menu, Files List, Structure List, Values List, and Batch Process.

SEQUENCE OF STEPS

    Application design screen menu bar: **Design**

    Design menu: [choose design option] ↵

    Objects menu: **<create>** | <object name> ↵

    Dialog box Name prompt: <file name> ↵

    Dialog box Description prompt: <description> ↵

    Dialog box Message Line prompt: <message> ↵

    Keyboard: **Ctrl-End** [to record choices]

USAGE

Select the type of object that you want to create. A submenu will appear displaying the option <create> and the names of any existing objects of that type. Select **<create>** to create a new object or the name of an existing object to modify it.

If you are creating a new object, a dialog box will appear asking for a name, a description, and a message line prompt (batch processes do not request a message line prompt). Enter a valid DOS file name, without an extension, after the Name prompt. You can enter any text after the Description prompt (but no quotation marks), or leave the option blank. The text you enter after the **Message Line** prompt will appear centered at the bottom of the screen when the user runs the application. Note, however, that any message line prompts that you specify at the Item level will override any message line prompts that you specify here.

After filling in the dialog box, press **Ctrl-End**. What happens next depends on the type of object you are creating, as discussed in the sections that follow.

Designing a Horizontal Bar Menu

If you are creating a new horizontal bar menu, an empty menu bar appears at the top of the screen with the cursor inside it.

SEQUENCE OF STEPS

To enter an option:

   Empty menu bar: F5 *<option name>*

   . . .

To move an existing option:

   Menu bar: [highlight option] **F7**
   Dialog box: **Item Only**
   Keyboard: [move item with arrow keys] ↵

To delete an option:

   Menu bar: [move cursor to first letter of option] **Ctrl-T |
   Del**

USAGE

To enter an option for your application, press **F5,** type in the option, and then press **F5** again. Use the **Space** bar or → to enter some space, press **F5,** type the next option, then press **F5** again. Repeat this process for as many options as you wish to place in the menu.

If you are modifying an existing menu, you can move an option by highlighting it and pressing **F7** (Move). Select

Item Only from the dialog box, use the arrow keys to move the item, and then press ↵.

To insert a new item, position the cursor at a blank space where you want the new item to appear. Make sure Insert mode is on; then press **F5**, type in the new item, and press **F5** again. To insert blank spaces, position the cursor, make sure Insert mode is on, and press the **Space** bar.

To delete a menu option, move the cursor to the first character in the option name and press the **Del** key repeatedly or press **Ctrl-T.**

To change the size of the horizontal bar menu, press **Shift-F7** (Size) and use the arrow keys to resize the menu. Press ↵ when you are done. To move the bar menu, press **F7** (Move), reposition the menu with the arrow keys, and press ↵.

Designing a Pop-Up or Pull-Down Menu

The Pop-Up Menu option on the Design menu is used to create both pop-up and pull-down menus. When you choose this option to create a new menu, an empty pop-up menu will appear on the screen.

SEQUENCE OF STEPS

Empty pop-up menu: [type in options]

Keyboard: **F7** [to resize frame]

USAGE

If necessary, use **Shift-F7** (Size) to enlarge the frame and then type in each menu option. Be sure to place each option on a separate line. Use Size after typing in all options to tighten the frame around them.

If you are modifying an existing pop-up menu, you can change any option by highlighting it and retyping the text. To insert a new option, enlarge the frame, if necessary, to make room for another option. Move the highlight to where you want the new option to appear and press **Ctrl-N**. Then type the new option. To delete an option, highlight it and press **Ctrl-Y**. The completed pop-up menu will look similar to the standard dBASE pull-down menus, except that it will not be attached to a menu bar.

Designing a Files List

A files list is an application object that presents a list of file names to the user. Use this object when you create an application that requires the user to select a file name.

USAGE

When you create a files list, an empty frame appears centered in the screen with a series of X's highlighted as an option. You can resize the frame and move it (keep in mind that the maximum width of a file name is 12 characters, so you cannot make the frame any narrower), but you cannot enter information into this frame, because the application uses the frame to present file names. Instead, to set the types of files to be displayed in the list, select **Identify Files in List** from the **List** pull-down menu (discussed later in this chapter). The user can scroll through the list of files using the usual ↑, ↓, PgUp, and PgDn keys and then select the currently highlighted item by pressing ↵.

The name of the selected file is stored in the variable &LISTVAL. You can use &LISTVAL in the dialog box that defines the action, in place of a specific file name, to have the action use the file that the user selected.

Designing a Structure List

The structure list object lets your application display a list of field names from the current database to the user. Use this object when you want the user to select field names from a database, such as when he or she is displaying database records or browsing.

When you create a structure list, you'll see a frame centered on the screen with a series of highlighted X's to help you determine the width of the frame. You can change the width of the frame or move it, but keep in mind that the frame must be wide enough to accommodate the largest possible field name (10 characters).

To determine which field names are to be included in the list, select **Identify Fields in List** from the **List** pull-down menu (discussed later in this chapter). The user can select field names from the structure list using the usual technique of highlighting and pressing ↵. These field names are stored in the &LISTVAL variable. The action you assign to the structure list should be one that supports a FIELD statement (such as Browse or Display/List). You can use the &LISTVAL variable in the FIELDS option of the dialog box in place of specific field names, so that the action displays only those fields that the user selected in the structure list.

Designing a Values List

A values list is an application object that presents a list of values from a single database field to the user. Use this option when you want your user to select an existing value from a database. For example, in an inventory application, if you want the user to specify an existing part number for some operation, you could use a values list to present all available part numbers. The user could then scroll through this list and select an item by highlighting it and pressing ↵.

When sizing the frame for the field values list, make sure that the frame is wide enough to accommodate the data in the field. For example, if the list is to display a field named Part-No, which is five characters wide, the frame too should be at least five characters wide. To determine which field from the current database (or view) the values list displays, select **Identify Field Values in List** from the **List** pull-down menu.

The value that the user selects from the values list is stored in the &LISTVAL variable, which you can use later when assigning an action to the values list object.

Designing a Batch Process

A batch process is an application object that performs a series of steps, or operations, for the user.

USAGE

When you create a new batch process, you'll see an empty frame centered on the screen. Type a plain-English description of each operation in the batch process. (The user will never see these descriptions, but you'll eventually assign an action to each item.)

If you are modifying an existing batch process, its description will appear centered on the screen. To delete an operation, highlight its description and press **Ctrl-Y**. To insert a new operation, first enlarge the frame, if necessary, to accommodate the new item using **Shift-F7** (Size) and ↓. Then position the highlight where you want the new operation to appear and press **Ctrl-N**. Type the plain-English description of the operation.

After filling in the descriptions of each step in the process, you can assign an action to each step using options from the **Item** pull-down menu (discussed later in this chapter).

The Application Menu

As discussed previously, the second option on the application design screen main menu changes to accommodate the type of object on which you are currently working. Table 12.3 shows which pull-down menu is available for each type of application object. This section discusses the options on the Application menu.

OBJECT	PULL-DOWN MENU
Sign-on banner	Application
Horizontal bar menu	Menu
Pop-up menu	Menu
Files list	List
Structure list	List
Values list	List
Batch process	Batch

Table 12.3: Pull-Down Menus for Application Objects

Changing the Application Name and Description

The Name and Describe option on the Application pull-down menu displays the name and description of the current application.

SEQUENCE OF STEPS

Application design screen menu bar: **Application**

Application menu: **Name and Describe** ↵

Dialog box Name prompt: *<name>* ↵

Dialog box Description prompt: *<description>* ↵

USAGE

You can change the application name and description, but remember that the name must be a valid file name, and the description should not contain quotation marks. Press **Ctrl-End** to save any changes or **Esc** to abandon them.

Assigning a Main Menu Type and Name

The Assign Main Menu option on the Application pull-down menu displays the type and name of the application main menu.

SEQUENCE OF STEPS

Application design screen menu bar: **Application**

Application menu: **Assign Main Menu** ⏎

Dialog box Main Menu Type prompt: **Bar** | **Pop-Up** | **Batch** [press space bar to cycle through options] ⏎

Dialog box Main Menu Name prompt: <*menu name*> | **Shift-F1** [highlight menu name] ⏎

Keyboard: **Ctrl-End** [to save changes]

USAGE

You can change the menu name or type, but remember that you must use a valid file name for the main menu name. Press **Ctrl-End** to save any changes or **Esc** to abandon them.

Displaying the Sign-On Banner

The Display Sign-On Banner option lets you decide whether the user sees the sign-on banner when he or she runs the application.

SEQUENCE OF STEPS

Application design screen menu bar: **Application**

Application menu: **Display Sign-On Banner** ⏎

Dialog box Display Sign-On Banner at Run Time
prompt: **Yes** | **No** ⏎

USAGE

When you select this option, you'll see a dialog box with the
options Yes and No. If you select **Yes,** the sign-on banner will
appear as soon as the user runs the application, with the instruction *Press ⏎ to continue* centered at the bottom of the
screen. After the user presses ⏎, the application main menu
appears on the screen. If you select **No,** the user is taken
directly to the application main menu.

Creating a Program Header

The Edit Program Header Comments option lets you modify
the heading in the generated application program. If you
plan to distribute your completed application and wish to
retain the copyright, you should fill in the dialog box with
your name, a copyright notice, and the version of dBASE
used to generate the application.

SEQUENCE OF STEPS

Application design screen menu bar: **Application**

Application menu: **Edit Program Header Comments** ⏎

Dialog box Application Author prompt: *<author name>* ⏎

Dialog box Copyright Notice prompt: *<copyright notice>* ⏎

Dialog box dBASE Version prompt: *<dBASE version>* ⏎

Keyboard: **Ctrl-End**

USAGE

Heading comments are entirely optional and do not affect the performance of the application in any way. The comments are simply placed at the top of the generated program to inform others who the author is and who has the right to make and distribute copies.

Modifying the Application Environment

The Modify Application Environment option lets you alter some predefined assumptions about the application environment. When selected, this option displays the following submenu: Display Options, Environment Settings, Search Path, View/Database and Index. Any options you select from this submenu affect the entire application, unless you specifically override them in a particular menu or menu option. The following sections describe each option.

Changing Display Options

When you select Display Options, you'll see a submenu that lets you change the border style and colors of the sign-on banner.

SEQUENCE OF STEPS

Application design screen menu bar: **Application**

Application menu: **Modify Application Environment** ↵

Modify Application Environment menu: **Display Options** ↵

Display Options menu: [highlight option] ↵

(Select colors and border styles)

USAGE

When **Object Border Style** is highlighted, you can press the Space bar to scroll through the options: **Double** (a double-line frame), **Single** (a single-line frame), **Panel** (a wide frame), or **None** (no frame). The remaining objects let you color the screen. The techniques you use to select colors are identical to those discussed in Chapter 11.

SEE ALSO

Customizing Your Environment/Display Options (Chapter 11)

Changing Environmental Settings

The Environment Settings option displays a submenu of dBASE IV settings that affect the entire application but can be overridden for a particular menu or option. The effects of each setting are described in Chapter 11. However, two items are unique to the Applications Generator, and these are described here.

SEQUENCE OF STEPS

Application design screen main menu: **Application**

Application menu: **Modify Application Environment** ↵

Modify Application Environment menu: **Environment Settings** ↵

Environment Settings menu: [highlight option and press **Space** bar to cycle through settings] ↵

Keyboard: **Ctrl-End** [to save settings]

USAGE

If the **Set Bell** setting is **On,** you can change the pitch and duration of the bell by entering values in the rightmost prompts. The first prompt, the frequency, can be any number in the range 19 to 10,000 cycles per second. The default frequency (which you normally hear when you use dBASE IV) is 512. (A lower number produces a lower pitch; a higher number produces a higher pitch.)

You can set the duration to from 2 to 19 *ticks* (a tick is approximately 0.055 second). The default setting is 2. For example, if you want your application to sound a lower, longer tone than the default tone used in dBASE IV, you can specify Set Bell ON (to 440,10) for the Set Bell option.

The **Set Escape** option lets you decide whether the user can leave the application (and return to dBASE IV). If Escape is On the user can leave the application by pressing Esc; if Escape is Off, the user cannot do so. When first developing and testing an application, you should leave this setting on, so you have the option of leaving the application by pressing Esc. After you've completed and thoroughly tested the application, you can turn this option off.

SEE ALSO

Customizing Your Workspace/Environmental Settings (Chapter 11)

Setting a Search Path

The Search Path option lets you determine a disk drive and directory that the completed application will search for database files, report formats, and other external application objects.

SEQUENCE OF STEPS

Application design screen main menu: **Application**
Application menu: **Modify Application Environment** ↵

Modify Application Environment menu: **Search Path** ↵

Dialog box Drive prompt: *<drive name>* | **Shift-F1** [highlight drive name] ↵

Dialog box Search Path prompt: *<search path>* ↵

Keyboard: **Ctrl-End** [to save settings]

USAGE

The Drive option determines the disk-drive name (for example, B or C), and the search path specifies one or more subdirectories.

If you place all application objects on a single subdirectory, you can leave both the **Drive** and **Search Path** options blank.

Changing the Database File, Index, and Sort Order

The View/Database and Index option lets you change the default database, index file, and sort order for the application.

SEQUENCE OF STEPS

Application design screen main menu: **Application**

Application menu: **Modify Application Environment** ↵

Modify Application Environment menu: **View/Database and Index** ↵

Dialog box Database/View prompt: *<database | view name>* | **Shift-F1** [highlight option] ↵

Dialog box Set Index To prompt: *<index file name>* | **Shift-F1** [highlight option] ↵

Dialog box Order prompt: *<index name>* ↵

Keyboard: **Ctrl-End** [to save changes]

When you select **View/Database and Index,** the screen displays the current default names. (You specified these in the Application Definition dialog box when you first entered the Applications Generator.) You can change these values from the Applications pull-down menu if you made a mistake when you first entered them.

Developing Quick Applications

The Generate Quick Application option on the Application pull-down menu creates a simple application that uses a single database file, sort order, custom screen, report format, and mailing label format.

Application design screen menu bar: **Application**

Application menu: **Generate Quick Application** ↵

Quick application form: [fill in]

Keyboard: **Ctrl-End** [to save form]

Dialog box: **Yes** ↵

Keyboard: [press any key]

Application design screen menu bar: **Exit**

Exit menu: **Save All Changes and Exit** ↵

Select **Generate Quick Application** from the **Application** pull-down menu. Fill in the quick application form using the names of a single database file, report format, label format, and index order (these must have already been created using the appropriate panels from the Control Center). Rather than typing file names, you can press **Shift-F1** (Pick) to select them from a submenu of all the files in the current catalog.

You can also fill in an author name and menu heading for the application. Press **Ctrl-End** after filling in the quick application form. Select **Yes** from the dialog box that appears. After the Applications Generator writes the program for the application, you'll see the prompt *Press any key to continue.* Do so. Finally, select **Save All Changes and Exit** from the **Exit** pull-down menu. When you return to the Control Center, you'll see the name of your application in the Applications panel.

Running a Quick Application

To run a quick application, follow these simple steps.

SEQUENCE OF STEPS

Control Center Applications panel: [highlight application name] ↵

Prompt box: **Run Application** ↵

Prompt box: **Yes** ↵

USAGE

Highlight the name of the application in the Applications panel and press ↵. Select **Run Application** from the prompt box that appears. Then select **Yes** when dBASE asks for verification.

After a few seconds the application main menu appears on the screen. The quick application technique does not create a menu bar with pull-down menus. Instead, it presents a smaller sign-on banner at the top of the screen and a single pop-up menu centered on the screen. The pop-up menu is identical to a pull-down menu, except that it is not directly attached to a menu-bar option.

Saving the Application Definition

The Save Current Application Definition option saves any changes to the current application.

SEQUENCE OF STEPS

Application design screen menu bar: **Application**

Application menu: **Save Current Application Definition** ↵

USAGE

This option saves your changes, but does not regenerate the application program.

Clearing the Work Surface

The Clear Work Surface option saves all menus and other application objects and clears them from the screen. (The sign-on banner, however, is never cleared from the screen.)

SEQUENCE OF STEPS

Application design screen menu bar: **Application**

Application menu: **Clear Work Surface** ↵

USAGE

Before dBASE IV saves any modified objects, it presents a dialog box asking if you want to save or abandon recent changes to each object. Select **Save Changes** to save new or modified objects. Note that this option is similar to the Put Away Current *<object>* option, except that it puts away all objects currently on the screen. To bring any object back to the design screen, select the appropriate object type from the Design pull-down menu and the object name from the submenu that appears.

The Menu Menu

Whenever you create or modify a horizontal bar or pull-down menu, the second option on the Applications Generator main menu changes to Menu. The Menu pull-down menu displays the following options (Attach Pull-Down Menus is available only when a horizontal bar menu is the current object): Name and Describe, Override Assigned Database or View, Write Help Text, Modify Display Options, Embed Code, Attach Pull-Down Menus, Save Current Menu, Put Away Current Menu, Clear Work Surface.

Changing the Menu Name and Description

This option is the same as the Name and Describe option on the Application menu, but is used to name and describe a single menu rather than the entire application.

SEQUENCE OF STEPS

Application design screen menu bar: **Menu**

Menu menu: **Name and Describe** ↵

Dialog box Name prompt: *<name>* ↵

Dialog box Description prompt: *<description>* ↵

Dialog box Message Line prompt: **<message>** ↵

Keyboard: **Ctrl-End**

USAGE ═══════════════

The **Name and Describe** option displays the name and description of the current menu and allows you to change either one. The name must be a valid DOS file name, and the description cannot contain any quotation marks. The Message Line prompt appears at the bottom of the screen whenever the current menu is displayed when the application is used. It can be up to 76 characters long and cannot contain quotation marks.

Overriding the Database or View

The Override Assigned Database or View option lets you assign a new database, view, index, or sort order to all options in the current menu.

SEQUENCE OF STEPS ═══════════════

Application design screen menu bar: **Menu**

Menu menu: **Override Assigned Database or View** ⏎

Dialog box For This Menu, You May Use Values prompt: **Above** | **Entered Below** | **In Effect at Run Time** [press **Space** bar to scroll through options] ⏎

Keyboard: **Ctrl-End** [to save changes]

USAGE ═══════════════

When you select **Override Assigned Database or View,** you'll see a dialog box with the name of the current database and index and options to assign different values. To change the assigned database or view for the menu, move the cursor to the **For This Menu, You May Use Values** prompt and press the **Space** bar to scroll through the options. Your options are

Option	Effect
Above	Menu will use the database, index, sort order specified above.
Entered Below	Menu will use the database, index, and sort order specified below.
In Effect at Run Time	Menu will use whatever database, index, and view are in use when the user selects the menu.

You can use the last option, **In Effect at Run Time**, to create a generic application that lets the user manage more than one database file. For example, your application could display a files list of all database files (*.DBF) before displaying the current menu. Whatever database the user selects from the files list would be used by all actions on the current menu.

If you specify **Below,** the current menu uses the database, index file, and sort order specified at the bottom of the dialog box. If you leave any of these options blank, dBASE uses the default values.

Note that changing the default values at this level affects all menu options in the current menu. When the user is done with the current menu, the default database and index defined at the Application level are put back into effect. To change the database, index, or sort order for a particular option within the current menu, select the Override Assigned Database or View option from the Item pull-down menu.

Writing Help Text

The Write Help Text option on the Menu pull-down menu lets you write a custom help screen for the current application menu.

SEQUENCE OF STEPS =========

Application design screen menu bar: **Menu**
Menu menu: **Write Help Text** ⏎
Editing frame: *<text>*
Keyboard: **Ctrl-End** [to save changes]

USAGE =========

When you select **Write Help Text,** dBASE presents a full-screen editing frame. You can type whatever text you wish into this frame and make changes and corrections using the usual dBASE IV editing keys. After creating your custom help screen, press **Ctrl-End** to return to the application design screen.

The user can press F1 to view the help screen any time the current application menu is on the screen. However, if you assign help screens to individual menu options (using the Item menu), these will be displayed rather than the help screen you define here. If you do not define a help screen for a menu or options within a menu, no help is displayed when the user presses F1. Instead, the user will see only the message *No help found for <object name>.*

Modifying Display Options

Modify Display Options on the Menu pull-down menu lets you assign a border style and colors to the current menu. The options are the same ones displayed by the Display Options option on the Application menu.

SEQUENCE OF STEPS =========

Application design screen menu bar: **Menu**
Menu menu: **Modify Display Options** ⏎
Display Options menu: [highlight option] ⏎

USAGE ==========

If you do not assign either a border style or colors, the current menu will use the display options specified on the Application pull-down menu.

SEE ALSO ==========

Customizing Your Environment/Display Options (Chapter 11)

Embedding Program Code in an Application

The Embed Code option allows you to add dBASE IV programming-language code to an application. This code can be executed either before or after the menu (or list) is displayed.

SEQUENCE OF STEPS ==========

Application design screen menu bar: **Menu**

Menu menu: **Embed Code** ⏎

Dialog box: **Before** | **After** [use ↑, ↓, and ⏎ to select option] ⏎

Editing frame: <*code*>

Keyboard: **Ctrl-End** [to save code]

USAGE ==========

When you select **Embed Code,** you'll be given a full screen in which to write your program. You can enter a maximum of 19 commands. Press **Ctrl-End** after writing your code.

Attaching Pull-Down Menus

The Attach Pull-Down Menus option is available on the Menu pull-down menu only if the current object is a horizontal bar menu.

SEQUENCE OF STEPS

Application design screen menu bar: **Menu**

Menu menu: **Attach Pull-Down Menus** ⏎

Dialog box: **Yes** | **No** [use ↑, ↓, ⏎ to select an option] ⏎

USAGE

When you select this option, you'll see a dialog box with the options **Yes** and **No** and the message *Pull down associated menus and assign this menu's attributes (such as colors, database/view, and code embeds) to them automatically?*

If you select **Yes,** the pop-up menus that are attached to main menu options will be displayed as soon as the user highlights the bar menu option. The pull-down menus will automatically inherit many attributes of the bar menu, as specified in the dialog box.

If you have already assigned unique attributes to the pull-down menus, these will be overridden when you change the **Attach Pull-Down Menus** setting to **Yes**. For this reason, it's best to set this option before you change any attributes on the pull-down menus. (That way, you won't have to go back and change them again.)

If you set **Attach Pull-Down Menus** to **No**, the pop-up menus are not displayed until the user highlights the main menu option and presses ⏎.

Saving the Current Menu

When you select the Save Current Menu option, the current menu is saved to disk but remains on screen so you can continue working with it.

Putting Away the Current Menu

The Put Away Current Menu option removes the current menu from the design screen. If the menu is new or has been modified, dBASE first presents options to save or abandon changes. If you need to bring back a menu that you've put away, select the appropriate menu type from the Design screen, and then the menu's name from the submenu that appears.

Clearing the Work Surface

The Clear Work Surface option on the Menu pull-down menu is identical to the Clear Work Surface option on the Application pull-down menu, discussed earlier in this chapter.

The List Menu

If the object you are currently working on is a files list, structure list, or values list, List appears as the second menu item on the design screen main menu. When selected, this menu displays the following options: Name and Describe, Override Assigned Database or View, Write Help Text, Modify Display Options, Embed Code, Identify Files in List, Save Current List, Put Away Current List, Clear Work Surface.

All options on this menu except Identify Files in List are identical to corresponding menu items on the Menu pull-down menu. These override any settings defined at the Preset or Application level for the current list only. The sixth menu option will vary, depending on the type of list object on which you are currently working, as summarized here:

Object	Menu Option Displayed
Files list	Identify Files in List
Structure list	Identify Fields in List
Values list	Identify Field Values in List

The sections below discuss these menu options.

Identifying Files in a List

The Identify Files in List option lets you determine which files are displayed in the files list object.

SEQUENCE OF STEPS ===============================

Application design screen menu bar: **List**

List menu: **Identify Files in List** ↵

Dialog box File Specification prompt: *<file specification>* ↵

USAGE ===============================

When you select this option, you'll be prompted to enter a file specification. Typically, you'll use a wildcard character to select a specific type of file in the files list. Here are some examples:

*.DBF	Displays only database (.DBF) files
*.MDX	Displays only index (.MDX) files
*.FRM	Displays only report format (.FRM) files
*.LBL	Displays only label format (.LBL) files
*.FMT	Displays only custom screen (.FMT) files
MAIL*.*	Displays only files beginning with MAIL

If you do not enter a file specification, all the files in the current subdirectory will be displayed in the files list when the user runs the application.

Identifying Fields in a List

If you are currently working on a structure list, the menu option Identify Fields in List is available on the List pull-down menu.

SEQUENCE OF STEPS

Application design screen menu bar: **List**

List menu: **Identify Fields in List** ↵

Dialog box Field Name prompt: *<field names>* | **Shift-F1** [highlight field names] ↵

Keyboard: **Ctrl-End** [to save field names]

USAGE

When you select **Identify Fields in List,** you'll be prompted to enter field names to include in the list. If you leave the prompt blank, all fields from the database will be displayed in the list when the user runs the application.

To limit the structure list to specific fields in the database, press **Shift-F1** (Pick) for a submenu of field names. Select each field you want displayed in the list by highlighting it and pressing ↵. Selected fields are marked with a triangle. If you change your mind, you can press ↵ to unselect a field name.

You can also type the field names directly into the prompt, separating each name with a comma (be sure to spell names correctly). After specifying the field names, press ↵ to return to the application design screen.

Identifying Field Values in a List

If the object you are currently working on is a values list, the Identify Field Values in List option will be available on the List pull-down menu.

SEQUENCE OF STEPS

Application design screen menu bar: **List**

List menu: **Identify Field Values in List** ↵

Dialog box Field Name prompt: *<field name>* | **Shift-F1** [highlight field name] ↵

Keyboard: **Ctrl-End** [to save field name]

USAGE

When you select this option, you'll be prompted to enter the name of the field for which you want to list values. Press **Shift-F1** (Pick) and select a field from the submenu that appears. Then press **Ctrl-End** to return to the List pull-down menu.

The index currently in use determines how the fields are displayed in the values list. For example, suppose you decide to list values in the State field of a database, and that database currently contains the records AZ, CA, WA, CA, AZ, and WA (in that order). If no index is in use, the fields list will be displayed in the following order: AZ, CA, WA, CA, AZ, WA. If an index of the State field is active when the user views the values list (and the **Duplicate Keys** option is set to **No**), the values list will display all the states, in alphabetical order, as follows: AZ, AZ, CA, CA, WA, WA. If an index of the State field, with the **Duplicate Values** option set to **Yes**, is active when the user views the values list, only unique states will be listed (in alphabetical order), as follows: AZ, CA, WA.

To select a database or index for the values list, use the Override Assigned Database or View option from the List menu or Reassign Index Order from the Item menu. (Remember, you create indexes outside the Applications Generator, at the database design screen.)

The Batch Menu

If the object you are creating or modifying is a batch process, you use the second option on the design screen pull-down menu, Batch. The Batch pull-down menu displays the following options: Name and Describe, Override Assigned Database or View, Embed Code, Save Current Batch Process, Put Away Current Batch Process, Clear Work Surface. All these options are identical to equivalent options on the Menu pull-down menu, described previously, except that they operate on the current batch process, rather than the current menu. There is no option for modifying the display characteristics, because batch processes are not presented to the user as objects. Instead, a batch process carries out a series of steps.

The Item Menu

The Item pull-down menu is available on the Applications Generator main menu whenever you are working on a menu, list, or batch process. This menu is used to assign *actions* and attributes to specific menu options, batch processes, and lists in your application.

SEQUENCE OF STEPS

Application design screen: [make object current]

Application design screen menu bar: **Item**

Item menu: [highlight option] ↵

USAGE ==============

To use the **Item** menu, first make current the object to which you want to assign attributes or actions. If the object is a menu, highlight the option to which you want to assign an action or attribute in your custom menu. (You can press **PgUp** and **PgDn** to scroll through your custom menu options or batch process operations.) Then press **F10** (Menu) and scroll to the **Item** pull-down menu. You'll notice that the option from your custom menu appears centered in the status bar near the bottom of the screen. If you are working on a batch process, the operation description will appear in the status bar.

If you are currently working on a list object, X's will appear in the status bar. You can assign only one action to be performed after the user selects an item from the list.

Although some options on the Item pull-down menu are identical to options on the Menu pull-down menu, options on the Menu menu affect the menu as a whole, whereas options on the Item menu affect individual menu options. Each option on the Item pull-down menu is discussed in the sections that follow.

Showing Information on an Item

The Show Item Information option displays the name of the current object, the item that is currently highlighted within that object, the database or view in use, and the action that is currently assigned to the item (but you can't change actions from the screen).

SEQUENCE OF STEPS ==============

Application design screen: [make object current]

Application design screen menu bar: **Item**

Item menu: **Show Item Information** ↵

Item information screen: [view information]

Keyboard: ↵ | **Esc** [to return to Item menu]

USAGE

To view the database, index order, and action assigned to a menu option, move the highlight to the menu option and select **Show Item Information** from the **Item** pull-down menu.

After viewing the item information, press **Ctrl-End** or **Esc** to return to the **Item** pull-down menu.

Assigning and Changing Actions

The Change Action option is the tool you use to assign and change actions that your application performs. When you create an application, you use Change Action to assign (or modify) an action for each option in your menus and each operation in a batch process. You can also assign a single action to each values list, structure list, and fields list; the action you assign to a list takes place immediately after the user selects an item from the list.

SEQUENCE OF STEPS

Application design screen: [make the object current]

Application design screen menu bar: **Item**

Item menu: **Change Action** ↵

Change Action menu: [select and define action]

Keyboard: **Esc** [to return to the design screen]

USAGE

Make the menu, batch process, or list the current object on the design screen. For a menu or batch process, highlight the option or plain-English description for which you want to assign (or change) an action. Press **F10** and highlight the

Item pull-down menu. Select **Change Action**. Then select an action and use submenus and dialog boxes to define it. To move to another option in a menu or another operation in a batch process, press **PgDn** or **PgUp** until the option or operation appears in the status bar. Optionally, press **Esc** to return to the design screen.

When you first select the **Change Action** option, you'll see the submenu that follows. (The uppercase options to the right of the menu options are the dBASE IV commands that the application will use.)

Text (No Action)

Open a Menu   ACTIVATE MENU

Browse (Add, Delete, Edit)   BROWSE

Edit Form (Add, Delete, Edit)   EDIT

Display or Print

Perform File Operation

Run Program

Quit

We'll return to these options, discussing each one in turn, after looking at the filter conditions you can use with many of them.

Entering Filter Conditions in Dialog Boxes

Many actions you assign to options in your application allow you to filter records from the database. In the Applications Generator, you need not use the query design screen to do this. Instead, you can enter filter conditions directly into dialog boxes that appear as you create the application.

The rules for defining data types in Applications Generator filter conditions are similar to those applicable to the query design screen. You must enclose character data in quotation marks, enclose date data in curly braces, and use numeric data without any delimiters. You can use the same operators in dialog boxes that you use in the query design screen. Similarly, you can use any dBASE function in a filter condition.

However, there are a few differences between the filter conditions you enter into the query design screen and those you enter into Applications Generator boxes. These are discussed in the sections that follow.

Complete Expressions

In a dialog box, you must use a *complete expression* as the filter condition. A complete expression is one that returns either a true or a false result.

In the query design screen, if you want to isolate records that have CA in the State field, you could place "CA" in the State box of the query. In an Applications Generator dialog box, the expression "CA" alone would not return a true or a false result. (In fact, it would return an error and stop the application running.) Instead, you would use the filter condition **State = "CA"**. This condition returns a true or false result, because a particular database record either *does* or *does not* have CA in the State field. Similarly, the filter conditions

    StartDate < {12/31/89} and Qty > 100

can return only a true or a false result.

Note that a filter condition consists of three components: a field name, an operator, and a comparison value. In the filter condition **Qty > 100**, Qty is the field name, > is the operator, and 100 is the comparison value. The one exception to the complete expression rule is the logical field, which does not require an operator or comparison value. We'll discuss this exception in a moment.

AND, OR, and NOT Operators

Unlike the query design screen, dialog boxes do not allow you to align or stagger expressions in rows to create AND and OR conditions. Instead, you use the operators .AND. and

.OR. In addition, you can use the .NOT. operator to specify conditions that are not true (or logical fields that contain .F. rather than .T.).

When using .AND., .OR., and .NOT. expressions, you must use complete expressions on both sides of the operator. For example, suppose StartDate is a date field, and you want to isolate records from the first quarter of 1989. You might think that you could use the filter condition

StartDate >= {01/01/89} .AND. <= {03/31/89}

to isolate the appropriate records. However, this expression will cause an error when you run the application, because the expression on the right side of the .AND. operator, <= {03/31/89}, is incomplete. dBASE can't determine that you mean **StartDate <= {03/31/89}**, so it doesn't know *what* to compare to {03/32/89}. (You and I can figure this out, but dBASE isn't quite so smart.) To isolate records from the first quarter of 1989, you should use the expression **StartDate >= {01/01/89} .AND. StartDate <= {03/31/89}**.

Logical fields do not require an operator or comparison value in a filter condition. The field name itself is a complete expression, because it refers to a value that is already .T. or .F. For example, if Current is the name of a logical field, the expression **Current** is identical to the expression **Current = .T.**. To isolate records that have .F. in a Logical field, use the .NOT. operator before the field name. For example, the expression **.NOT. Current** is identical to the expression **Current = .F.**

Refining Filter-Condition Logic

You can use parentheses to refine the meanings of .AND. and .OR. in filter condition expressions. For example, suppose a database contains State as a character field and Paid as a logical field, and you want to isolate the records of New York and New Jersey residents who have paid.

If you use the filter condition

State = "NY" .OR. State = "NJ" .AND. Paid

there is some ambiguity about whether you want records on New York and New Jersey residents who have paid, or records on New York residents (regardless of whether they've paid), and New Jersey residents who have paid.

By default, dBASE interprets all .NOT. expressions first, then .AND. expressions, and then .OR. expressions. You can eliminate any ambiguity in a filter condition by using parentheses to isolate portions it. dBASE always interprets an expression from the innermost parentheses outward. For example, the filter condition

(State = "NY" .OR. State = "NJ") .AND. Paid

isolates the .OR. portion of the filter condition and executes that first. If the State field holds either NY or NJ, the next condition, the member has Paid, must also be met.

When you use parentheses to refine the logic of a filter condition, be sure the parentheses are *balanced;* That is, that the expression contains an equal number of opening and closing parentheses.

&LISTVAL in Filter Conditions   The Applications Generator lets your application display lists of values from a database field. (These are discussed in "Values Lists" later in this chapter.) When the user selects a value from a values list, this selection is stored in a variable named &LISTVAL.

You can use &LISTVAL instead of a specific comparison value in any Applications Generator dialog box filter condition. However, you must enclose the &LISTVAL variable name in the symbols for the data type. For example, if the values list displays data from a character field named Part-Code, the filter condition to isolate records that have that part code would be PartCode = "&LISTVAL."

Note that you cannot test a query that uses &LISTVAL through the query design screen. Instead, test it using a real comparison value (for example, LastName = "Smith") and then substitute &LISTVAL for the comparison value when you create the application. That is, enter **LastName = "&LISTVAL"** in the dialog box.

FILTER, FOR, SCOPE, and WHILE

In your application, many of the actions you assign will provide up to four different ways to filter records: FILTER, FOR, SCOPE, and WHILE.

FOR and FILTER Conditions   In most situations, you will want to place your application filter condition after the FOR prompt. FOR accepts any valid filter condition, as long as it fits in the space provided. For example, if you enter the filter condition **State = "NY"** in the FOR section of a Print a Report dialog box, the report will print letters for only New York residents.

The FILTER option, which is available in some dialog boxes, is virtually identical to the FOR option. You can place any valid filter condition in the FILTER section, and the operation will limit the operation to records that meet the filter criterion. For example, if you enter **MONTH(StartDate) = 12** as the FILTER condition in the Print a Report dialog box, the printed report includes only records that have December start dates.

If you use both a FOR and a FILTER condition in a dialog box, the conditions are combined using .AND. logic. For example, if the FILTER condition in a Print a Report dialog box is **State = "NJ"** and the FOR condition in that same dialog box is **MONTH(StartDate) = 12**, the report prints only records with NJ in the state field and December start dates. Note that you could achieve the same results by placing the filter condition **State = "NJ" .AND. MONTH(StartDate) = 12** in either the FOR or the FILTER section.

SCOPE Conditions   The SCOPE option in an Applications Generator dialog box lets you define the number of records to be included in an operation. Your options are summarized in Table 12.4.

The default scope for most operations is ALL. Three exceptions are Substitute Field Values, Mark Records for Deletion, and Unmark Records, which operate only on the current record, unless you specify an ALL or FOR scope condition in the dialog box.

WHILE Conditions   The WHILE condition limits a group
of records that are adjacent in the database and meet a filter
condition. dBASE executes WHILE operators faster than FOR
or FILTER operators, but WHILE operators can be used only
if two criteria are met. The database must be indexed (or
sorted) on the field being searched, and the current record in
the database must already meet the filter condition.

To meet these criteria, an application must first make sure
the appropriate index is in use (using the Reassign Index
Order option on the Item menu if necessary) and then locate
the first record that meets the filter condition (using the Item
menu's Position Record Pointer option, before the WHILE
condition is executed).

OPTION	EFFECT
ALL	Includes all records in the database.
RECORD \<n\>	Isolates a specific record, based on its position in the database. For example, entering RECORD 5 limits an operation to record number 5 in the database.
NEXT \<n\>	Isolates a group of records, starting from the current record. For example, entering NEXT 3 limits the operation to the current record and the two that follow. (If an index is active, NEXT 3 means the next three records in the current sort order.)
REST	Isolates records from the current record, to the end of the database file. If an index is active, REST refers to the rest of the database records in the current sort order.

Table 12.4: SCOPE Options

WHILE is faster than FOR and FILTER because both FOR and FILTER look at every record in the database and isolate records that meet the filter conditions. A WHILE condition, on the other hand, uses an index to find the first record that matches the filter condition, then looks at records *until* it encounters a record that does not meet the filter condition; it wastes no time looking at other records.

WHILE searches can be tricky to set up. Therefore, until you've had some experience in programming with the dBASE IV programming language, your best bet is to use FOR and FILTER search conditions when developing applications.

SEE ALSO ══════════════

Chapter 5: Searching a Database

The Change Action Submenu

The sections that follow describe each action and each submenu item and dialog box in the Change Action submenu.

Assigning No Action

If you assign the Text (No Action) action to a menu option, the user cannot highlight the option when he or she runs the application.

SEQUENCE OF STEPS ══════════════

Change Action menu: **Text (No Action)** ⏎ ⏎
Keyboard: **Ctrl-End** [to return to the design screen]

USAGE ══════════════

Text (No Action) is the default setting initially assigned to all menu options, batch processes, and list selections.

Opening a Menu

If you assign the action Open a Menu to an application item, a submenu appears asking for the type and name of the menu to display.

SEQUENCE OF STEPS

Change Action menu: **Open a Menu** ↵

Dialog box Menu Type prompt: **Bar** | **Pop-Up** | **Files** | **Structure** | **Values** [press **Space** bar to scroll through options]

Dialog box Menu Name prompt: <*name*> | **Shift-F1** [highlight option] ↵

Keyboard: **Ctrl-End** [to return to the design screen]

USAGE

You can press the **Space** bar to scroll through the menu type options, which are **Bar** (a horizontal bar menu), **Pop-Up** (a pop-up or pull-down menu), **Files** (a files list), **Structure** (a structure list), and **Values** (a values list). After you select the menu type, move the cursor to the **Menu Name** option and type the name of the menu (or list) that you want the option to display. You can also press **Shift-F1** (Pick) to see a submenu of existing object names and select the appropriate name.

When the user later runs the application and selects the option to which you've assigned the Open a Menu action, he or she will see the menu (or list object) you've specified. Note that if a menu option displays a list, you will also need to assign an action to that list. The action you assign will occur immediately after the user selects a list item.

Displaying Data in a Browse Screen

The Browse (Add, Delete, Edit) action displays data from the current database or view in a browse screen.

SEQUENCE OF STEPS

Change Action menu: **Browse (Add, Delete, Edit)** ↵

Dialog box Fields prompt: *<fields>* | **Shift-F1** [highlight names] ↵ ·

Dialog box Filter prompt: *<filter condition>* ↵

Dialog box Fields to Lock Onscreen prompt: *<number>* ↵

Dialog box Freeze Edit Field prompt: *<field>* | **Shift-F1** [highlight name] ↵

Dialog box Maximum Column Width prompt: *<number>* ↵

Dialog box Format File prompt: *<file name>* ↵

Dialog box Allow Record Add? prompt: **Yes** | **No** [scroll through options with **Space** bar] ↵

Dialog box Allow Record Edit? prompt: **Yes** | **No** [scroll through options with **Space** bar] ↵

Dialog box Allow Record Delete? prompt: **Yes** | **No** [scroll through options with **Space** bar] ↵

Dialog box Keep Image on Exit? prompt: **Yes** | **No** [scroll through options with **Space** bar] ↵

Dialog box Display Browse Menu? prompt: **Yes** | **No** [scroll through options with **Space** bar] ↵

Dialog box Use Previous Browse Table? prompt: **Yes** | **No** [scroll through options with **Space** bar] ↵

Dialog box Follow Record After Update? prompt: **Yes** | **No** [scroll through options with **Space** bar] ↵

Dialog box Compress Display? prompt: **Yes** | **No** [scroll through options with **Space** bar] ↵

Keyboard: **Ctrl-End** [to save settings]

USAGE

When you assign the **Browse (Add, Delete, Edit)** action to one of your menu options, you'll first see the dialog box with the options summarized below.

Fields: If you do not specify fields, the browse screen displays all fields from the database or view. If you want, you can specify that only certain fields be displayed. The order in which you specify the fields determines the order used by the browse screen when specifying multiple fields. Separate each field name by a comma. You can also select field names from a submenu by pressing **Shift-F1** (Pick).

Filter: If you do not specify any filter conditions, the browse screen displays all records in the database or view. If you enter a valid filter condition, only records that meet it are displayed.

Fields to Lock Onscreen: If you use the default setting, zero, for the **Fields to Lock Onscreen** option, no fields are locked. You can enter a number indicating how many adjacent fields at the left side of the browse screen you want to remain stationary as the user scrolls to the right.

Freeze Edit Field: If you do not specify a field to freeze, the user can move the highlight to any field in the browse screen. If you enter (or Pick) a field name, the highlight will be confined to the field you specify.

Maximum Column Width: If you do not specify the maximum column width, all fields are displayed in columns that match their widths, as defined in the database structure. If you enter a number, no column will be wider than the number you specify. Fields that are longer than the maximum column width will be truncated on the browse screen.

Format File: If you do not specify a format file, the browse screen imposes no restrictions on data entered into the database. If you enter the name of a custom form, field templates, default values, and other special features of the custom form are applied to the browse screen.

Allow Record Add?: If you specify **Yes** for this option, the user can add new records through the browse screen. If you specify **No,** the user cannot.

Allow Record Edit?: If you specify **Yes** for this option, the user can change any data in the browse screen. If you specify **No,** the user can view data through the browse screen but cannot make any changes.

Allow Record Delete?: If you specify **Yes** for this option, the user can mark records for deletion through the browse screen (using Ctrl-U). If you specify **No,** the user cannot.

Keep Image on Exit?: If you specify **No** for this option, the browse screen disappears when the user stops using it. If you specify **Yes,** an image of the browse screen remains on the screen. (It will be tucked behind your application's custom menus.)

Display Browse Menu?: If you specify **Yes** for this option, the user can access the Browse menu by pressing F10. If you specify **No,** the user cannot access the Browse menu.

Use Previous Browse Table?: If you specify **No** for this option, a new browse screen is constructed each time the user browses records. If you specify **Yes,** settings from the previous browse screen are used in the current browse screen.

Follow Record after Update?: If you specify **Yes** for this option, the highlight follows a record to its new position in a database if a change affects the sort order. If you specify **No,** the highlight does not follow a record to its new sort-order position. (This option is effective only when an index is in use.)

Compress Display?: If you specify **No** for this option, the standard browse screen is used, displaying 17 records at a time. If you specify **Yes,** some text surrounding the standard browse screen is removed, and the browse screen displays 19 records.

After completing the browse screen dialog box, press **Ctrl-End** to return to the Item pull-down menu.

SEE ALSO

The Browse Screen (Chapter 3)

Displaying Data in a Custom Form

Assign the Edit Form action to a menu option, values list, or batch process operation if you want to display a single record from the database on a custom form.

SEQUENCE OF STEPS

Change Action menu: **Edit Form (Add, Delete, Edit)** ↵

Dialog box Format File prompt: *<file name>* ↵

Dialog box Mode prompt: **Edit** | **Append** [scroll through options with **Space** bar] ↵

Dialog box Fields prompt: *<fields>* | **Shift-F1** [highlight names] ↵

Dialog box FILTER, SCOPE, FOR, and WHILE prompts: *<filter condition>* ↵

Dialog box Allow Record Add? prompt: **Yes** | **No** [scroll through options with **Space** bar] ↵

Dialog box Allow Record Edit? prompt: **Yes** | **No** [scroll through options with **Space** bar] ↵

Dialog box Allow Record Delete? prompt: **Yes** | **No** [scroll through options with **Space** bar] ↵

Dialog box Keep Image on Exit? prompt: **Yes** | **No** [scroll through options with **Space** bar] ↵

Dialog box Display Edit Menu? prompt: **Yes** | **No** [scroll through options with **Space** bar] ↵

Dialog box Use Previous Edit form? prompt: **Yes** | **No** [scroll through options with **Space** bar] ↵

Dialog box Follow Record After Update? prompt: **Yes** | **No** [scroll through options with **Space** bar] ↵

Keyboard: **Ctrl-End** [to save settings]

USAGE

When you select the **Edit Form (Add, Delete, Edit)** action, a dialog box appears with the options summarized below:

Format File: Press **Shift-F1** (Pick) and select the name of the custom form to use. You can select **<create>** to create a custom form on the spur of the moment. If you leave this option blank, the application displays the standard edit screen.

Mode: If you specify **Edit** mode, the current database record will be displayed when the user selects the menu option. If you specify **Append** mode, the user will be able to add new records immediately.

Fields: If a custom form is not in use, you can limit the edit screen display to only certain fields. Press **Shift-F1** (Pick) and select fields to display on the edit screen.

FILTER, SCOPE, FOR, and WHILE: See the section Generator Filter Conditions at the beginning of this chapter.

Allow Record Add?: If you specify **Yes** for this option, the user may add new records. If you specify **No,** the user may not add new records through this custom form.

Allow Record Edit?: If you specify **Yes** for this option, the user can edit data through this custom form. If you specify **No,** the user can view but not change data.

Allow Record Delete?: If you specify **Yes** for this option, the user can mark records for deletion (using Ctrl-U) through this form. If you specify **No,** the user cannot mark records for deletion.

Keep Image on Exit?: If you specify **No** for this option, the custom form disappears from the screen when the user is finished with it. If you specify **Yes,** an image of the form remains on the screen after the user exits.

Display Edit Menu?: If you specify **Yes** for this option, the user can access the edit menu by pressing **F10** (Menu). If you specify **No,** the user cannot do so.

Use Previous Edit form?: If you specify **No** for this option, a new browse table is constructed when the user presses F2 to switch to the browse screen. If you specify **Yes,** the previously defined browse screen is reinstated.

Follow Record after Update?: If you specify **Yes** for this option, and an index is in use, the cursor follows the record to its new position if the user changes a field that affects the sort order. If you specify **No,** the cursor does not follow the record.

After filling in the Edit form dialog box, press **Ctrl-End** to return to the Item pull-down menu.

SEE ALSO

Chapter 7: Custom Forms

Displaying or Printing Data

Selecting this option allows you to display data on the screen or printer. When Display or Print is selected, the following submenu appears:

Report	REPORT FORM
Labels	LABEL FORM
Display/List	DISPLAY/LIST

SEQUENCE OF STEPS

Application design screen: [make the object current]

Application design screen menu bar: **Item**

Item menu: **Change Action** ⏎

Change Action menu: **Display or Print** ⏎

Print menu: **Report** *or* **Labels** *or* **Display/List** ⏎

Printing Reports The Report option lets you define a report format to use for printing data from the database. When selected, the **Report** option displays a dialog box with the options summarized below:

Form Name: Press **Shift-F1** (Pick) and specify the report format for printing the report. You can also select **<create>** from the Pick submenu to create a report format on the spur of the moment.

Heading: In the Heading box, you can enter text to be displayed on the first line of each printed page in the report. Enclose the heading in brackets ([]) or single quotation marks ('). Do not use double quotation marks (") in the report heading.

Report Format: Press the **Space** bar to move between the options **Full Detail** (to print all records used to obtain totals and subtotals) and **Summary Only** (to print only subtotals and totals, without detail lines).

Heading Format: Select **Plain** (to not print the date and page number in the report heading) or **Include Date and Page** (to display them).

Before Printing: To eject the page currently in the printer before printing a report, select **Skip to New Page.** Otherwise, press the **Space** bar to scroll to the **Do Not Eject** option.

Send Output To: Press the **Space** bar to scroll through the options **Printer, Disk File, Screen,** and **Ask at Run Time.** If you choose **Ask at Run Time,** the application displays a submenu with the options Printer, Screen, and Disk File when the user runs the application and opts to print the report.

FILTER, SCOPE, FOR, and WHILE: (See the section "Applications Generator Filter Conditions" earlier in this chapter.)

After filling in the Print a Report dialog box, press **Ctrl-End** to return to the Item pull-down menu.

SEE ALSO

Printing Labels and Reports (Chapter 6)

Printing Labels   Use the Labels action when you want your
application to print labels. When you select **Labels,** you'll see
a dialog box with the options summarized below:

Form Name: To specify the format to use for printing
labels, press **Shift-F1** (Pick) while the cursor is in the
Form Name box and then select the label format name
from the displayed submenu. You can also select
<create> to create a mailing label format on the spur of
the moment.

Send Output To: Press the **Space** bar to scroll through
the options **Printer, Disk File, Screen,** and **Ask at Run
Time.** If you choose **Ask at Run Time,** the application
will present the options Printer, Screen, and Disk File
when the user runs the application and opts to print
labels.

Print Sample?: If you specify **Yes** for this option, the application prints samples to help the user align the labels
in the printer. If you specify **No,** the application prints
labels immediately, without first printing any samples.

After filling in the Print Labels dialog box, press **Ctrl-End**
to return to the Items menu.

SEE ALSO

Printing Labels and Reports (Chapter 6)

Displaying Records Without a Report Format   The
Display/List option allows your application to display database records without using a report format. Selecting **Dis-
play/List** presents a dialog box with the options summarized
below:

Pause at Full Page/Screen: If you specify **Yes** for this option, the display pauses for a key press after displaying 20 lines of text. If you specify **No,** all records are displayed without any pauses.

Send Output To: Press the **Space** bar to scroll through the options **Printer, Disk File, Screen,** and **Ask at Run Time.** If you choose **Ask at Run Time,** the application presents the options Printer, Screen, and Disk File when the user runs the application and opts to display or list records.

Include Record Numbers?: If you specify **Yes** for this option, the record number is printed to the left of each record. If you specify **No,** record numbers are omitted.

Fields: If you do not specify a field, all fields from the database are displayed. To limit the display to specific fields, press **Shift-F1** (Pick) and select the fields to display. You can also type field names in the order in which you want them to appear in the display, separating the names with a comma.

FILTER, SCOPE, FOR, and WHILE: (See the section "Applications Generator Filter Conditions" earlier in this chapter.)

After completing the Display/List dialog box, press **Ctrl-End** to return to the Item menu.

Performing File Operations

When you select Perform File Operation as the action for an application, dBASE displays a submenu with the options shown here:

File Copy	COPY FILE
Add Records from File	APPEND FROM
Copy Records to File	COPY TO
Substitute Field Values	REPLACE
Mark Records for Deletion	DELETE
Unmark Records	RECALL

Discard Marked Records	PACK
Generate Index	INDEX ON
Reindex Database	REINDEX
Physically Sort Database	SORT TO
Import Foreign File	IMPORT
Export Foreign File	EXPORT

SEQUENCE OF STEPS

Application design screen: [make the object current]

Application design screen menu bar: **Item**

Item menu: **Change Action** ↵

Change Action menu: **Perform File Operation** ↵

Copying Files   Select the File Copy action when you want your application to copy a file. Note that this option can be used to copy any file, but it requires both the source and destination file names to use extensions. Wildcard characters are not permitted.

When you select **File Copy,** you are prompted to enter the name of the file to copy from and the name of the file to copy to. If a file with the name specified in the To box already exists, it will be overwritten when the user selects this option from your application.

If you want your application to allow the user to pick the name of the file to copy, assign the File Copy option as the action for a files list object. Then specify &LISTVAL in the dialog box as the name of the file to copy. For more information, see "Copying, Moving, Renaming, and Deleting Files" / "Copying Files" in Chapter 10.

Adding Records from a File   Select the **Add Records from File** option when you want your application to add records from one database file to the database that is in use when the user selects the option. You'll see a dialog box with the following choices:

Add Records from File/Array: Enter the name of the file to copy records from, either by pressing Pick or by typing the file name. An array refers to data stored in RAM. It is an advanced structure primarily used by experienced dBASE IV programmers. The Copy Records to File option, discussed in the next section, lets you copy records to an array. You cannot select an array name from the Pick submenu.

Of Type: Press the space bar to specify the type of file that records will be copied from. Your options are **DBF** (a dBASE IV database file), **dBASE II, FW2** (Framework II), **RPD** (RapidFile), **Delimited** (delimited ASCII text file), **Array** (data in memory), **SDF** (structured ASCII text file), DIF (data interchange format), **SYLK** (Multiplan Sylk format), and **WKS** (Lotus 1-2-3 format).

Delimiter: Specify a delimiter if you are importing a delimited text file that does not use double quotation marks to delimit character strings.

FOR: (See the section "Applications Generator Filter Conditions" earlier in this chapter.)

After completing the dialog box, press **Ctrl-End** to return to the Item pull-down menu. For more information, see "Importing and Exporting Data" in Chapter 10.

Copying Records to a File   Use the Copy Records to File option when you want your application to copy records from the database file in use (when the user selects the option) to a new file. Note that, unlike the File Copy option discussed earlier, this option copies only database records. Also, this option can isolate specific records for copying, whereas File Copy can copy only an entire file. When you select **Copy Records to File,** you'll see a dialog box with the options summarized below:

Copy Record to File/Array: Specify the name of the file to copy records to. If you are copying records to an array, do not include a file name extension.

Of Type: Select a type of file to copy records to (see "Of Type" in the preceding section).

Delimiter: Specify a delimiter (if you want to use a character other than double quotation marks) if you are exporting copied records to a delimited ASCII file.

Fields: If you do not specify a field, all fields in the database will be copied to the new file. You can select specific fields by pressing **Shift-F1** (Pick) or by typing field names, separating them with a comma.

SCOPE, FOR, and WHILE: (See the section "Applications Generator Filter Conditions" earlier in this chapter.)

Press **Ctrl-End** after completing the dialog box. For more information see "Importing and Exporting Data" in Chapter 10.

Substituting Field Values   Select the Substitute Field Values option when you want your application to change values in a database field. Note that only the current database is affected by the operation. When you select **Substitute Field Values,** dBASE displays a dialog box with the options summarized below:

SCOPE, FOR, and WHILE: If you do not specify any SCOPE, FOR, or WHILE conditions, the substitution is effective only in the current database record. To change values in all database records, specify **ALL** as the SCOPE condition. To change values in specific records, enter a filter condition in the **FOR** box. (See "Applications Generator Filter Conditions" earlier in this chapter.)

The Field Named: Enter the name of each field in which you want to change or replace some value. You can select field names from a submenu by pressing **Shift-F1** (Pick).

With This Value: For each field you specify for a change, enter an expression that defines the new value. For example, to increase a field named UnitPrice by 15 percent, enter the expression **UnitPrice** ∗ **1.15**. To change all values in a logical field named UPDATED to .T., specify

ALL as the SCOPE condition, UPDATED as the field to replace the contents of, and .T. as the replacement value.

Additive Option?: This option applies only to memo fields. If you specify **Yes** for this option, the value in the With This Value box is added to the bottom of any existing text in the memo field. If you leave this option set to **No,** new text replaces any existing text in the memo field.

Press **Ctrl-End** after completing the dialog box.

Marking Records for Deletion   The Mark Records for Deletion option allows an application option to mark records for deletion. When you select **Mark Records for Deletion,** you'll see a dialog box with the options **SCOPE, FOR,** and **WHILE.** If you leave all three options blank, only the current record is marked for deletion. To mark all records in the database for deletion, enter **ALL** as the SCOPE condition. To mark specific records for deletion, enter a filter condition in the **FOR** box. See "Applications Generator Filter Conditions" earlier in this chapter and "Deleting Records" in Chapter 3.

Unmarking Records   Use the Unmark Records option when you want your application to unmark (recall) records that are marked for deletion. When you select the option **Unmark Records,** dBASE displays a dialog box that presents the options **SCOPE, FOR,** and **WHILE.** If you leave all three options blank, only the current record is unmarked. To unmark all the records in the database, enter **ALL** as the SCOPE condition. To unmark records that meet a search criterion, enter a filter condition in the **FOR** box. See the section "Applications Generator Filter Conditions" earlier in this chapter and "Deleting Records" in Chapter 3.

Discarding Marked Records   The **Discard Marked Records** option packs the database, thereby permanently removing all records that are marked for deletion. When you select this option, you'll see the message *This selection will cause all records marked for deletion to be removed from the database. OK?* Press **Ctrl-End** to accept the action, or **Esc** if you change your mind. For more information see "Deleting Records" in Chapter 3.

Generating an Index   Use the Generate Index option when you want your application to create a new index. (However, it is more efficient to create all indexes through the database design screen *before* you enter the Applications Generator.) When you select **Generate Index,** dBASE displays a dialog box with the options summarized below. For more information see Chapter 4: Sorting a Database.

Index Key Expression: Enter the index key expression, using the rules discussed in Chapter 4. You can base the index on a single field, such as LastName, or on an expression, such as UPPER (LastName + FirstName).

Index First Key Expression Only (Unique)?: If you specify **No** for this option, the index will display all database records when activated. If you specify **Yes,** the index will limit all displays to the first occurrence of each unique value in the database.

Index in Descending Order? If you specify **No** for this option, records are displayed in ascending sorted order. If you specify **Yes,** records are displayed in descending sorted order.

Generate Index to Index File: Enter the name of the index file to create if you are *not* going to use the standard dBASE IV index file (which uses the extension .MDX). The index will be stored under the file name you specify, with the extension .NDX. (To use the indexing techniques described in Chapter 4, leave the Index File prompt blank.)

Or Tag: Use this option to create a standard dBASE IV index, which is stored with other indexes in the .MDX index file. The name can be up to eight characters long and cannot contain any spaces, punctuation, or file name extension.

Of MDX File: By default, the standard dBASE IV index file is stored in a file with the same name as the database file, but with the extension .MDX. To add the new index to the standard index file, enter the database name in this prompt, either with no extension or with the .MDX extension (but do not use .DBF or any other extension in this entry).

For more information, see Chapter 4: Sorting a Database.

Reindexing a Database

Use the **Reindex Database** option when you want your application to allow the user to rebuild indexes. Indexes generally need to be rebuilt only if a power outage or some other problem corrupts index files that are stored in RAM. Because such problems occur from time to time, your applications should provide an option to rebuild all indexes. When you assign this action to an option in your application, you'll see the message *This selection will cause all active index files for the currently selected database or view to be rebuilt. OK?* Press ↵ to accept the action or **Esc** to cancel it.

Sorting a Database   Select the Physically Sort Database option when you want your application to create a separate, sorted copy of the database currently in use. (As discussed in Chapter 4, it's much simpler to present records in sorted order using indexes.) When you select **Physically Sort Database,** dBASE displays a dialog box with the options summarized below:

To File: Enter the name of the file you want to copy the sorted records to. If a file of that name already exists when the user selects this option from your application, that file will be overwritten by the new data.

SCOPE, FOR, and WHILE: If you leave the **SCOPE, FOR,** and **WHILE** options blank, all records in the current database will be copied to the sorted file. To limit the copy to specific records, you can enter a filter condition. (See the section "Applications Generator Filter Conditions" earlier in this chapter.)

Sort Fields: Enter the names of fields used for sorting in order of importance. For example, to sort records by Last-Name and by FirstName within identical last names, enter LASTNAME as sort field 1, and FIRSTNAME as sort field 2. You can select field names from a submenu by pressing **Shift-F1** (Pick).

Ascending: When the cursor is in the **Ascending** field, press the **Space** bar to scroll through the options **Ascending** and **Descending.**

Ignore Case: When the cursor is in the **Ignore Case** field, press the **Space** bar to scroll through the options **Ignore Case** (uppercase and lowercase distinctions do not affect the sort order) and **Use Case** (all lowercase letters appear after uppercase letters in the sort order).

Press **Ctrl-End** after completing the dialog box. For more information, see Chapter 4: Sorting a Database.

Importing Files   Use the Import Foreign File option when you want your application to import data from a foreign data format. When you select **Import Foreign File,** you'll be given two options in a dialog box:

From File: Enter the name of the file to import records from in this box. You can press **Shift-F1** (Pick) to select a file name from the current catalog or directory. If you want the application user to select the name of the foreign file, create a files list that displays the appropriate file names. Then assign the Import File action to the files list and enter &LISTVAL as the FROM file.

Of Type: Use the **Space** bar to scroll through foreign file types. Your options are **PFS, dBASE II, RPD** (RapidFile), **FW2** (Framework II), and **WK1** (Lotus 1-2-3).

Press **Ctrl-End** after completing the dialog box. For more information see "Importing and Exporting Data" in Chapter 10.

Exporting Files   Assign the Export Foreign File action when you want your application to export records from the current database to the format required by a software product other than dBASE IV. When you select **Export Foreign File,** dBASE displays a dialog box with the options summarized below:

To File: Specify the name of the file to export database records to at this prompt. If a file with the name you provide already exists when the user selects this option, that file will automatically be overwritten with new data.

Of Type: Use the **Space** bar to scroll through foreign file formats in this prompt. Your options are **PFS, dBASE II, FW2** (Framework II), and **RPD** (RapidFile).

Fields: If you do not specify a field, all fields from the current database will be exported to the foreign file. To limit the exportation to particular fields, press **Shift-F1** (Pick) and select fields to export from the submenu that appears. You can also type the names of fields to export, separating them with a comma, in the order in which you want them to appear in the exported file.

SCOPE, FOR, and WHILE: If you do not specify a **SCOPE, FOR,** or **WHILE** condition, all records from the current database file will be exported to the foreign file. Specify a condition to limit the exportation to records that meet some search criterion. (See the section "Applications Generator Filter Conditions" earlier in this chapter.)

Press **Ctrl-End** after filling in the dialog box. For more information see "Importing and Exporting Data" in Chapter 10.

Running Programs

The **Run Program** option allows you to add actions to your application that run programs, including dBASE III PLUS and dBASE IV programs, batch processes, and DOS programs and commands. When you select this option from the Item pull-down menu, dBASE displays a submenu with the following options:

Do dBASE Program   DO
Execute Batch Process

Insert dBASE Code

Run DOS Program   RUN

Load/Call Binary File   LOAD/CALL

Play Back Macro   PLAY MACRO

SEQUENCE OF STEPS

Application design screen menu bar: **Item**

Item menu: **Run Program** ↵

Run Program menu: *<option>* ↵

Keyboard: **Ctrl-End**

Executing a dBASE Program   Select the **Do dBASE Program** option when you want your application to execute a custom dBASE program. You'll be prompted to enter a program name and parameters to pass to the program. The name must be that of an existing dBASE III PLUS or dBASE IV program. The parameters must match the order and data types of parameters expected by the PARAMETERS command in the program being run.

Executing a Batch Process   When you want an option in your application to execute a batch process, assign the **Execute Batch Process** action to the menu option. You'll be prompted to enter the name of the batch process to execute.Type the name or press **Shift-F1** (Pick) to select it from a submenu.

Inserting dBASE Code   The **Insert dBASE Code** option lets you create a series of dBASE IV programming commands to be executed when the user selects the attached menu option. When you select this option, you'll be prompted to enter the programming commands.

Running a DOS Program   The **Run DOS Program** action causes dBASE IV to send a command to DOS. When you select this option, you'll be given the options **Program** and **Parameters.** Enter the program (or command) name in the first box (for example, COPY or DIR). Enter any additional parameters in the **Parameters** box.

For example, to display the names of all database files on the current directory, enter DIR as the program and *.DBF as the parameter. To copy all files with the name JULYGL to the diskette in drive A, enter **COPY** as the program name and **JULYGL.* A:** as the parameter. After the application completes the DOS operation, dBASE will return the user to your custom application. For more information, see "Accessing DOS" in Chapter 10.

Executing a Binary File   The **Load/Call Binary File** option loads a binary file into RAM, if it has not already been loaded, and then executes that file. If the binary file has already been loaded, this option only calls it. Binary files can be used only by programmers who are familiar with assembly language programming.

Playing Back a Macro   The **Play Back** Macro action causes your application to play back a series of recorded keystrokes (a macro). When prompted, enter the macro name and press **Ctrl-End.** For more information about macros, see "Keystroke Macros" in Chapter 11.

Exiting the Application

The Quit option on the Item submenu allows the user to exit your application, either back to dBASE IV or all the way back to DOS. **Quit** offers two options:

Return to Calling Program	RETURN
Quit to DOS	QUIT

Select **Return to Calling Program** if you want the application to return to the dBASE IV Control Center when the user exits. Select **Quit to DOS** if you want your application to leave dBASE IV and return to DOS when the user exits. Press ↵ to select OK after selecting an option.

Overriding a Database or View

The Override Assigned Database or View option on the Item
pull-down menu lets you select a new database, view, index,
or index sort order for a specific menu option.

SEQUENCE OF STEPS

Application design screen menu bar: **Item**

Item menu: **Override Assigned Database or View** ⏎

USAGE

This option works in the same manner as the Override Assigned Database or View option on the Menu pull-down
menu, but assigns a new default value to the current menu
option only (rather than to all options in the current menu).

The dialog box that appears when you select this option is
identical to the one displayed by the Menu pull-down menu.
Note that as soon as the application completes the action, the
default database, view, index, and order assigned at the Menu
or Application level go back into effect.

Attaching Code to a Menu Option

The Embed Code option allows you to add dBASE IV programming language code to a specific menu option in an
application.

SEQUENCE OF STEPS

Application design screen menu bar: **Item**

Item menu: **Embed Code** ⏎

Submenu: **Before | After** ⏎

USAGE

This option is identical to the Embed Code option on the Menu pull-down menu, except that the dBASE IV code is executed before or after (or both before and after) the user selects the associated menu option.

Shading Menu Items

In your experience with dBASE IV, you've undoubtedly noticed that sometimes menu items are shaded, indicating that they are unavailable because of some condition that makes them meaningless. For example, the Remove Highlighted File from Catalog option is shaded and unavailable from the Control Center Catalog pull-down menu if no file name is highlighted in the Control Center. The Bypass Item on Condition option on the Applications Generator Item pull-down menu lets you add a similar feature to your own applications.

SEQUENCE OF STEPS

Application design screen menu bar: **Item**

Item menu: **Bypass Item on Condition** ↵

Dialog box Skip This Item If prompt: *<expression>* ↵

USAGE

When you select **Bypass Item on Condition,** a dialog box appears that presents the prompt *Skip this item if:* and a space for entering a valid dBASE IV expression. You can use the **Bypass Item on Condition** feature only in application pop-up and pull-down menus. Also, you cannot assign this action to menu options that have already been assigned the Text (No Action) action.

Positioning the Record Pointer

The Position Record Pointer option lets you move the record pointer (that is, define the current record in the database file) before the action assigned to an application menu option takes place. If you used a WHILE condition in a dialog box, you would almost certainly need to use this option to position the record pointer at the first record in the database that matches the condition.

SEQUENCE OF STEPS

Application design screen menu bar: **Item**

Item menu: **Position Record Pointer** ↵

Dialog box Display Positioning Menu at Run Time? prompt:
Yes | No [scroll through options with **Space** bar] ↵

Dialog box Seek First Occurrence of Key prompt:
<value> ↵

Dialog box GoTo prompt: **Top | Bottom |** *<record number>* ↵

Dialog box Locate prompt: *<filter condition>* ↵

Keyboard: **Ctrl-End** [to save settings]

USAGE

When you select **Position Record Pointer** from the Applications Generator Item pull-down menu, dBASE displays a dialog box with the options summarized in the next section.

Displaying the Positioning Menu at Run Time

At the **Display the Positioning Menu at Run Time?** prompt, use the **Space** bar to select either **Yes** or **No.** If you select **Yes,** when the user selects the menu option to which you've assigned this action your application automatically displays the following options: Position By, Seek Record, GoTo Record, Locate Record, Return.

If an index is not active at the moment, the **Seek Record** option will be shaded and unavailable. If an index is active, the user can select **Seek Record** and enter a value to search for. (You can use a WHILE condition, rather than a FOR condition, in an operation that allows the user to seek a record in an indexed database.)

If the user selects **Goto Record,** the application presents the options **Top** (to position the record pointer at the first record), **Bottom** (to position the pointer at the last record, and **Record #** (which allows the user to type a record number and then positions the pointer at the appropriate record).

If the user selects **Locate Record,** your application will show a submenu with the **SCOPE, FOR,** and **WHILE** options. (See the section "Applications Generator Filter Conditions" earlier in this chapter.)

After the user selects an option from the submenu, the action you assigned to the application menu option through the Change Action option will be executed. If you specify **No** as the Display Positioning Menu at Run Time? setting, the positioning menu will not be displayed to the user.

Searching for an Index Value

If an index is in use when the user selects the current menu option from your application, you can specify a value to search for in that index. Fill in the **Seek First Occurrence of Key** option with the starting value that you want to search for. Use proper delimiters for the data type.

Moving the Record Pointer to a Specific Position

Use the **GoTo** option if you want your application to begin the action that follows with the record pointer at a specific position in the database. Your options are **Top** or **Bottom** or a particular record number.

Locating a Value in a Field

The **Locate (Scope, For, and While)** option searches for a value in any field in the database (an index is not required). Enter a scope or filter condition in the **FOR** or **WHILE** box. (See the section "Applications Generator Filter Conditions" earlier in this chapter.) Press **Ctrl-End** after filling in the dialog box.

Reassigning the Index Order

Select the Reassign Index Order option from the Item pull-down menu to specify a new sort order for the current application menu option.

SEQUENCE OF STEPS

Application design screen menu bar: **Item**

Item menu: **Reassign Index Order** ⏎

Dialog box Set Order To prompt: *<index name>* ⏎

USAGE

When you select this option, a dialog box with the prompt *Set ORDER to:* appears. Enter the name of the index required for the current sort order.

Note that when you select **Reassign Index Order** for a particular menu option in your application, the new index order is used only while that option performs its action. As soon as that action is complete, dBASE reinstates the default index (or the one defined for the current menu).

Defining a Logical Window

If an action in your application displays data on the screen, you can create a *window* to limit that display to a smaller portion of the screen.

SEQUENCE OF STEPS

Application design screen menu bar: **Item**

Item menu: **Define Logical Window** ⏎

Dialog box Window Name prompt: *<window name>* ⏎

Dialog box Display Border As prompt: **Single | Double | Panel | Custom | None** [scroll through options with space bar] ⏎

Dialog box Border Characters prompt: *<character codes>* ⏎

Dialog box Colors prompt: *<color codes>* ⏎

Dialog box Upper-Left Corner prompt: *<row and column>* ⏎

Dialog box Lower-Right Corner prompt: *<row and column>* ⏎

Keyboard: **Ctrl-End**

USAGE

When you select **Define Logical Window,** dBASE displays a dialog box with the options discussed below.

Entering the Window Name

Enter a valid DOS file name as the window name.

Defining a Border Style

The **Display Border As** option determines the style of the border surrounding the window. Press the **Space** bar to scroll through the options: **Single** (single-line), **Double** (double-line), **Panel** (wide line), **Custom** (to use characters defined in the Border Characters box), and **None.**

Using Border Characters

If you specify **Custom** as the display border, you can enter ASCII character codes for the top horizontal border, bottom horizontal border, left vertical border, right vertical border, upper-left corner, upper-right corner, lower-left corner, and lower-right corner (in that order).

Using Colors

To change the colors for the logical window, enter the appropriate color codes (listed in Table 12.5) for the standard, enhanced, border, and background colors (in that order). For example, entering GR+/B, W/R, BG displays standard text as yellow on blue, highlighted text as white on red, and the border as cyan.

Specifying the Upper-Left Corner

Specify the row (from 0 to 23) and column (from 0 to 78) position of the upper-left corner of the box.

COLOR	CODE	COLOR	CODE
Black	N	Green	G
Blank	X	High intensity	+
Blinking	*	Magenta	RB
Blue	B	Red	R
Brown	GR	White	W
Cyan	BG	Yellow	GR+
Underline	U (Monochrome only)		
Inverse	I (Monochrome only)		

Table 12.5: Color Codes

Specifying the Lower-Right Corner

Specify the row (from 1 to 24) and column (from 1 to 79) for the lower-right corner of the box.

Writing Help Text

The Write Help Text option lets you define help text for a specific menu option in your application. The user sees this help text when he or she highlights the menu option and presses F1. If you do not assign help text to a specific menu option, dBASE displays any help text defined for the overall menu when the user presses F1. (If you do not define help text for the menu, dBASE displays the message *No help found* when the user presses F1.)

SEQUENCE OF STEPS

Application design screen menu bar: **Item**

Item menu: **Write Help Text** ↵

Editing frame: [write help text]

Keyboard: **Ctrl-End** [to save help text]

USAGE

When you select **Write Help Text,** you'll be taken to a full-screen editing frame. Type your help text and use the standard dBASE IV editing keys to make changes and corrections. Press **Ctrl-End** when you are done.

Assigning a Message Line Prompt

The Assign Message Line Prompt option lets you define a message line prompt, which the user will see at the bottom of the screen when he or she highlights the current application menu option.

SEQUENCE OF STEPS

Application design screen menu bar: **Item**

Item menu: **Assign Message Line Prompt** ↵

Dialog box: <*prompt*> ↵

USAGE .

When you select this option, a dialog box displays the message line prompt currently assigned to the menu (if any). You'll also be prompted to enter a new message line prompt. If you leave the message line prompt for the current menu option blank, dBASE displays any message-line prompt assigned to the overall menu. If you type a new message line prompt, dBASE displays that prompt when the user highlights the current menu option.

The Generate Menu

The Generate pull-down menu lets you produce the dBASE IV code required to run your application. You can also use the Generate menu to create documentation for your application. The menu offers three options, as discussed in the following sections.

Generating Code and Documentation

The Begin Generating option generates the application code or documentation, depending on the template defined by the Select Template option (discussed in the the next section). Before selecting Begin Generating, you should select Clear Work Surface from the second menu option to save and put away all objects currently on the screen.

SEQUENCE OF STEPS

Application design screen menu bar: **Generate**
Generate menu: **Begin Generating** ⏎
Application design screen menu bar: **Exit**
Exit menu: **Save Changes and Exit** ⏎

USAGE

If you make any changes whatsoever to an existing application, you must select **Begin Generating** to regenerate the
code before you exit the Applications Generator. If you do not
regenerate the code, your changes will not appear when you
run the application. When regenerating an existing application, the screen displays the prompt *Program <application
name> already exists...Overwrite (Y/N)?* Enter **Y** to overwrite
the previous version of the application or **N** to cancel the
regeneration. It takes dBASE some time to develop an application, so do not attempt to exit the Applications Generator until you see the message-line prompt *Generation is
complete -- press any key to continue.* After generating the application code, select **Save Changes and Exit** from the **Exit**
pull-down menu to return to the Control Center.

Note that if you select Begin Generating before you've
defined a main menu for the application, you'll be prompted
to specify the main menu. Press the space bar to select a
menu type (Bar, Pop-Up, or Batch), and then type the menu
name, or press Pick (Shift-F1) and select a menu name.

Selecting a Template

The Applications Generator uses templates to create application code and documentation. The template is a skeletal version of the application you are developing. When you select
Begin Generating, the application fills in the blanks in the
template to produce your specific application.

SEQUENCE OF STEPS

Application design screen menu bar: **Generate**

Generate menu: **Select Template** ⏎

Template prompt: **MENU.GEN** | **DOCUMENT.GEN** | **QUICKAPP.GEN** ⏎

USAGE

The dBASE IV package comes with three templates, named MENU.GEN, DOCUMENT.GEN, and QUICKAPP.GEN. When you select **Select Template** from the **Generate** pull-down menu, you can specify which template to use for the current generation. To generate application code, use **MENU.GEN**. To generate documentation, use **DOCUMENT.GEN**. **QUICK-APP.GEN** is used automatically by the Generate Quick Application option on the Application pull-down menu, so you need not select this template.

Note that if you select DOCUMENT.GEN to generate documentation, the document is stored in a text file with the same name as the application, but the extension .DOC. You can use any word processor, or the DOS TYPE or PRINT command to print the documentation.

Displaying Code or Documentation during Generation

The Display during Generation option provides two choices: Yes and No.

SEQUENCE OF STEPS

Application design screen menu bar: **Generate**

Generate menu: **Display during Generation** ⏎

Prompt box: **Yes** | **No** ⏎

| USAGE |

If you select **Yes,** you'll be able to see the generated code or documentation on the screen as the Applications Generator creates it. (It goes by much too quickly to read, but it can be interesting to watch nonetheless.) If you select **No,** no code or text is shown on the screen.

The Preset Menu

The Preset menu provides options for changing default settings that affect the current application and any applications you develop in the future. You can override the Preset default values for a specific application by using options from the Application pull-down menu.

Specifying Sign-On Defaults

When you select the Sign-On Defaults option, you'll see a dialog box with three options: Application Author, Copyright Notice, and dBASE Version.

| SEQUENCE OF STEPS |

Application design screen menu bar: **Preset**

Preset menu: **Sign-On Defaults** ↵

Dialog box Application Author prompt: <*author name*> ↵

Dialog box Copyright Notice prompt: <*copyright notice*> ↵

Dialog box dBASE Version prompt: <*version number*> ↵

Keyboard: **Ctrl-End** [to save settings]

USAGE

You can enter any text (but no quotation marks) after the prompts. Use the usual dBASE editing keys, if necessary, to make changes and corrections. Press **Ctrl-End** after filling in the dialog box.

The text you enter as the sign-on default display will automatically appear in the sign-on banner whenever you create a new application. You can still, however, change the sign-on banner for any new application. Also, remember that your application will display the sign-on banner only if you select Display Sign-On Banner from the Application pull-down menu.

Choosing Display Options

The Display Options option on the Preset pull-down menu lets you select a default border and coloring scheme for all future applications.

SEQUENCE OF STEPS

Application design screen menu bar: **Preset**

Preset menu: **Display Options** ↵

USAGE

The border style and colors you define here can be overridden in any application by selecting Modify Application Environment from the Application pull-down menu and Display Options from the submenu that appears.

Choosing Environment Settings

The Environment Settings option on the Preset pull-down menu lets you define default settings for all future applications.

SEQUENCE OF STEPS

Application design screen menu bar: **Preset**

Preset menu: **Environment Settings** ↵

USAGE

You can scroll through **Yes** and **No** options by pressing the **Space** bar. To override the default settings in a specific application, select Modify Application Environment from the Application pull-down menu and Environment Settings from the submenu.

Specifying an Application Drive and Directory Path

The Application Drive/Path option on the Preset menu lets you define a disk drive and directory path for all future applications. You can override the default drive and search path for a specific application by selecting Modify Application Environment from the Application pull-down menu and Search Path from the submenu.

SEQUENCE OF STEPS

Application design screen menu bar: **Preset**

Preset menu: **Application Drive/Path** ↵

Dialog box Drive prompt: *<drive name>* ↵

Dialog box Search path prompt: *<search path>* ↵

Keyboard: **Ctrl-End** [to save settings]

USAGE

In the Drive box, enter the name of the drive (for example, B or C) that applications should search for database, report format, label format, and custom form files. In the Search Path box, enter the file search path. (The search path can contain a maximum of 60 characters.) You can include one or more subdirectory names, separating each with a comma or semicolon.

For example, if you specify C as the search drive and \DBASE;\DBASE\MEMBERS;\DBASE\AR as the path, all applications will search the three subdirectories for database objects. That is, when the application needs to find a file, it will first search C:\DBASE. If the file cannot be found, the application will search C:\DBASE\MEMBERS. If the file is still not found, the application will search C:\DBASE\AR.

The Exit Menu

The Exit menu lets you leave the Applications Generator and return to the Control Center. It provides two options, Save All Changes and Exit and Abandon All Changes and Exit.

Saving Changes and Exiting

The Save All Changes and Exit option saves all new and recently changed objects on the application design screen and then returns you to the Control Center.

SEQUENCE OF STEPS

Application design screen menu bar: **Exit**

Exit menu: **Save All Changes and Exit** ⏎

USAGE

Note that selecting this option does not generate application code. If you create an application and do not generate the code (using options on the Generate pull-down menu), you will not be able to run the application. If you modify an existing application and select **Save All Changes and Exit** without regenerating the application code, you will not see your changes when you run the application.

When you select **Save All Changes and Exit,** the objects you created are stored in a file with the name you provide and the extension .APP.

Abandoning Changes and Exiting

The Abandon All Changes and Exit option on the Exit pull-down menu discards all current changes to objects on the application design screen and returns you to the Control Center.

SEQUENCE OF STEPS

Application design screen menu bar: **Exit**

Exit menu: **Abandon All Changes and Exit** ↵

USAGE

If any objects where changed on the application design screen, this option presents the prompt *Are you sure you want to exit from Application Design without saving any changes?*. Select **Yes** to abandon changes or **No** to retain changes and stay in the design screen.

Running a Completed Application

To run a completed application from the Control Center, highlight the name of the application in the Applications panel, press ↵, select Run Application, and Yes. Optionally, from the DOS prompt, you can enter the DBASE command, followed by a single blank space and the application name, to start dBASE and the application simultaneously.